ISBN 0-17-617676-4

TABLE OF CONTENTS

PREFACE

There is much to be proud of with regard to our Canadian business environment. A report produced by the Economist Intelligence Unit (EIU) indicated that Canada is expected to be the best country in the world in which to conduct business in the coming years. The report included rankings among the world's 60 largest countries based on the quality or attractiveness of the business environment and its key components. In the report, Canada jumped three places from its ranking in the 1998–2002 study, to achieve the top position for the first time, ahead of the Netherlands. Finland, the United Kingdom, and the United States rounded out the top five. Canada earned particularly high scores in the quality of its infrastructure, its approach to foreign trade and capital, favourable market opportunities, and political environment.[1]

Canada is indeed poised to earn a distinguished reputation on the world scene. At the same time, it is important to consider how we can maintain and strengthen such a reputation. Perhaps central among the factors to consider is the manner in which we conduct business in this country—the integrity of our business environment. Unfortunately, we have witnessed that Canada, like any other country, is not immune to scandal and corruption. In recent years, both the private and public sectors have been forced to confront a host of misdeeds that speak to the issue of corporate governance, social responsibility, and business ethics. The challenge for Canadian business leaders is to ensure that, along with our industrial development, comes an equally well-developed sense of corporate ethics and social responsibility.

The Responsibilities of Business: Managing Stakeholders and Ethics, employs a stakeholder management framework, emphasizing business's social and ethical responsibilities to both external and internal stakeholder groups. A managerial perspective is embedded within the book's dual themes of business ethics and stakeholder management. The ethics dimension is central because it is becoming increasingly clear that ethical or moral considerations are woven into the fabric of the public issues that organizations face.

The stakeholder management perspective is essential because it requires managers to (1) identify the various groups or individuals who have stakes in the firm or its actions, decisions, and practices, and (2) incorporate the stakeholders' concerns into the firm's strategic plans and operations. Stakeholder management is an approach that increases the likelihood that decision makers will integrate ethical wisdom with management wisdom in all that they do.

OBJECTIVES

Taken as a whole, this book strives to take the reader through a building-block arrangement of basic concepts and ideas that are vital to the business/society relationship and to explore the nature of social and ethical issues and stakeholder groups with which management must interact. It considers the external and internal stakeholder groups in some depth.

Among the specific objectives of this book are:

1. To raise awareness of the demands that emanate from stakeholders and are placed on business firms.

2. To help prospective managers understand appropriate business responses and management approaches for dealing with social, political, and global issues and stakeholders.

3. To promote an appreciation of ethical issues and the influence these issues have on management decision making, behaviour, policies, and practices in the Canadian business context.

i

4. To examine the broad question of business's legitimacy as an institution in a global society from both a business and societal perspective.

5. To draw attention to the increasing extent to which social, ethical, political and global issues must be considered from a strategic business perspective.

FOCUS OF THE BOOK

This book takes a *managerial approach* to the business/society relationship. The managerial approach emphasizes two major themes that are important today: stakeholder management and business ethics. First, let us discuss the managerial focus.

MANAGERIAL APPROACH

Managers are practical, and they have begun to deal with social and ethical concerns in ways similar to those they have used to deal with traditional business functions—operations, marketing, finance, and so forth—in a rational, systematic, and administratively rigorous fashion. By viewing issues of social concern from a managerial frame of reference, managers have been able to reduce seemingly unmanageable social concerns to ones that can be dealt with in a rational and fair fashion. Yet, at the same time, managers have had to integrate traditional economic considerations with ethical or moral considerations.

Our managerial approach, then, will be one that (1) clarifies the nature of the social or ethical issues that affect organizations and (2) suggests alternative managerial responses to these issues in a rational and ethical fashion. The test of success will be the extent to which we can improve an organization's social performance by taking a managerial approach rather than dealing with the issues on an ad hoc basis.

STAKEHOLDER MANAGEMENT & ETHICS THEME

Stakeholders are individuals or groups with which business interacts who have a "stake," or vested interest, in the firm. We consider two broad groups of stakeholders in this book.

The first broad grouping of stakeholders is composed of *internal stakeholders*. Business owners and employees are the principal groups of internal stakeholders. We live in an organizational society, and many people think that their roles as employees are just as important as their roles as investors or owners. Both of these groups have legitimate claims on the organization, and management's task is to address their needs and balance these needs against those of the firm and of other stakeholder groups.

Second, we consider *external stakeholders*, which include the members of the global context, government, consumers, and community members. Much of business operates globally and it is critical to identify stakeholder challenges in this global context. It is also helpful to understand the role and workings of government in order to best appreciate business's relationships with other groups. Consumers may be business's most important stakeholders. In addition, members of the community are crucial, and two major community issues include business giving (or corporate philanthropy) and plant closings (including downsizing).

As hard as one might try to extricate business from the major ethical issues of the day, it just cannot be done. The managerial focus attempts to take a practical look at the social issues and expectations business faces, but ethical questions inevitably come into play. Ethics basically refers to issues of right, wrong, fairness, and justice, and business ethics focuses on ethical issues that arise in the commercial realm. Ethical threads run throughout our discussion because questions of right, wrong, fairness, and justice, no matter how slippery they are to deal with, permeate business's activities as it attempts to interact effectively with major stakeholder groups: employees, customers, owners, government, and the community. Chapter 10 identifies the nature of ethical, stakeholder organizations and sources of influence on organizational morality.

The inevitable task of management is not only to deal with the various stakeholder groups in an ethical fashion but also to reconcile the conflicts of interest that occur between the organization and the stakeholder groups. Implicit in this challenge is the ethical dimension present in practically all business decision making where stakeholders are concerned. In addition to the challenge of treating fairly the groups with which business interacts, management faces the equally important task of creating an organizational climate in which all employees make decisions with the interests of the public, as well as those of the organization, in mind. At stake is not only the firm's reputation but also the reputation of the business community in general.

STRUCTURE OF THE BOOK

The structure of this book is illustrated in Figure 1.

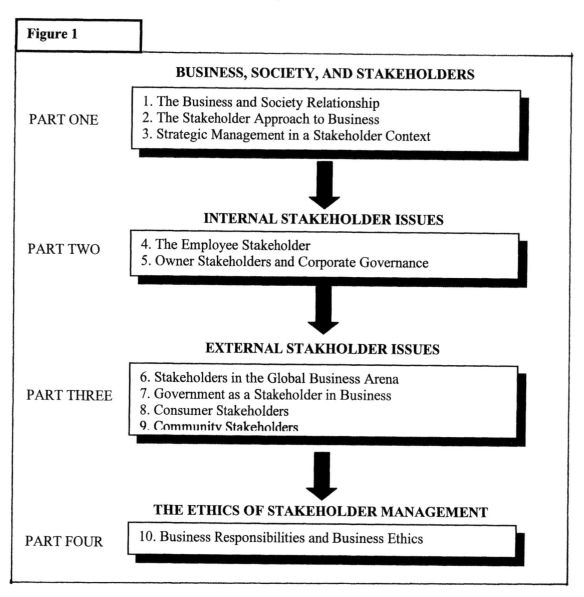

Figure 1

BUSINESS, SOCIETY, AND STAKEHOLDERS

PART ONE
1. The Business and Society Relationship
2. The Stakeholder Approach to Business
3. Strategic Management in a Stakeholder Context

INTERNAL STAKEHOLDER ISSUES

PART TWO
4. The Employee Stakeholder
5. Owner Stakeholders and Corporate Governance

EXTERNAL STAKHOLDER ISSUES

PART THREE
6. Stakeholders in the Global Business Arena
7. Government as a Stakeholder in Business
8. Consumer Stakeholders
9. Community Stakeholders

THE ETHICS OF STAKEHOLDER MANAGEMENT

PART FOUR
10. Business Responsibilities and Business Ethics

In Part 1, entitled "Business, Society, and Stakeholders," there are two chapters. Chapter 1 provides an overview of the business/society relationship, and discusses the notion of corporate citizenship or social responsibility. Chapter 2 addresses the stakeholder management concept and, together with Chapter 1, provides a crucial basis for understanding all of the discussions that follow. They provide the context for the business/society relationship. Chapter 3 examines the challenges of management as strategic planners in a stakeholder context. Topics include strategic management, corporate public affairs, issues management and crisis management.

Part 2 is entitled "Internal Stakeholder Issues". This section includes an examination of employee, owner and managerial stakeholders. Chapter 4 considers issues of critical importance to the manager-employee relationship and emphasizes managerial responsibilities toward employee stakeholders. This discussion of major workplace issues includes such areas as employee rights, employment equity and discrimination. Chapter 5 explores corporate governance and the management/shareholder relationship. Clearly owners have a major stake in the organization and consequently it is useful to consider the nature of current controversies surrounding the control, ownership and management of today's organizations.

Part 3, "External Stakeholder Issues," addresses the major external stakeholders of business. Chapter 6 identifies critical stakeholder issues in the global context along with current management challenges. Given that government is an active player in all the stakeholder groups, we offer specific attention to the business/government relationship in Chapter 7. Chapters 8 explores the notion of consumer stakeholders – what are the interests of consumer stakeholders and what challenges exist for management to adequately address these needs? Chapter 9 looks at community stakeholder issues and discusses a number of important issues for organizations in the context of the community.

Part 4, "The Ethics of Stakeholder Management," focuses on the ethical implications of business and stakeholder management. Although ethical issues cut through and permeate many of the discussions in this book, this chapter explores in some detail the approaches to understanding the concept of business ethics. Business ethics fundamentals are presented in Chapter 10 and we explore the factors that influence the ethical orientation or climate of business.

ACKNOWLEDGMENTS

There are many people to acknowledge for their contributions to and support of this book. First, we would like to express gratitude to those individuals at Thomson Nelson who were responsible for making this book a reality. This text would not have been possible without the guidance and expertise offered by Anthony Rezek, Acquisitions Editor, and Karina Hope, Senior Developmental Editor. Mary Stangolis, Senior Editorial Assistant, deserves much credit for her dedicated attention to and valuable work on preparing this book for publication. Thanks must also go to Bob Kohlmeier, Senior Production Editor and Valerie Adams, Copyeditor for their invaluable contributions.

We wish to thank our colleagues for their insights and suggestions, including Professors Diane Jurkowski, Joanne Magee, Ken McBey, Julia Richardson, Louise Ripley, Gary Spraakman, and Mark Schwartz. Our thanks also go to Rosenda Brown, Ruth Davis, Dana Myers, Mordechai Rothman, and Billie West, whose input and assistance were much appreciated.

Finally, we wish to express appreciation to our family members for their patience, understanding, and encouragement. We dedicate this book to you.

Len Karakowsky
Archie B. Carroll
Ann K. Buchholtz

ABOUT THE AUTHORS

Len Karakowsky is an associate professor of management at York University. He earned his Ph.D. from the Joseph L. Rotman School of Management at the University of Toronto, his M.B.A from the Schulich School of Business at York University, and his Bachelor of Commerce from the University of Toronto. He has served on the faculty of York University since 1997.

Professor Karakowsky's research has been published in the *Journal of Applied Psychology, Administration and Society, Journal of Management Studies, Group and Organization Management, Small Group Research, Journal of Management Systems, International Business Review*, and many other publications. He has authored and co-authored award-winning papers for academic conferences hosted by the Academy of Management as well as for the Administrative Sciences Association of Canada (ASAC). He is also the author of *The Nature of Management and Organizations: Challenges in the Canadian Context*, published by Captus Press.

Professor Karakowsky's teaching, research, and consulting interests are in organizational development, business and society, diversity in the workplace, business ethics, and human resource management. In 2003, he received the best paper award from the Organizational Behaviour division of the ASAC for his research that addressed the issue of managing demographic diversity in organizations. His most recent research efforts focus on how organizations, teams, and leaders can establish and build a culture of trust among their work force. In 2002 and 2003, Dr. Karakowsky received the York University Merit Award for achievements in research, teaching, and service to the university.

Archie B. Carroll is professor of management and holder of the Robert W. Scherer Chair of Management and Corporate Public Affairs in the Terry College of Business at the University of Georgia. He has served on the faculty of the University of Georgia since 1972. Dr. Carroll received his three academic degrees from the Florida State University in Tallahassee.

Professor Carroll has published numerous books and articles. His research has appeared in the *Academy of Management Journal, Academy of Management Review, Business and Society, Journal of Business Ethics, Business Ethics Quarterly*, and many others.

His teaching, research, and consulting interests are in business and society, business ethics, corporate social performance, global stakeholder management, and strategic management. He is currently serving on the editorial review boards of *Business and Society, Business Ethics Quarterly*, and the *Journal of Public Affairs*. He is former division chair of the Social Issues in Management (SIM) Division of the Academy of Management and a founding board member of the International Association for Business and Society (IABS). He is a Fellow of the Southern Management Association.

In 1992, Dr. Carroll was awarded the Sumner Marcus Award for Distinguished Service by the SIM Division of the Academy of Management; and in 1993, he was awarded the Terry College of Business, University of Georgia, Distinguished Research Award for his 20 years of work in corporate social performance, business ethics, and strategic planning. From 1995 to 2000, he served as chairman of the Department of Management at the University of Georgia. In 1998–1999, he served as president of the Society for Business Ethics. In 2000, he was appointed director of the Nonprofit Management and Community Service Program in the Terry College of Business.

Ann K. Buchholtz is an associate professor of strategic management in the Terry College of Business at the University of Georgia. She has served on the faculty of the University of Georgia since 1997. Dr. Buchholtz received her Ph.D. from the Leonard N. Stern School of Business at New York University. Professor Buchholtz's teaching, research, and consulting interests are in business ethics, social issues, strategic management, and corporate governance. Her work has been published in *Business and Society, Business Ethics Quarterly, Academy of Management Journal, Academy of Management Review, Organization Science, Journal of Management, Business Horizons, Journal of General Management, and Human Resource Management Review*. She has served as a reviewer for the *Academy of Management Journal, Academy of Management Review, Journal of Management, Journal of Management Inquiry,*

Academy of Management Executive, and numerous national and international conferences. She serves on the board of the Social Issues in Management Division (SIM) of the Academy of Management. Prior to entering academe, Dr. Buchholtz's work focused on the educational, vocational, and residential needs of individuals with disabilities. She has worked in a variety of organizations, in both managerial and consultative capacities, and has consulted with numerous public and private firms.

1

THE BUSINESS AND SOCIETY RELATIONSHIP

CHAPTER OBJECTIVES

After studying this chapter, you should be able to:

1   Characterize business and society and their interrelationships.

2   Define corporate social responsibility (CSR) and its four components.

3   Explain the value of viewing CSR as a "pyramid".

4   Provide arguments for and against CSR.

5   Discuss the relationship between social performance and financial performance.

For many years now, news stories have brought to the attention of the public countless social and ethical issues that have framed the business and society relationship. Because the news media have a flair for the dramatic, it is not surprising that the reporting of these issues has been highlighted by criticisms of various actions, decisions, and practices on the part of business management. However the growing reports of corporate misconduct cannot be entirely blamed on the press. In fact, in very recent times we have witnessed an astounding flood of corporate scandals and crimes that can only be blamed on corrupt business practices, not on the dramatic flair of the news media. If recent years are any indication of the health of the business and society relationship, then there is cause for grave concern. For many observers, the rapidly expanding list of corporate wrongdoers has all but caused a breach in society's trust for business leaders.

While many have grown accustomed to reading reports that highlight criticisms of the actions, decisions, and practices on the part of business management, no one was prepared for the onslaught of business scandals that we came to read about in recent years. Among the biggest headline grabbers was Enron—an organization that, in 15 years, grew from being an obscure entity to the seventh largest company in the United States. Sadly, Enron's success was largely the product of an elaborate scam of falsely reported profits and debts perpetrated by Enron management and its auditor, public accounting firm Arthur Anderson. Ultimately, this led to Enron's collapse in 2001 and the subsequent demise of Arthur Anderson. It appears that the Enron disaster heralded the arrival of a massive list of subsequent corporate misdeeds.

In 2001, WorldCom, the second-largest long-distance telephone company in the U.S. went into bankruptcy as a result of corporate corruption. WorldCom's chief executive Bernard J. Ebbers was among the participants of WorldCom's fraudulent activities, including falsely reporting the company's revenues in order to meet shareholder expectations. This fraud and the consequent bankruptcy, the largest in U.S. history, ultimately cost shareholders US$180 billion as a result of the drop in the stock's value.

Numerous other companies worldwide have recently been exposed for falsely reporting their financial status, including such well-known U.S. players as Tyco International, Conseco, Adelphia Cable, Global Crossing, Xerox, and HealthSouth. Elsewhere, recent allegations of fraudulent activities have been levelled at the Dutch food distributor and retailer Royal Ahold, France's Vivendi, Britain's Marconi, SK Corp. in South Korea, and Tokyo Electric Power in Japan.

Anyone who has attended to recent news reports understands that Canadian business is no less immune to corporate scandal and wrongdoing than any other business sector in the world. Consider the following examples reported between 2002-2004:

- Canadian media mogul Conrad Black was fired as chairman of Hollinger International Inc., which, in turn, controls Hollinger newspaper assets such as London's *Daily Telegraph* and Chicago's *Sun-Times*. A US$200 million lawsuit directed at Black alleged that he was responsible for altering the company's financial records, and for diverting company funds to himself, to an associate, and to other companies that he controlled.[1]

- Canada earned the distinction of being home to a company that became the first multinational corporation to be fined ($2.2 million) for bribing a government official involved in a World Bank–funded dam project designed to provide water to South Africa. Acres International, an Ontario-based engineering firm, was found guilty of paying a bribe of $266 000 to the former chief executive of the Lesotho Highlands Water Project in Africa as a means to obtain a $21.5 million technical assistance contract for a multi-dam construction program.

- The Montreal family-entertainment company, Cinar, paid a total of $25 million in lawsuits stemming from fraudulent business ventures.

- Following a four-year investigation, the RCMP filed criminal charges against four former executives of Livent Inc., a well-known Toronto-based theatre-production company. The charges allege that the executives falsified accounting records and defrauded investors of approximately $500 million during the 1990s.

- The Ontario Securities Commission passed down a series of fines and penalties on the former directors of the Canadian YBM Magnex International Inc. for a number of corporate misdeeds involving financial reporting. YBM Magnex had collapsed in 1998 with allegations that it had served as a front for the Russian mafia.

- A managing director of equity investments at the CIBC unit Canadian Imperial Holdings Inc. was arrested and charged in an investigation into illegal U.S. mutual fund trading.

- The Canadian government, together with a number of Canadian businesses, faced charges of corruption stemming from a government advertising and corporate sponsorship program managed by the federal Public Works Department. The federal auditor general's report indicated that $100 million was paid to a number of communications agencies in the form of fees and commissions, and the program was essentially designed to generate commissions for these companies rather than to produce any benefit for Canadians.

- The Canadian Imperial Bank of Commerce agreed to pay a penalty of US$80 million to settle charges of aiding and abetting the Enron Corporation's accounting fraud.

In addition to these specific incidents of corporate wrongdoing, many common issues that carry social or ethical implications have arisen within the relationship between business and society. Some of these general issues included corporate abuse of the environment, sweatshop conditions employed by multinational corporations, sexual harassment in the workplace, corporate power, toxic waste disposal, minority rights, drug testing, insider trading, whistle blowing, product liability crises, and the use of political action committees by business to influence the outcome of legislation. Other ongoing issues include business's alleged lack of concern for the welfare of consumers, which is reflected in the growing criticism of fast food companies that encourage the consumption of unhealthy products and lawsuits against the tobacco industry for manufacturing and marketing an inherently dangerous product. Questions continue to be raised about the safety of many products. The litany of such issues could go on and on, but these examples illustrate the continuing tensions between business and society.

These samples of both specific corporate incidents and general issues typify the kinds of stories about business and society that one finds today in newspapers, magazines, and on television. We offer these issues as illustrations of the widespread interactions between business and society that capture the headlines almost daily. Most of these corporate episodes are situations in which the public or some segment of the public believes that a firm has done wrong or treated some individual or group unfairly. In some cases, major laws have been broken. In virtually all of these episodes, questions of whether or not business firms have behaved properly have arisen—whether they have been socially responsible or ethical. Ethical questions are typically present in these kinds of situations. In today's socially aware environment, a business firm frequently finds itself on the defensive—that is, it finds itself being criticized for some action it has taken or failed to take. For example, the spate of corporate accounting scandals has put much greater onus on firms to report their financial status in a fair and accurate manner.

At a general level, we are discussing the role of business in society. Many debates on this issue have taken place. In this book we will address some of these concerns—what a firm must do to be considered socially responsible, and what managers must do to be considered ethical. The issues we mentioned earlier are anything but abstract. They require immediate attention and definite courses of action, which quite often become the next subject of debate on the roles and responsibilities of business in society.

Many economic, legal, ethical, and technological questions and issues about business and society are under debate. This period is turbulent in the sense that it has been characterized by significant changes in the economy, in society, in technology, and in global relationships. Against this continuing turbulence in the business/society relationship, we want to set forth and discuss some ideas that are fundamental to an understanding of where we are, how we got here, and where we may be heading.

WHAT IS BUSINESS AND SOCIETY?

Business may be defined as the collection of private, commercially oriented (profit-oriented) organizations, ranging in size from one-person proprietorships (such as Benny K's Surplus Store) to corporate giants (such as Nortel, Bombardier, Coca-Cola, and Canadian Tire). Between these extremes, of course, are many medium-sized proprietorships, partnerships, and corporations. When we discuss business in this collective sense, we refer to businesses of all sizes and in all types of industries.

Society may be defined as a community, a nation, or a broad grouping of people having common traditions, values, institutions, and collective activities and interests. As such, when we speak of business/society relationships, we may in fact mean business and the local community (such as business and Alberta), business and Canada as a whole, or business and a specific group of people (consumers, minorities, shareholders).

When we refer to business and the entire society, we think of society as being composed of numerous interest groups, more or less formalized organizations, and a variety of institutions. Each of these groups, organizations, and institutions is a purposeful aggregation of people who have banded together because they represent a common cause or share a set of common beliefs about a particular issue. Examples of interest groups or purposeful organizations are numerous: Canadian Business for Social Responsibility, Ethics Practitioners Association of Canada, Canadian Chamber of Commerce, Friends of the Earth, People for the Ethical Treatment of Animals, and Consumer's Association of Canada.

When we speak of business/society relationships, we usually refer either to particular segments or subgroups of society (consumerists, women, minorities, environmentalists, youth) or to business and some system in our society (politics, law, custom, religion, economics). These groups of people or systems may also be referred to in an institutional form (business and the courts, business and consumers, business and labour, business and the government regulators).

Figure 1–1 displays in graphic form the points of interface between business and some of these multiple publics, systems, or stakeholders, with which business has social relationships. Stakeholders are those groups or individuals with whom an organization interacts or has interdependencies. Note that each of the stakeholder groups may be further subdivided into more specific subgroups.

Figure 1-1

Business and Selected Stakeholder Relationships

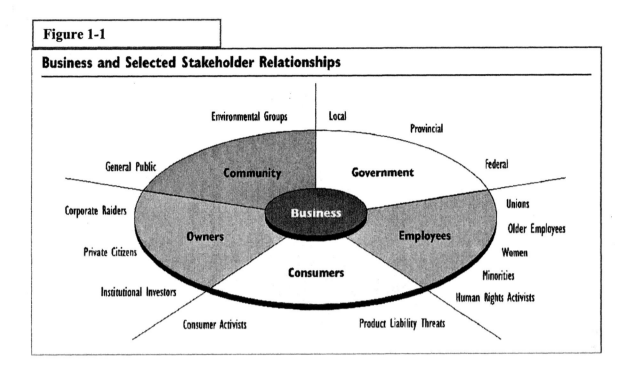

BUSINESS IN SOCIETY: CORPORATE SOCIAL RESPONSIBILITY

What is the role of business in society? What role should business play in society? While we typically think of businesses as money-making machines, does business have any responsibilities beyond the profit objective? Clearly, these questions contain no simple answers. To help shed light on this issue, it is useful to consider the notion of corporate social responsibility and the logic behind such a notion.

Keith Davis and Robert Blomstrom defined **corporate social responsibility** as follows:

> Social responsibility is the obligation of decision makers to take actions which protect and improve the welfare of society as a whole along with their own interests.[2]

This definition suggests two active aspects of social responsibility—*protecting* and *improving*. To protect the welfare of society implies the avoidance of negative impacts on society. To improve the welfare of society implies the creation of positive benefits for society.

Archie Carroll's four-part definition of CSR focuses on the types of social responsibilities that business arguably possess. Carroll's definition helps us to understand the component parts that make up CSR:

> The social responsibility of business encompasses the economic, legal, ethical, and discretionary (philanthropic) expectations that society has of organizations at a given point in time.[3]

Carroll's four-part definition attempts to place economic and legal expectations of business in context by relating them to more socially oriented concerns. These social concerns include ethical responsibilities and philanthropic (voluntary/discretionary) responsibilities.

ECONOMIC RESPONSIBILITIES

First, there are business's **economic responsibilities**. It may seem odd to call an economic responsibility a social responsibility, but, in effect, this is what it is. First and foremost, our social system calls for business to be an economic institution. That is, it should be an institution whose orientation is to produce goods and services that society wants and to sell them at fair prices—prices that society thinks represent the true values of the goods and services delivered and that provide business with profits adequate to ensure its perpetuation and growth and to reward its investors. While thinking about its economic responsibilities, business employs many management concepts that are directed towards financial effectiveness—attention to revenues, costs, strategic decision making, and the host of business concepts focused on maximizing the long-term financial performance of the organization.

LEGAL RESPONSIBILITIES

Second, there are business's **legal responsibilities**. Just as society has sanctioned our economic system by permitting business to assume the productive role mentioned earlier, as a partial fulfillment of the social contract, it has also laid down the ground rules—the laws—under which business is expected to operate. Legal responsibilities reflect society's view of "codified ethics" in the sense that they embody basic notions of fair practices as established by our lawmakers. It is business's responsibility to society to comply with these laws. If business does not agree with laws that have been passed or are about to be passed, our society has provided a mechanism by which dissenters can be heard through the political process. In the past 30 years, our society has witnessed a proliferation of laws and regulations striving to control business behaviour. This aspect of the business and society relationship will be developed in more detail in later chapters.

As important as legal responsibilities are, legal responsibilities do not cover the full range of behaviours expected of business by society. The law is inadequate for at least three reasons. First, the law cannot possibly address all the topics, areas, or issues that business may face. New topics continually emerge such as Internet-based business (e-commerce) and genetically engineered foods. Second, the law often lags behind more recent concepts of what is considered appropriate behaviour. For example, as technology permits more exact measurements of environmental contamination, laws based on measures made by obsolete equipment become outdated but not frequently changed. Third, laws are made by lawmakers and may reflect the personal interests and political motivations of legislators rather than appropriate ethical justifications. A wise sage once said: "Never go to see how sausages or laws are made." It may not be a pretty picture.

ETHICAL RESPONSIBILITIES

Because laws are important but not adequate, **ethical responsibilities** embrace those activities and practices that are expected or prohibited by societal members even though they are not codified into law. Ethical responsibilities embody the full scope of norms, standards, and expectations that reflect a belief of what consumers, employees, shareholders, and the community regard as fair, just, and in keeping with the respect for or protection of stakeholders' moral rights.[4]

In one sense, changes in ethics or values precede the establishment of laws because they become the driving forces behind the initial creation of laws and regulations. For example, the civil rights, environmental, and consumer movements reflected basic alterations in societal values and thus may be seen as ethical bellwethers foreshadowing and leading to later legislation. In another sense, ethical responsibilities may be seen as embracing and reflecting newly emerging values and norms that society expects business to meet, even though they may reflect a higher standard of performance than that currently required by law. Ethical responsibilities in this sense are often ill defined or continually under public scrutiny and debate as to their legitimacy and, thus, are frequently difficult for business to agree upon. Regardless, business is expected to be responsive to newly emerging concepts of what constitutes ethical practices.

Superimposed on these ethical expectations emanating from societal and stakeholder groups are the implied levels of ethical performance suggested by a consideration of the great ethical principles of moral philosophy, such as justice, rights, and utilitarianism.[5]

Ethical responsibilities encompass those areas in which society expects certain levels of moral or principled performance but for which it has not yet articulated or codified into law.

PHILANTHROPIC RESPONSIBILITIES

Fourth, there are business's voluntary/discretionary or **philanthropic responsibilities**. These are viewed as responsibilities because they reflect current expectations of business by the public. These activities are voluntary, guided only by business's desire to engage in social activities that are not mandated, not required by law, and not generally expected of business in an ethical sense. Nevertheless, the public has an expectation that business will engage in **philanthropy** and thus this category has become a part of the social contract between business and society. Such activities might include corporate giving, product and service donations, volunteerism, partnerships with local government and other organizations, and any other kind of voluntary involvement of the organization and its employees with the community or other stakeholders. Examples of companies fulfilling their philanthropic responsibilities are many:

- CIBC sponsors such charitable events as Run for the Cure to raise funds for combating cancer.

- Microsoft Canada Inc. donates millions of dollars to areas such as youth, education, and community programs.

- Bell Canada has spent millions funding a partnership with universities and governments in Ontario and Quebec that supports student research in communications technology.

- Bombardier Inc. established the J. Armand Bombardier Foundation, a Canadian charitable organization which donates funds to such causes as shelters, food banks, and outreach programs.

The distinction between ethical responsibilities and philanthropic responsibilities is that the latter typically are not expected in a moral or an ethical sense. Communities desire and expect business to contribute its money, facilities, and employee time to humanitarian programs or purposes, but they do not regard firms as unethical if they do not provide these services at the desired levels. Therefore, these responsibilities are more discretionary, or voluntary, on business's part, although the societal expectation that they be provided is always present. This category of responsibilities is often referred to as good **"corporate citizenship."**

In essence, then, our definition forms a four-part conceptualization of corporate social responsibility that encompasses the economic, legal, ethical, and philanthropic expectations placed on organizations by society at a given point in time. Figure 1–2 summarizes the four components, society's expectation regarding each component, and examples. The implication is that business has accountability for these areas of responsibility and performance. This four-part definition provides us with categories within which to place the various expectations that society has of business. With each of these categories considered as indispensable facets of the total social responsibility of business, we have a conceptual model that more completely describes the kinds of expectations that society expects of business. One advantage of this model is that it can accommodate those who have argued against CSR by characterizing an economic emphasis as separate from a social emphasis. This model offers these two facets along with others that collectively make up corporate social responsibility.

Figure 1-2

Understanding the Four Components of Corporate Social Responsibility

Type of Responsibility	Societal Expectation	Examples
Economic	*Required* of business by society	Be profitable. Maximize sales, minimize costs. Make sound strategic decisions. Be attentive to dividend policy.
Legal	*Required* of business by society	Obey all laws, adhere to all regulations. Environmental and consumer laws. Laws protecting employees. Obey the Criminal Code, the Income Tax Act, and the Corruption of Foreign Public Officials Act. Fulfill all contractual obligations. Honour warranties and guarantees.
Ethical	*Expected* of business by society	Avoid questionable practices. Respond to spirit as well as letter of law. Assume law is a floor on behaviour, operate above minimum required. Do what is right, fair, and just. Assert ethical leadership.
Philanthropic	*Desired/expected* of business by society	Be a good corporate citizen. Make corporate contributions. Provide programs supporting community—education, health/human services, culture and arts, civic. Provide for community betterment. Engage in volunteerism.

THE PYRAMID OF CORPORATE SOCIAL RESPONSIBILITY

A helpful way of graphically depicting the four-part definition is envisioning a pyramid composed of four layers. This **Pyramid of Corporate Social Responsibility** is shown in Figure 1-3.[6]

The pyramid portrays the four components of CSR, beginning with the basic building block of economic performance, at the base. At the same time, business is expected to obey the law, because the law is society's codification of acceptable and unacceptable behaviour. Next is business's responsibility to be ethical. At its most basic level, this is the obligation to do what is right, just, and fair and to avoid or minimize harm to stakeholders (employees, consumers, community, the environment, and others). Finally, business is expected to be a good corporate citizen—to fulfill its voluntary/discretionary or philanthropic responsibility to contribute financial and human resources to the community and to improve the quality of life.

No metaphor is perfect, and the Pyramid of CSR is no exception. It is intended to illustrate that the total social responsibility of business is composed of distinct components that, when taken together, make up the whole. Although the components have been treated as separate concepts for discussion purposes, they are not mutually exclusive and are not intended to juxtapose a firm's economic responsibilities with its other responsibilities. At the same time, a consideration of the separate components helps the manager to see that the different types or kinds of obligations are in constant and dynamic tension with one another.

Figure 1-3

The Pyramid of Corporate Social Responsibility

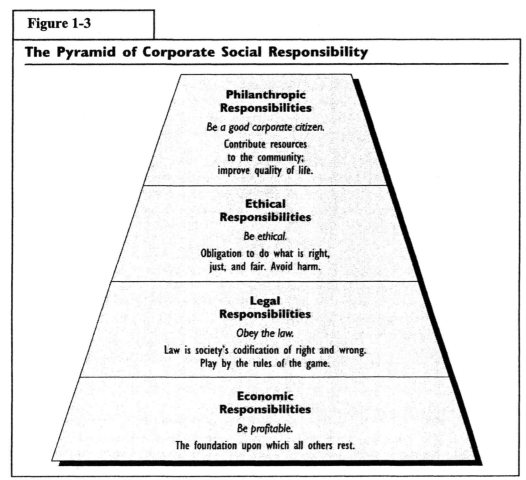

Philanthropic Responsibilities

Be a good corporate citizen.

Contribute resources to the community; improve quality of life.

Ethical Responsibilities

Be ethical.

Obligation to do what is right, just, and fair. Avoid harm.

Legal Responsibilities

Obey the law.

Law is society's codification of right and wrong. Play by the rules of the game.

Economic Responsibilities

Be profitable.

The foundation upon which all others rest.

Source: Archie B. Carroll, "The Pyramid of Corporate Social Responsibility: Toward the Moral Management of Organizational Stakeholders," *Business Horizons* (July–August 1991), 42. Copyright © 1991 by the Trustees at Indiana University, Kelley School of Business.

The most critical tensions, of course, are those between economic and legal, economic and ethical, and economic and philanthropic. The traditionalist might see this as a conflict between a firm's "concern for profits" and its "concern for society," but it is suggested here that this is an oversimplification. A CSR or stakeholder perspective would recognize these tensions as organizational realities but would focus on the total pyramid as a unified whole and on how the firm might engage in decisions, actions, policies, and practices that simultaneously fulfill all its component parts. This pyramid should not be interpreted to mean that business is expected to fulfill its social responsibilities in some sequential fashion, starting at the base. Rather, business is expected to fulfill all its responsibilities simultaneously.

In summary, the total social responsibility of business entails the concurrent fulfillment of the firm's economic, legal, ethical, and philanthropic responsibilities. In equation form, this might be expressed as follows:

Economic Responsibilities + Legal Responsibilities + Ethical Responsibilities

+ Philanthropic Responsibilities

= Total Corporate Social Responsibility

Stated in more practical and managerial terms, the socially responsible firm should strive to:

- Make a profit.

- Obey the law.

- Be ethical.

- Be a good corporate citizen.

It is especially important to note that the four-part CSR definition and the Pyramid of CSR represent a stakeholder model. That is, each of the four components of responsibility addresses different stakeholders in terms of the varying priorities in which the stakeholders are affected. Economic responsibilities most dramatically impact owners and employees (because if the business is not financially successful, owners and employees will be directly affected). Legal responsibilities are certainly crucial with respect to owners, but in today's society the threat of litigation against businesses emanates frequently from employees and consumer stakeholders. Ethical responsibilities affect all stakeholder groups, but an examination of the ethical issues business faces today suggests that they involve consumers and employees most frequently. Finally, philanthropic responsibilities most affect the community, but it could be reasoned that employees are next affected because some research has suggested that a company's philanthropic performance significantly affects its employees' morale.

As we study the evolution of business's major areas of social concern, as presented in various chapters, we will see how our model's four facets (economic, legal, ethical, and philanthropic) provide us with a useful framework for conceptualizing the issue of corporate social responsibility. The social contract between business and society is to a large extent formulated from mutual understandings that exist in each area of our basic model. But, it should be noted that the ethical and philanthropic categories, taken together, more nearly capture the essence of what people generally mean today when they speak of the social responsibility of business. Situating these two categories relative to the legal and economic obligations, however, keeps them in proper perspective.

ARGUMENTS AGAINST AND FOR CORPORATE SOCIAL RESPONSIBILITY

In an effort to provide a balanced view of CSR, we will consider the arguments that traditionally have been raised against and for it. We should state clearly at the outset, however, that those who argue against corporate social responsibility are not using in their considerations the comprehensive CSR definition and model presented here. Rather, it appears that the critics are viewing CSR more narrowly— as only the efforts of the organization to pursue social, noneconomic/nonlegal goals (our ethical and philanthropic categories). Some critics equate CSR with only the philanthropic category. We should also state that only a very few businesspeople and academics continue to argue against the fundamental notion of CSR today. The debate among businesspeople more often centres on the kinds and degrees of CSR and on subtle ethical questions, rather than on the basic question of whether or not business should be socially responsible.

ARGUMENTS AGAINST CSR

Let us first look at the arguments that have surfaced over the years from the anti-CSR school of thought. Most notable has been the classical economic argument. This traditional view holds that management has one responsibility: to maximize the profits of its owners or shareholders. This classical economic school, led by economist Milton Friedman, argues that social issues are not the concern of businesspeople and that these problems should be resolved by the unfettered workings of the free market system.[7] Further, this view holds that if the free market cannot solve the social problem, then it falls upon government and legislation to do the job. Friedman softens his argument somewhat by his assertion that management is "to make as much money as possible while conforming to the basic rules of society, both those embodied in the law and those embodied in ethical customs."[8] When Friedman's entire statement is considered, it appears that he accepts three of the four categories of the four-part model—economic, legal, and ethical. The only item not specifically embraced in his quote is the voluntary or philanthropic category. In any event, it is clear that the economic argument views corporate social responsibility more narrowly than we have in our conceptual model.

A second major objection to CSR has been that business is not equipped to handle social activities. This position holds that managers are oriented toward finance and operations and do not have the necessary expertise (social skills) to make social decisions.[9] Although this may have been true at one point in time, it is less true today. Closely related to this argument is a third: If managers were to pursue corporate social responsibility vigorously, it would tend to dilute the business's primary purpose.[10] The objection here is that CSR would put business into fields not related, as F. A. Hayek has stated, to their "proper aim."[11]

A fourth argument against CSR is that business already has enough power—economic, environmental, and technological—and so why should we place in its hands the opportunity to wield additional power?[12] In reality, today, business has this social power regardless of the argument. Further, this view tends to ignore the potential use of business's social power for the public good.

One other argument that merits mention is that by encouraging business to assume social responsibilities we might be placing it in a deleterious position in terms of the international balance of payments. One consequence of being socially responsible is that business must internalize costs that it formerly passed on to society in the form of dirty air, unsafe products, consequences of discrimination, and so on. The increase in the costs of products caused by including social considerations in the price structure would necessitate raising the prices of products, making them less competitive in international markets. The net effect might be to dissipate the country's advantages gained previously through technological advances. This argument weakens somewhat when we consider the reality that social responsibility is quickly becoming a global concern, not one restricted to North American firms and operations.

The arguments presented here constitute the principal claims made by those who oppose the CSR concept, as it once was narrowly conceived. Many of the reasons given appear quite rational. Value choices as to the type of society the citizenry would like to have, at some point, become part of the total social responsibility question. Whereas some of these objections might have had validity at one point in time, it is doubtful that they carry much weight today.

ARGUMENTS FOR CSR

Thomas Petit's perspective is useful as our point of departure in discussing support of the CSR doctrine. He says that authorities have agreed upon two fundamental points: "(1) Industrial society faces serious human and social problems brought on largely by the rise of the large corporations, and (2) managers must conduct the affairs of the corporation in ways to solve or at least ameliorate these problems."[13]

This generalized justification of corporate social responsibility is appealing. It actually comes close to what we might suggest as a first argument for CSR—namely, that it is in business's long-range self-interest to be socially responsible. Petit's argument provides an additional dimension by suggesting that it was partially business's fault that many of today's social problems arose in the first place and, consequently, that business should assume a role in remedying these problems. It may be inferred from this that deterioration of the social condition must be halted if business is to survive and prosper in the future.

The long-range self-interest view holds that if business is to have a healthy climate in which to exist in the future, it must take actions now that will ensure its long-term viability. Perhaps the reasoning behind this view is that society's expectations are such that if business does not respond on its own, its role in society may be altered by the public—for example, through government regulation or, more dramatically, through alternative economic systems for the production and distribution of goods and services.

It is sometimes difficult for managers who have a short-term orientation to appreciate that their rights and roles in the economic system are determined by society. Business must be responsive to society's expectations over the long term if it is to survive in its current form or in a less restrained form.

One of the most practical reasons for business to be socially responsible is to ward off future government intervention and regulation. Today there are numerous areas in which government intrudes with an expensive, elaborate regulatory apparatus to fill a void left by business's inaction. To the extent that business polices itself with self-disciplined standards and guidelines, future government intervention can be somewhat forestalled.

Keith Davis has presented two additional supporting arguments that deserve mention together: "Business has the resources" and "Let business try."[14] These two views maintain that because business has a reservoir of management talent, functional expertise, and capital, and because so many others have tried and failed to solve general social problems, business should be given a chance. These arguments have some merit, because there are some social problems that can be handled, in the final analysis, only by business. Examples include a fair workplace, providing safe products, and engaging in fair advertising. Admittedly, government can and does assume a role in these areas, but business must make the final decisions.

Another argument is that "proacting is better than reacting." This position holds that proacting (anticipating and initiating) is more practical and less costly than simply reacting to problems once they have developed. Environmental pollution is a good example, particularly business's experience with attempting to clean up rivers, lakes, and other waterways that were neglected for years. In the long run, it would have been wiser to prevent the environmental deterioration from occurring in the first place. A final argument in favour of CSR is that the public strongly supports it. A 2003 poll sponsored by Environics International indicates that the public believes that companies should not only focus on profits for shareholders but that they should be responsible to their workers and communities, even if making things better for workers and communities requires companies to sacrifice some profits.

ASSESSING THE STATE OF CORPORATE SOCIAL RESPONSIBILITY

The 2003 CSR Monitor survey sponsored by Environics International/GlobeScan assessed responses from over 21 000 consumers, shareholders, and corporate employees in 21 countries. This representative survey revealed that corporate social responsibility is critically important to the citizens of the world. The survey also indicated that more than eight in ten Canadians believe companies should contribute to more than the health of the economy.[15] The survey echoed the findings of the previous annual survey with regard to expectations that major companies should do more than make profits in the twenty-first century.[16]

According to a Conference Board of Canada survey, 77 percent of Canadians are most likely to invest in, and 79 percent to work for, companies they view as socially responsible.[17] In addition, a 2003 Ipsos-Reid poll showed that 55 percent of Canadians surveyed consciously decided to buy a product or service from one company over another because they felt the company was a good corporate citizen.[18] Another survey sponsored by Environics highlighted critical expectations held of corporate behaviour for the coming years. In the twenty-first century, major companies will be expected to do all the following:

- Demonstrate their commitment to society's values and their contribution to society's social, environmental, and economic goals through actions.

- Fully insulate society from the negative impacts of company operations and its products and services.

- Share the benefits of company activities with key stakeholders as well as with shareholders.

- Demonstrate that the company can make more money by doing the right thing, in some cases reinventing its business strategy. This "doing well by doing good" will reassure stakeholders that the new behavior will outlast good intentions.[19]

Added together, these annual surveys strongly suggest that CSR is fast becoming a global expectation that requires a comprehensive strategic response. Ethics and CSR need to be made a core business value integrated into all aspects of the firm. However, what is striking in the 2003 survey is that significant proportions of respondents in most countries were unable to name a socially responsible company, despite the consistently high expectations for companies to be socially responsible.[20]

SOCIAL PERFORMANCE AND FINANCIAL PERFORMANCE

One issue that comes up frequently in considerations of corporate social performance is whether or not there is a demonstrable relationship between a firm's social responsibility or performance and its financial performance. Unfortunately, attempts to measure this relationship are typically hampered by measurement problems. The appropriate performance criteria for measuring financial performance and social responsibility are subject to debate. Furthermore, the measurement of social responsibility is fraught with definitional problems. Even if a definition of CSR could be agreed on, there still would remain the complex task of operationalizing the definition.

There have been at least three different views, hypotheses, or perspectives that have dominated these discussions and research. Perhaps the most popular view, which we will call *Perspective 1*, is built on the belief that socially responsible firms are more financially profitable. To those who advocate the concept of social performance, it is apparent why they would like to think that social performance is a driver of financial performance and, ultimately, a corporation's reputation. If it could be demonstrated that socially responsible firms, in general, are more financially successful and have better reputations, this would significantly bolster the CSP view, even in the eyes of its critics.

Perspective 1 has been studied extensively. Unfortunately, most of the studies that have sought to demonstrate this relationship have failed to produce conclusive results. In spite of this, some studies have claimed to have successfully established this linkage. For example, a study by Covenant Investment Management concluded that social concern pays. This study found that 200 companies ranking highest on Covenant's overall social responsibility scale had outperformed the Standard & Poor's 500-stock index during the five years studied.[21] To be considered a valid finding, however, the Covenant research would have to be subjected to careful scrutiny. Part of the problem with Perspective 1 is that positive correlations made be found but causality is not clearly established.

Perspective 2, which has not been studied as extensively, argues that a firm's financial performance is a driver of its social performance. This perspective is built somewhat on the notion that social responsibility is a "fair-weather" concept; that is, when times are good and companies are enjoying financial success, we witness higher levels of social performance. In their study, Preston and O'Bannon found the strongest evidence that financial performance either precedes, or is contemporaneous with, social performance. This evidence supports the view that social–financial performance correlations are best explained by positive synergies or by "available funding."[22]

Perspective 3 argues that there is an interactive relationship among social performance, financial performance, and corporate reputation. In this symbiotic view, the three major factors influence each other, and, because they are so interrelated, it is not easy to identify which factor is driving the process.

Regardless of the perspective taken, each view advocates a significant role for CSP, and it is expected that researchers will continue to explore these perspectives for years to come. Figure 1–4 depicts the essentials of each of these views.

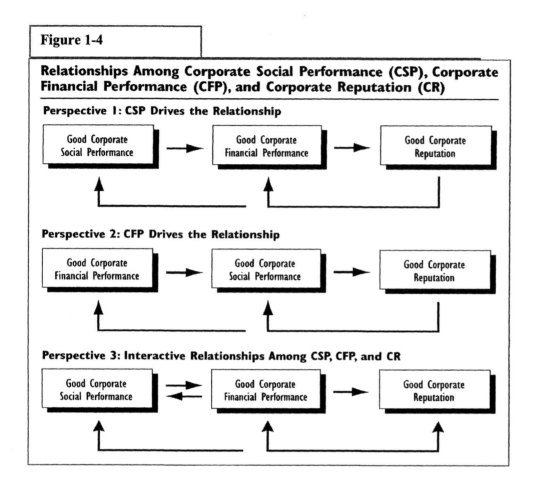

Figure 1-4

Relationships Among Corporate Social Performance (CSP), Corporate Financial Performance (CFP), and Corporate Reputation (CR)

Perspective 1: CSP Drives the Relationship

Good Corporate Social Performance → Good Corporate Financial Performance → Good Corporate Reputation

Perspective 2: CFP Drives the Relationship

Good Corporate Financial Performance → Good Corporate Social Performance → Good Corporate Reputation

Perspective 3: Interactive Relationships Among CSP, CFP, and CR

Good Corporate Social Performance ⇄ Good Corporate Financial Performance → Good Corporate Reputation

A MULTIPLE BOTTOM-LINE PERSPECTIVE

A basic premise of all these perspectives is that there is only one "bottom line"—a corporate bottom line that addresses primarily the shareholders', or owners', investments in the firm. An alternative view is that the firm has "multiple bottom lines" that benefit from corporate social performance. This stakeholder-bottom-line perspective argues that the impacts or benefits of CSP cannot be fully measured or appreciated by considering only the impact of the firm's financial bottom line.

To truly operate with a stakeholder perspective, companies need to accept the multiple-bottom-line view. Thus, CSP cannot be fully comprehended unless we also consider that its impacts on stakeholders, such as consumers, employees, the community, and other stakeholder groups, are noted, measured, and considered. Research may never conclusively demonstrate a relationship between CSP and financial performance. If a stakeholder perspective is taken, however, it may be more straightforward to assess the impact of CSP on multiple stakeholders' bottom lines. This model of CSP and stakeholders' bottom lines might be depicted as shown in Figure 1–5.

Figure 1-5

Relationship Between Corporate Social Performance (CSP) and Stakeholders' "Multiple Bottom Lines"

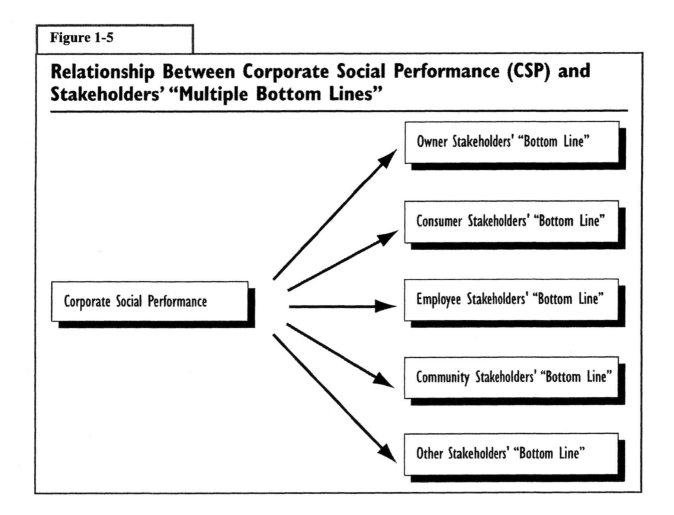

SUMMARY

Within the context of the pluralistic business system in Canada, business firms must deal with a multitude of stakeholders and an increasingly diverse society. The recognition that business operates within the societal context leads us to consider the social responsibilities of business. The corporate social responsibility concept has a rich history. It has grown out of many diverse views and even today does not enjoy a consensus of definition. A four-part conceptualization was presented that broadly conceives CSR as encompassing economic, legal, ethical, and philanthropic components. The four parts were presented as part of the Pyramid of CSR. The identification of social issues has blossomed into a field now called "stakeholder management." Studies of the relationship between social responsibility and economic performance do not yield consistent results, but social efforts are nevertheless expected and are of value to both the firm and the business community. In the final analysis, sound corporate social (stakeholder) performance is associated with a "multiple-bottom-line effect" in which a number of different stakeholder groups experience enhanced bottom lines.

KEY TERMS

business (page 4)

corporate citizenship (page 7)

corporate social responsibility (page 5)

economic responsibilities (page 6)

ethical responsibilities (page 7)

legal responsibilities (page 6)

philanthropic responsibilities (page 7)

philanthropy (page 7)

Pyramid of CSR (page 8)

society (page 4)

DISCUSSION QUESTIONS

1. Identify and explain the Pyramid of Corporate Social Responsibility. Provide several examples of each "layer" of the pyramid. Identify and discuss some of the tensions among the layers or components.

2. In your view, what is the single strongest argument *against* the idea of corporate social responsibility? Briefly explain.

3. In your view, what is the single strongest argument *for* corporate social responsibility? Briefly explain.

4. Discuss the interrelationships among the concepts of corporate social performance, corporate financial performance, and corporate reputation. Which perspective on these relationships seems most valid to you? Explain why.

ENDNOTES

1. Theresa Tedesco and Barbara Shecter, "Black Heads to Court for Selloff Protection *CanWest News Service* (January 20, 2004) http://www.canada.com/national/nationalpost/index.html; Theresa Tedesco and Barbara Shecter, "Conrad Black Sells Hollinger, Lashes Out," *CanWest News Service* (January 19, 2004).

2. Keith Davis and Robert L. Blomstrom, *Business and Society: Environment and Responsibility*, 3rd ed. (New York: McGraw-Hill, 1975), 39.

3. Archie B. Carroll, "A Three-Dimensional Conceptual Model of Corporate Social Performance," *Academy of Management Review* (Vol. 4, No. 4, 1979), 497–505.

4. Archie B. Carroll, "The Pyramid of Corporate Social Responsibility: Toward the Moral Management of Organizational Stakeholders," *Business Horizons* (July–August 1991), 39–48. Also see Archie B. Carroll, "The Four Faces of Corporate Citizenship," *Business and Society Review* (Vol. 100-101, 1998), 1–7.

5. *Ibid.*

6. *Ibid.*

7. Milton Friedman, "The Social Responsibility of Business Is to Increase Its Profits," *New York Times* (September 1962), 126.

8. *Ibid.*, 33 (emphasis added).

9. Christopher D. Stone, *Where the Law Ends* (New York: Harper Colophon Books, 1975), 77.

10. Keith Davis, "The Case For and Against Business Assumption of Social Responsibilities," *Academy of Management Journal* (June 1973), 312–322.

11. F. A. Hayek, "The Corporation in a Democratic Society: In Whose Interest Ought It and Will It Be Run?" in H. Ansoff (ed.), *Business Strategy* (Middlesex: Penguin, 1969), 225.

12. Davis, 320.

13. Thomas A. Petit, *The Moral Crisis in Management* (New York: McGraw-Hill, 1967), 58.

14. Davis, 316.

15. http://www.globescan.com.

16. The Millennium Poll on Corporate Social Responsibility (Environics, Intl., Ltd., Prince of Wales Business Leaders Forum, The Conference Board, 1999), http://www.Environics.net.

17. Conference Board of Canada, http://www.conferenceboard.ca/GCSR.

18. "Poll Rates Corporate Canada on CSR," P. 26, http://www.ipsos-reid.com.

19. The Millennium Poll on Corporate Social Responsibility (Environics, Intl., Ltd., Prince of Wales Business Forum, The Conference Board, 1999), http://www.Environics.net.

20. Conference Board of Canada, http://www.conferenceboard.ca.

21. *Chicago Tribune*, "Social Concern Pays, Study Suggests," *The Atlanta Journal* (June 7, 1993), E4.

22. Preston and O'Bannon, 428.

2

THE STAKEHOLDER
APPROACH TO BUSINESS

CHAPTER OBJECTIVES

After studying this chapter, you should be able to:

1   Define *stake* and *stakeholder* and describe the origins of these concepts.

2   Differentiate among the production, managerial, and stakeholder views of the firm.

3   Explain the three values of the stakeholder model.

4   Discuss the concept of stakeholder management.

5   Identify and discuss the five major questions that capture the essence of stakeholder management.

Life in business organizations was once simpler. First, there were the investors who put up the money to get the business started. This was in the precorporate period, so there was only one person, or a few at most, financing the business. Next, the owners needed employees to do the productive work of the firm. Because the owners themselves were frequently the managers, another group—the employees—was needed to get the business going. Then the owners needed suppliers to make raw materials available for production and customers to purchase the products or services they were providing. All in all, it was a less complex period, with minimal and understood expectations among the various parties.

The business organization today, especially the modern corporation, is the institutional centrepiece of a complex society. Our society today consists of many people with a multitude of interests, expectations, and demands as to what major organizations ought to provide to accommodate people's lifestyles. We have seen business respond to the many expectations placed on it. We have seen many assorted legal, ethical, and philanthropic expectations and demands being met by organizations willing to change as long as the economic incentive was still present. What was once viewed as a specialized means of providing profit through the manufacture and distribution of goods and services has become a multipurpose social institution that many people and groups depend on for their livelihood, prosperity, and fulfillment.

In a society conscious of an always-improving lifestyle, with more groups every day laying claims to their pieces of the good life, business organizations today need to be responsive to individuals and groups they once viewed as powerless and unable to make such claims on them. We call these individuals and groups *stakeholders*.

It is becoming apparent that business organizations must address the legitimate needs and expectations of stakeholders if they want to be successful in the long run.[1] Business must also address stakeholders because it is the ethical course of action to take. Stakeholders have claims, rights, and expectations that should be honoured, and the stakeholder approach encourages that pursuit. It is for these reasons that the stakeholder concept and orientation have become an essential part of the vocabulary and thinking in the arena of business, society, and ethics.

ORIGINS OF THE STAKEHOLDER CONCEPT

The stakeholder concept has become a central idea in understanding business and society relationships. The term "stakeholder" is a variant of the more familiar and traditional idea of *stockholders* or *shareholders*—the investors in or owners of businesses. Just as a private individual might own his or her house, automobile, or video recorder, a shareholder owns a portion or a share of one or more businesses. Thus, a shareholder is also called a stakeholder. However, shareholders are just one group of many legitimate stakeholders that business and organizations must address today to be effective.

WHAT IS A STAKE?

To appreciate the concept of stakeholders, it helps to understand the idea of a stake. A **stake** is an interest or a share in an undertaking. If a group is planning to go out to dinner and a show for the evening, each person in the group has a stake, or interest, in the group's decision. No money has yet been spent, but each member sees his or her interest (preference, taste, priority) in the decision. A stake is also a claim. A claim is an assertion to a title or a right to something. A claim is a demand for something due or believed to be due. We can see clearly that an owner or a shareholder has an interest in and an ownership of a share of a business.

The idea of a stake, therefore, can range from simply an interest in an undertaking at one extreme to a legal claim of ownership at the other extreme. In between these two extremes is a "right" to something. This right might be a legal right to certain treatment rather than a legal claim of ownership, such as that of a shareholder. Legal rights might include the right to fair treatment (e.g., not to be discriminated against) or the right to privacy (not to have one's privacy invaded or abridged). The right might be thought of as a moral right, such as that expressed by an employee: "I've got a right not to be fired because I've worked here 30 years, and I've given this firm the best years of my life." Or a consumer might say, "I've got a right to a safe product after all I've paid for this."

As we have seen, there are several different types of stakes. Figure 2–1 summarizes various categories or types of stakes.

Figure 2-1

Types of Stakes

An Interest	A Right	Ownership
When a person or group will be affected by a decision, it has an interest in that decision.	Legal Right: When a person or group has a legal claim to be treated in a certain way or to have a particular right protected.	When a person or group has a legal title to an asset or a property.
Examples: This plant closing will affect the community. This TV commercial demeans women, and I'm a woman.	Examples: Employees expect due process, privacy; customers or creditors have certain legal rights.	Examples: "This company is mine, I founded it, and I own it," or, "I own 1000 shares of this corporation."
	Moral Right: When a person or group thinks it has a moral right to be treated in a certain way or to have a particular right protected.	
	Examples: Fairness, justice, equity.	

WHAT IS A STAKEHOLDER?

A **stakeholder**, then, is an individual or a group that has one or more of the various kinds of stakes in a business. Just as stakeholders may be affected by the actions, decisions, policies, or practices of the business firm, these stakeholders also may affect the organization's actions, decisions, policies, or practices. With stakeholders, therefore, there is a potential two-way interaction or exchange of influence. In short, a stakeholder may be thought of as "any individual or group who can affect or is affected by the actions, decisions, policies, practices, or goals of the organization."[2]

WHO ARE BUSINESS'S STAKEHOLDERS?

In today's competitive, global business environment, there are many individuals and groups who are business's stakeholders. From the business point of view, there are certain individuals and groups that have **legitimacy** in the eyes of management. That is, they have a legitimate interest in, or claim on, the operations of the firm. The most obvious of these groups are shareholders, employees, and customers. From the point of view of a highly pluralistic society, stakeholders include not only these groups, but other groups as well. These other groups include competitors, suppliers, the community, special-interest groups, the media, and society or the public at large. It has also been strongly argued by Mark Starik that the natural environment, nonhuman species, and future generations should be considered among business's important stakeholders.[3]

PRODUCTION →MANAGERIAL → STAKEHOLDER VIEWS

The evolution and progress of the stakeholder concept parallels the evolution of the business enterprise. In what has been termed the traditional **production view of the firm**, owners thought of stakeholders as only those individuals or groups that supplied resources or bought products or services.[4] As time passed and we witnessed the growth of corporations and the resulting separation of ownership from control, business firms began to see the need for interaction with major constituent groups if they were to be managed successfully. Thus, we witnessed the evolution of the **managerial view of the firm**. Finally, as major internal and external changes occurred in business, managers were required to undergo a revolutionary conceptual shift in how they perceived the firm and its multilateral relationships with constituent or stakeholder groups. The result was the **stakeholder view of the firm**.[5] In actual practice, however, some managers have not yet come to appreciate the need for the stakeholder view. Figure 2–2 depicts the evolution from the production view to the managerial view of the firm, and Figure 2–3 illustrates the stakeholder view of the firm.

Figure 2-2

The Production and Managerial Views of the Firm

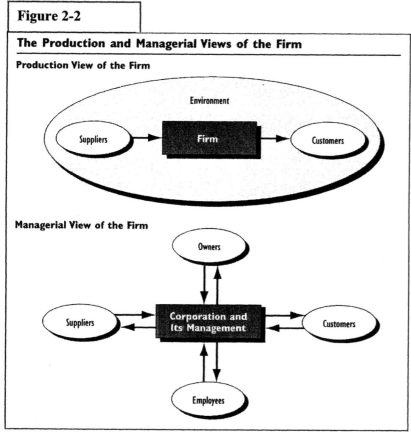

Production View of the Firm

Managerial View of the Firm

Source: From Freeman's *Strategic Management: A Stakeholder Approach*, Copyright © 1984 by R. Edward Freeman. Reprinted with permission from Pittman Publishing Company.

Figure 2-3

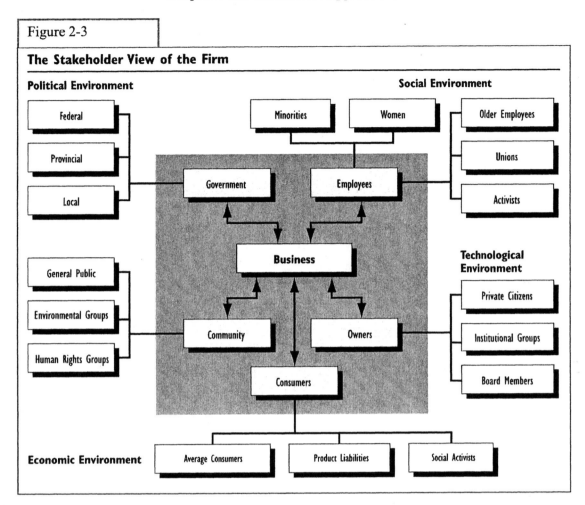

The Stakeholder View of the Firm

In the stakeholder view of the firm, management must perceive its stakeholders as not only those groups that management thinks have some stake in the firm but also as those groups that themselves think or perceive they have a stake in the firm. This must be the perspective that management takes at the outset, at least until it has had a chance to weigh very carefully the legitimacy of the claims and the power of the various stakeholders. We should note here that each stakeholder group is composed of subgroups. For example, the government stakeholder group includes federal, provincial, and municipal government stakeholders.

PRIMARY AND SECONDARY STAKEHOLDERS

Wheeler and Sillanpää have presented a useful way to categorize stakeholders. Using such categories as primary and secondary and social and nonsocial, they propose defining stakeholders as follows:[6]

Primary social stakeholders include:
- Shareholders and investors
- Employees and managers
- Customers
- Local communities
- Suppliers and other business partners
- Government and regulators

Secondary social stakeholders include:
- Social pressure groups
- Media and academic commentators
- Trade bodies
- Competitors

Primary social stakeholders have a direct stake in the organization and its success and, therefore, are influential. Secondary social stakeholders may be extremely influential as well, especially in affecting reputation and public standing, but their stake in the organization is more representational of public or special interests than direct. Therefore, the level of accountability to a secondary stakeholder tends to be lower, but these groups may wield significant power and quite often represent legitimate public concerns.[7]

Primary nonsocial stakeholders include:

- The natural environment
- Future generations
- Nonhuman species

Secondary nonsocial stakeholders include:

- Environmental pressure groups
- Animal welfare organizations

It should be kept in mind that secondary stakeholders can quickly become primary ones. This often occurs with the media or special-interest groups when the urgency of a claim (as in a boycott or demonstration) takes precedence over the legitimacy of that claim. In today's business environment, the media have the power to instantaneously transform a stakeholder's status with coverage on the evening news. Thus, it may be useful to think of primary and secondary classes of stakeholders for discussion purposes, but we should understand how easily and quickly those categories can shift.

LEGITIMACY, POWER, URGENCY: A TYPOLOGY OF STAKEHOLDER ATTRIBUTES

Expanding on the idea that stakeholders have such attributes as legitimacy, power, and urgency, Mitchell, Agle, and Wood generated a typology of stakeholders based on these three attributes.[8] When these three attributes are superimposed, as depicted in Figure 2–4, seven stakeholder categories result.

Figure 2-4

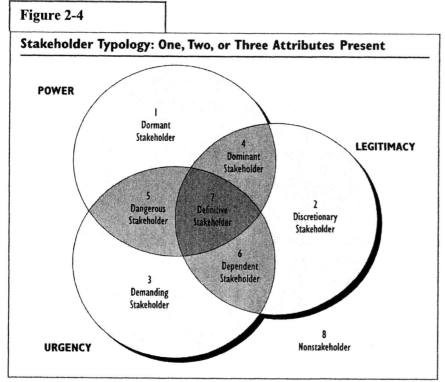

Stakeholder Typology: One, Two, or Three Attributes Present

POWER

1 Dormant Stakeholder

4 Dominant Stakeholder

LEGITIMACY

5 Dangerous Stakeholder

7 Definitive Stakeholder

2 Discretionary Stakeholder

6 Dependent Stakeholder

3 Demanding Stakeholder

URGENCY

8 Nonstakeholder

A brief look at the three attributes of legitimacy, power, and urgency helps us to see how stakeholders may be thought of and analyzed in these key terms. Legitimacy refers to the perceived validity or appropriateness of a stakeholder's claim to a stake. Therefore, owners, employees, and customers represent a high degree of legitimacy due to their explicit, formal, and direct relationships with a company. Stakeholders that are more distant from the firm, such as social activist groups, competitors, or the media, might be thought to have less legitimacy.

Power refers to the ability or capacity to produce an effect—to get something done that otherwise may not be done. Therefore, whether one has legitimacy or not, power means that the stakeholder could affect the business. For example, with the help of the media, a large, vocal, social activist group such as People for the Ethical Treatment of Animals (PETA) could wield extraordinary power over a business firm.

Urgency refers to the degree to which the stakeholder claim on the business calls for the business's immediate attention or response. Urgency may imply that something is critical—it really needs to get done. Or, it may imply that something needs to be done immediately, or on a timely basis. A management group may perceive a union strike, a consumer boycott, or a social activist group picketing outside headquarters as urgent.

An interesting example of a stakeholder action that illustrates both power and urgency occurred recently in several dozen Home Depot stores in the United States. In each of the stores, strange announcements began blaring from the intercom systems: "Attention shoppers, on aisle seven you'll find mahogany ripped from the heart of the Amazon." Shocked store managers raced through the aisles trying to apprehend the environmental activists who were behind the stunt. The activists had apparently gotten the access codes to the intercoms. After months of similar antics, Home Depot bowed to the demands of the environmental group and announced that it would stop selling wood chopped from endangered forests and, instead, stock wood products certified by a new organization called the Forest Stewardship Council (FSC).[9] This newly founded group wasn't even on Home Depot's radar screen and then, all of a sudden, it had to capitulate to selling only wood certified by the FSC.

Mitchell, Agle, and Wood take the position that managers must attend to stakeholders based on their assessment of the extent to which competing stakeholder claims are characterized by legitimacy, power, and urgency. Using the categories in Figure 2–4, therefore, the stakeholder groups represented by overlapping circles (for example, those with two or three attributes, such as Categories 4, 5, 6, and 7) are highly "salient" to management and would likely receive priority attention.

STRATEGIC, MULTIFIDUCIARY, AND SYNTHESIS VIEWS

One challenge embedded in the stakeholder approach is to determine whether it should be perceived primarily as a way to *manage better* those groups known as stakeholders or as a way to *treat more ethically* those groups known as stakeholders. Kenneth Goodpaster has addressed this issue by distinguishing among the strategic approach, the multifiduciary approach, and the stakeholder synthesis approach.[10] Goodpaster uses the term "strategic" in a sense slightly different from that in which it was used in the previous discussion.

The *strategic approach* views stakeholders primarily as factors to be taken into consideration and managed while the firm is pursuing profits for its shareholders. In this view, managers might take stakeholders into account because offended stakeholders might resist or retaliate (for example, through political action, protest, or boycott). This approach sees stakeholders as instruments that may facilitate or impede the firm's pursuit of its strategic objectives. Thus, it is an instrumental view.

The *multifiduciary approach* views stakeholders as more than just individuals or groups who can wield economic or legal power. This view holds that management has a fiduciary responsibility to stakeholders just as it has this responsibility to shareholders. Here, management's traditional fiduciary, or trust, duty is expanded to embrace stakeholders on roughly equal footing with shareholders. Thus, shareholders are no longer of exclusive importance as they would be under the strategic approach. This view expands the idea of a fiduciary responsibility to include shareholders and other important stakeholders.

Goodpaster recommends that business organizations take neither of these extreme postures but rather pursue a new *stakeholder synthesis approach*. This new view holds that business does have moral responsibilities to stakeholders but that they should not be seen as part of a fiduciary obligation. Thus, management's basic fiduciary responsibility to shareholders is kept intact, but it is also expected to be implemented within a context of ethical responsibility. This ethical responsibility is its duty not to harm, coerce, lie, cheat, steal, and so on.[11] Thus, the result is the same in the multifiduciary and stakeholder synthesis views. However, the reasoning is different.

As we continue our discussion of stakeholder management, it should be clear that we are pursuing it from a balanced perspective. This balanced perspective suggests that we are integrating the strategic approach with the stakeholder synthesis approach such that they are compatible. We should be managing strategically and morally at the same time. The stakeholder approach should not be just a better way to manage, it also should be a more ethical way to manage.

THREE VALUES OF THE STAKEHOLDER MODEL

As an alternative to Goodpaster's strategic, multifiduciary, and stakeholder synthesis views, Donaldson and Preston have articulated three aspects or values of the stakeholder model of the firm. These three aspects, although interrelated, are distinct. They differentiate among the descriptive, instrumental, and normative aspects of stakeholder theory or the stakeholder model.[12]

First, the stakeholder model is *descriptive*. That is, it provides language and concepts to effectively describe the corporation or organization. The corporation is a constellation of cooperative and competitive interests possessing both instrumental and intrinsic value. Understanding organizations in this way allows us to have a fuller description or explanation of how they function. The language and terms used in stakeholder theory are useful in helping us to understand organizations.

Second, the stakeholder model is *instrumental*. It is useful in establishing the connections between the practice of stakeholder management and the resulting achievement of corporate performance goals. The fundamental premise here is that practising effective stakeholder management should lead to the achievement of traditional goals, such as profitability, stability, and growth.

Third, the stakeholder model is *normative*. In the normative perspective, stakeholders are identified by their interest in the organization whether or not the organization has any corresponding interest in them. Thus, the interests of all stakeholders are of intrinsic value. Stakeholders are seen as possessing value irrespective of their instrumental use to management. The normative view is often thought of as the moral or ethical view because it emphasizes how stakeholders *should* be regarded.

Stakeholder management necessitates the simultaneous attention to the legitimate interests of all appropriate stakeholders in the creation of organizational structures and policies.[13]

KEY QUESTIONS IN STAKEHOLDER MANAGEMENT

The managers of a business firm have the responsibility of establishing the firm's overall direction (its strategies, goals, and policies) and seeing to it that these plans are carried out. As a consequence, managers have some long-term responsibilities and many that are of more immediate concern. Before the stakeholder environment became as turbulent and rapidly changing as it now is, the managerial task was relatively straightforward and the external environment was stable. As we have evolved to the stakeholder view of the firm, however, we see the managerial task as an inevitable consequence of the trends and developments we described in our first two chapters.

Stakeholder management has become important as managers have discovered the many groups that have to be relatively satisfied for the firm to meet its objectives. Without question, we still recognize the significance and necessity of profits as a return on the shareholders' investments, but we also see the growing claims of other stakeholder groups and the success they have had in getting what they want.

The challenge of stakeholder management, therefore, is to see to it that the firm's primary stakeholders achieve their objectives and that other stakeholders are dealt with ethically and are also satisfied. At the same time, the firm is expected to be profitable. This is the classic "win-win" situation. It does not always occur, but it is a legitimate goal for management to pursue to protect its long-term best interests. Management's second-best alternative is to meet the goals of its primary stakeholders, keeping in mind the important role of its owner-investors. Without economic viability, all other stakeholders' interests are lost.

With these perspectives in mind, let us approach stakeholder management with the idea that managers can become successful stewards of their stakeholders' resources by gaining knowledge about stakeholders and using this knowledge to predict and deal with their behaviour and actions. Ultimately, we should manage the situation in such a way that we achieve our objectives ethically and effectively. Thus, the important functions of stakeholder management are to describe, to understand, to analyze, and, finally, to manage.

The quest for stakeholder management embraces social, ethical, and economic considerations. Normative as well as instrumental objectives and perspectives are essential. Five major questions must be asked if we are to capture the essential information we need for stakeholder management:

1. *Who* are our stakeholders?
2. What are our stakeholders' *stakes*?
3. What *opportunities and challenges* do our stakeholders present to the firm?
4. What *responsibilities* (economic, legal, ethical, and philanthropic) does the firm have to its stakeholders?
5. What *strategies* or *actions* should the firm take to best handle stakeholder challenges and opportunities?[14]

1. WHO ARE OUR STAKEHOLDERS?

To this point, we have described the likely primary and secondary stakeholder groups of a business organization. To manage them effectively, each firm and its management group must ask and answer this question for itself: Who are our stakeholders? To answer this question fully, management must identify not only generic stakeholder groups but also the specific subgroups. A generic stakeholder group is simply a broad grouping, such as employees, shareholders, environmental groups, or consumers. Within each of these generic categories there may be a few or many specific subgroups. Figure 2–5 illustrates some of the generic and specific stakeholder subgroups of a very large organization.

Figure 2-5

Some Generic and Specific Stakeholders of a Large Firm

Owners	Employees	Governments	Customers
Trusts	Young employees	Federal	Business purchasers
Foundations	Middle-aged employees	Provincial	Government purchasers
Mutual funds	Older employees	Municipal	Educational institutions
Board members	Women	Special-interest groups	
Management owners	Minority groups		
Employee pension funds	Special needs		
Individual owners	Special-interest groups		
	Unions		

Community	Competitors	Social Activist Groups
General fund-raising	Firm A	Greenpeace
Charities	Firm B	National Citizens' Coalition
Schools	Firm C	Council of Canadians
Hospitals		Friends of the Earth
Residents who live close by		Mothers Against Drunk Driving (MADD)
All other residents		Animal Alliance of Canada
Neighbourhood associations		Consumer's Association of Canada
Local media		Canadian Civil Liberties Association
		People for the Ethical Treatment of Animals (PETA)

To illustrate the process of stakeholder identification, we will consider some events in the life of the McDonald's Corporation that resulted in their broadening significantly who were considered their stakeholders. The case study starts in the fall of 1999 when the social-activist group PETA (People for the Ethical Treatment of Animals), which claims 700 000 members, decided it was dissatisfied with some of McDonald's practices and decided it would launch a billboard and bumper-sticker campaign against the hamburger giant.[15] PETA felt McDonald's was dragging its feet on animal welfare issues, and so PETA went on the attack. PETA announced it would put up billboards saying "The animals deserve a break today" and "McDonald's: Cruelty to Go" in Norfolk, Virginia, PETA's home city. The ad campaign was announced when talks broke down between PETA and McDonald's on the subject of ways the company might foster animal-rights issues within the fast-food industry. Using concepts introduced earlier, PETA was a secondary social or nonsocial stakeholder and, therefore, had low legitimacy. However, its power and urgency were high as it was threatening the company with a highly visible, potentially destructive campaign that was being favourably reported by a cooperative media.

It's not clear what all took place over the ensuing year, but it is evident that PETA's pressure tactics continued and escalated. In the fall of 2000, McDonald's announced significant changes in the demands it began placing on its chicken and egg suppliers. McDonald's announced that its egg suppliers must now improve the living conditions of its chickens. Specifically, McDonald's is now insisting that its suppliers no longer cage its chickens wing-tip to wing-tip. Suppliers must now increase the space allotted to each hen from 48 square inches to 72 square inches (approximately 310 square centimetres to 456 square centimetres) per hen. Suppliers will also be required to stop "forced molting," a process that increases egg production by denying hens food and water for up to two weeks.[16]

It came out that during the ensuing year, PETA escalated its pressure tactics against the firm. PETA began distributing "unhappy meals" at restaurant playgrounds and outside the company's shareholder meeting. The kits, which came in boxes similar to McDonald's Happy Meals that it sells to children, were covered with pictures of slaughtered animals. It also depicted a bloody, knife-wielding "Son of Ron" doll that resembled the Ronald McDonald clown, as well as toy farm animals with slashed throats. One image featured a bloody cow's head and the familiar fast-food phrase "Do you want fries with that?"[17]

As a result of this example, we can see how the set of stakeholders that McDonald's had to deal with grew significantly from its traditional stakeholders to include powerful groups such as PETA. With the aid of the media, especially major newspapers and magazines, PETA moved from being a secondary stakeholder to a primary stakeholder in McDonald's life.

In 2001, members of PETA and the Animal Rights Foundation of Florida (ARFF) began an attack on Burger King, similar to the attack on McDonald's. They greeted Burger King's new CEO with signs and banners reading "Burger King: King of Cruelty," while showing a video documenting the abuses that PETA hopes Burger King will put a stop to. The organizations also planned a full-page ad in *The Miami Herald* asking the new CEO to take action to reduce the suffering of chickens, pigs, and other animals on farms that supply the company's meat and eggs. This is the latest volley in PETA's "Murder King" campaign, in which hundreds of demonstrations against Burger King have taken place in more than a dozen countries and in every U.S. state.[18]

The purpose of this discussion has been to illustrate the evolving nature of the question, "Who are our stakeholders?" In actuality, stakeholder identification is an unfolding process. However, by recognizing early the potential of failure if one does not think in stakeholder terms, the value and usefulness of stakeholder thinking can be readily seen. Had McDonald's perceived PETA as a stakeholder earlier on, perhaps it could have dealt with this situation more effectively.

Many businesses do not carefully identify their generic stakeholder groups, much less their specific stakeholder groups. This must be done, however, if management is to be in a position to answer the second major question, "What are our stakeholders' stakes?"

2. WHAT ARE OUR STAKEHOLDERS' STAKES?

Once stakeholders have been identified, the next step is to answer the question: What are our stakeholder's stakes? Even groups in the same generic category frequently have different specific interests, concerns, perceptions of rights, and expectations. Management's challenge here is to identify the nature and legitimacy of a group's stake(s) and the group's power to affect the organization. As we discussed earlier, urgency is another critical factor.

IDENTIFYING THE NATURE/LEGITIMACY OF A GROUP'S STAKES. Let's consider an example of stakeholders who possess varying stakes. Assume that we are considering corporate owners as a generic group of stakeholders and that the corporation is large, with several million shares of stock outstanding. Among the ownership population are these more specific subgroups:

1. Institutional owners (trusts, foundations, churches, universities)
2. Large mutual fund organizations
3. Board of director members who own shares
4. Members of management who own shares
5. Tens of thousands of small, individual shareholders

For all these groups, the nature of stakeholder claims on this corporation is ownership. All these groups have legitimate claims—they are all owners.

IDENTIFYING THE POWER OF A GROUP'S STAKES. When we examine power, we see significant differences. Which of the groups in the previous list are the most powerful? Certainly not the thousands of small, individual investors, unless they have found a way to organize and thus wield considerable power. The powerful stakeholders in this case are (1) the institutional owners and mutual fund organizations, because of the sheer magnitude of their investments, and (2) the board and management shareholders, because of their dual roles of ownership and management (control). However, if the individual shareholders could somehow form a coalition based on some interest they have in common, they could exert significant influence on management decisions.

IDENTIFYING SPECIFIC GROUPS WITHIN A GENERIC GROUP. Consider, for example, a manufacturing firm in an industry in Vancouver that is faced with a generic group of environmental stakeholders. Within the generic group of environmental stakeholders might be the following specific groups:

1. Residents who live within a 25-kilometre radius of the plant
2. Other residents in the city
3. Residents who live in the path of the jet stream hundreds of kilometres away who are being impacted by acid rain
4. Environment Canada (federal government)
5. Provincial Ministry of the Environment (provincial government)
6. Friends of the Earth (social activist group)
7. The Wilderness Society (social activist group)
8. Pollution Probe (social activist group)

It would require some degree of care to identify the nature, legitimacy, power, and urgency of each of these specific groups. However, it could and should be done if the firm wants to get a handle on its environmental stakeholders. Furthermore, we should stress that companies have an ethical responsibility to be sensitive to legitimate stakeholder claims even if the stakeholders have no power or leverage with management.

If we return for a moment to the McDonald's example, we would have to conclude that PETA, as a special-interest, animal-welfare group, did not have much legitimacy vis-à-vis McDonald's. PETA did claim animal's rights and treatment as a moral issue, however, and thus had some general legitimacy through the concerns it represented. Unfortunately for PETA, not all of the public shares its concerns or degree of concern with these issues. However, PETA had tremendous power and urgency. It was this power, wielded in the form of adverse publicity and media attention, that doubtless played a significant role in bringing about changes in McDonald's policies.

3. WHAT OPPORTUNITIES AND CHALLENGES DO OUR STAKEHOLDERS PRESENT TO THE FIRM?

In many respects, opportunities and challenges represent opposite sides of the coin when it comes to stakeholders. Essentially, the opportunities are to build good working relationships with the stakeholders. Challenges, on the other hand, usually present themselves in such a way that the firm must handle the stakeholders well or be hurt in some way—financially (short term or long term) or in terms of its public image or reputation in the community. Therefore, it is understandable why our emphasis is on challenges rather than on opportunities posed by stakeholders.

These challenges typically take the form of varying degrees of expectations or demands. In most instances, they arise because stakeholders think or believe that their needs are not being met adequately.

The challenges also arise when stakeholder groups think that any crisis that occurs is the responsibility of the firm or that the firm caused the crisis in some way. Examples of some stakeholder crises include:[19]

- *Coca-Cola.* Coke faced a major crisis when reports came in that their world-famous product was causing illnesses among consumers in Europe. Dozens of consumers who drank the soft drinks became sick. The governments of France, Belgium, Luxembourg, and The Netherlands ordered Coca-Cola products off their shelves as a result of the reports. Coke executives later pinpointed the problem along two points in its bottling system controlled by Coca-Cola Enterprises in Belgium. The crisis occurred at a time when Coke products were already suffering declining sales in some regions. The biggest recall in Coke's history hurt its reputation in European markets.

- *Home Depot.* Under pressure from social activist groups such as Rainforest Action Network and staged "Days of Action" by protestors, the Atlanta-based chain agreed to stop selling products made from old-growth wood. The environmentalists threatened to follow up with newspaper ads, frequent pickets, and civil disobedience if the company did not agree.

If one looks at the business experiences of the past couple of decades, including the crises mentioned here, it is evident that there is a need to think in stakeholder terms to fully understand the potential threats that businesses of all kinds face on a daily basis.

Opportunities and challenges might also be viewed in terms of potential for cooperation and potential for threat. Savage and his colleagues have argued that such assessments of cooperation and threat are necessary so that managers might identify strategies for dealing with stakeholders.[20] In terms of potential for threat, Savage et al. assert that managers need to consider the stakeholder's relative power and its relevance to a particular issue confronting the organization. In terms of potential for cooperation, the firm needs to be sensitive to the possibility of joining forces with other stakeholders for the advantage of all parties involved.

Figure 2–6 presents a list of the factors that Savage and his colleagues claim will increase or decrease a stakeholder's potential for threat or cooperation. By carefully analyzing these factors, managers should be able to better assess such potentials.

Figure 2-6

Factors Affecting Potential for Stakeholder Threat and Cooperation

	Increases or Decreases Stakeholder's Potential for Threat?	Increases or Decreases Stakeholder's Potential for Cooperation?
Stakeholder controls key resources (needed by organization)	Increases	Increases
Stakeholder does not control key resources	Decreases	Either
Stakeholder more powerful than organization	Increases	Either
Stakeholder as powerful as organization	Either	Either
Stakeholder less powerful than organization	Decreases	Increases
Stakeholder likely to take action (supportive of the organization)	Decreases	Increases
Stakeholder likely to take nonsupportive action	Increases	Decreases
Stakeholder unlikely to take any action	Decreases	Decreases
Stakeholder likely to form coalition with other stakeholders	Increases	Either
Stakeholder likely to form coalition with organization	Decreases	Increases
Stakeholder unlikely to form any coalition	Decreases	Decreases

Source: Grant T. Savage, Timothy W. Nix, Carlton J. Whitehead, and John D. Blair, "Strategies for Assessing and Managing Organizational Stakeholders," *Academy of Management Executive* (Vol. V, No. 2, May 1991), 64. Reprinted with permission.

4. WHAT RESPONSIBILITIES DOES THE FIRM HAVE TO ITS STAKEHOLDERS?

Once threats and opportunities of stakeholders have been identified and understood, the next logical question is, "What responsibilities does the firm have in its relationships with all stakeholders?" What economic, legal, ethical, and philanthropic responsibilities does management have to each stakeholder? Because most of the firm's economic responsibilities are principally to itself, the analysis really begins to focus on legal, ethical, and philanthropic questions. The most pressing threats present themselves as legal and ethical questions.

We should stress, however, that the firm itself has an economic stake in the legal and ethical issues it faces. For example, when Johnson & Johnson (J&J) was faced with the Tylenol poisoning incident, it had to decide what legal and ethical actions to take and what actions were in the firm's best economic interests. J&J probably judged that recalling the Tylenol products was not only the ethical action to take but also would ensure its reputation for being concerned about consumers' health and well-being. Figure 2–7 illustrates the stakeholder/responsibility matrix that management faces when assessing the firm's responsibilities to stakeholders. The matrix may be seen as a template that managers might use to systematically think through its array of responsibilities.

Figure 2-7

Stakeholder/Responsibility Matrix

Stakeholders	Types of Responsibilities			
	Economic	Legal	Ethical	Philanthropic
Owners				
Customers				
Employees				
Community				
Public at Large				
Social Activist Groups				
Others				

5. WHAT STRATEGIES OR ACTIONS SHOULD MANAGEMENT TAKE?

Once responsibilities have been assessed, a business must contemplate strategies and actions for dealing with its stakeholders. In almost every decision situation, a multitude of alternative courses of action are available, and management must choose one or several that seem best. MacMillan and Jones suggest that management has before it a number of basic strategies or approaches in dealing with stakeholders. Important questions or decision choices include:

- Do we deal *directly* or *indirectly* with stakeholders?

- Do we take the *offence* or the *defence* in dealing with stakeholders?

- Do we *accommodate, negotiate, manipulate,* or *resist* stakeholder overtures?

- Do we employ a *combination of the above* strategies or pursue a *singular course* of action?[21]

Savage et al. argue that development of specific strategies may be based on a classification of stakeholders according to the classification of the potentials for cooperation and threat. If we use these two dimensions, four stakeholder types and resultant generic strategies emerge.[22] These stakeholder types and corresponding strategies are shown in Figure 2–8.

Figure 2-8

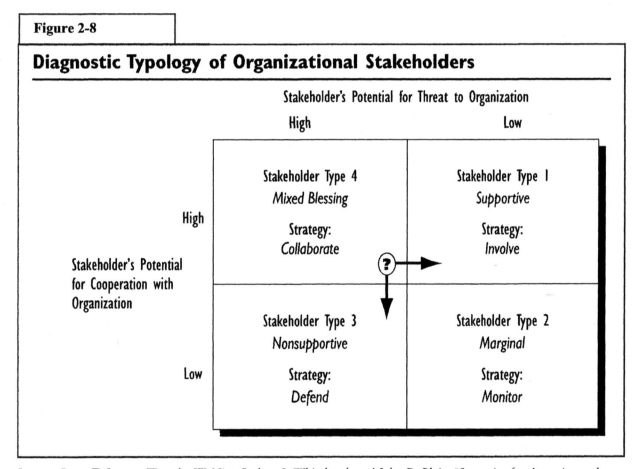

Diagnostic Typology of Organizational Stakeholders

Stakeholder's Potential for Threat to Organization

	High	Low
High — Stakeholder's Potential for Cooperation with Organization	Stakeholder Type 4 *Mixed Blessing* Strategy: *Collaborate*	Stakeholder Type 1 *Supportive* Strategy: *Involve*
Low	Stakeholder Type 3 *Nonsupportive* Strategy: *Defend*	Stakeholder Type 2 *Marginal* Strategy: *Monitor*

Source: Grant T. Savage, Timothy W. Nix, Carlton J. Whitehead, and John D. Blair, "Strategies for Assessing and Managing Organizational Stakeholders," *Academy of Management Executive* (Vol. V, No. 2, May 1991), 64. Reprinted with permission.

Stakeholder Type 1—the supportive stakeholder—is high on potential for cooperation and low on potential for threat. This is the ideal stakeholder. To a well-managed organization, supportive stakeholders might include its board, managers, employees, and customers. Others might be suppliers and service providers. The strategy here is one of involvement. An example of this might be the strategy of involving employee stakeholders through participative management or decentralization of authority.

Stakeholder Type 2—the marginal stakeholder—is low on both potential for threat and potential for cooperation. For large organizations, these stakeholders might include professional associations of employees, consumer interest groups, or shareholders—especially those who are not organized. The strategy here is for the organization to monitor the marginal stakeholder. Monitoring is especially called for to make sure circumstances do not change. Careful monitoring could avert later problems.

Stakeholder Type 3—the nonsupportive stakeholder—is high on potential for threat but low on potential for cooperation. Examples of this group could include competing organizations, unions, federal or other levels of government, and the media. The authors' recommended strategy here is to defend against the nonsupportive stakeholder.

Stakeholder Type 4—the mixed blessing stakeholder—is high on both potential for threat and potential for cooperation. Examples of this group, in a well-managed organization, might include employees who are in short supply, clients, or customers. A mixed blessing stakeholder could become a supportive or a nonsupportive stakeholder. The recommended strategy here is to collaborate with the mixed blessing stakeholder. By maximizing collaboration, the likelihood is enhanced that this stakeholder will remain supportive.

The authors summarize their position regarding these four stakeholder types as follows:[23]

> ... managers should attempt to satisfy minimally the needs of marginal stakeholders and to satisfy maximally the needs of supportive and mixed blessing stakeholders, enhancing the latter's support for the organization.

Effective stakeholder management requires the careful assessment of the five core questions we have posed. To deal successfully with those who assert claims on the organization, managers must understand these core questions at least at a basic level. It is tempting to wish that none of this was necessary. However, such wishing would require management to accept the production or managerial view of the firm, and these views are no longer tenable. Business today cannot turn back the clock to a simpler period. Business has been and will continue to be subjected to careful scrutiny of its actions, practices, policies, and ethics. This is the real world in which management lives, and management must accept it and deal with it. Criticisms of business and calls for better corporate citizenship have been the consequences of the changes in the business/society relationship, and the stakeholder approach to viewing the organization has become one needed response. To do less is to decline to accept the realities of business's plight in the modern world and to fail to see the kinds of adaptations that are essential if businesses are to prosper in the present and in the future.

SUMMARY

A stakeholder is an individual or a group that claims to have one or more stakes in an organization. Stakeholders may affect the organization and, in turn, be affected by the organization's actions, policies, practices, and decisions. The stakeholder approach extends beyond the traditional production and managerial views of the firm and warrants a much broader conception of the parties involved in the organization's functioning and success. Both primary and secondary social and nonsocial stakeholders assume important roles in the eyes of management. A typology of stakeholders suggests that three attributes are especially important: legitimacy, power, and urgency.

Strategic, multifiduciary, and stakeholder synthesis views help us appreciate the perspectives that may be adopted with regard to stakeholders. The stakeholder synthesis perspective is recommended because it highlights the ethical responsibility business has to its stakeholders. The stakeholder model of the firm has three values: descriptive, instrumental, and normative.

Five key questions aid managers in stakeholder management: (1) Who are our stakeholders? (2) What are our stakeholders' stakes? (3) What challenges or opportunities are presented to our firm by our stakeholders? (4) What responsibilities does our firm have to its stakeholders? (5) What strategies or actions should our firm take with respect to our stakeholders? Although the stakeholder management approach is quite complex and time-consuming, it is a way of managing that is in tune with the complex environment that business organizations face today.

KEY TERMS

legitimacy (page 21)

managerial view of the firm (page 22)

production view of the firm (page 22)

stake (page 20)

stakeholder (page 21)

stakeholder view of the firm (page 22)

strategic approach (page 25)

multifiduciary approach (page 26)

stakeholder synthesis approach (page 26)

DISCUSSION QUESTIONS

1. Explain the concepts of stake and stakeholder from your perspective as an individual. What kinds of stakes and stakeholders do you have? Discuss.

2. Differentiate between primary and secondary social and nonsocial stakeholders in a corporate situation.

3. Explain in your own words the differences among the production, managerial, and stakeholder views of the firm.

4. Is the stakeholder corporation a realistic model for business firms? Why or why not?

ENDNOTES

1. Jeanne M. Logsdon, Donna J. Wood, and Lee E. Benson, "Research in Stakeholder Theory, 1997–1998: The Sloan Foundation Minigrant Project" (Toronto: The Clarkson Centre for Business Ethics, 2000).

2. This definition is similar to that of R. Edward Freeman in *Strategic Management: A Stakeholder Approach* (Boston: Pitman, 1984), 25.

3. Mark Starik, "Is the Environment an Organizational Stakeholder? Naturally!" *International Association for Business and Society (IABS) 1993 Proceedings*, 466–471.

4. Freeman, 5.

5. *Ibid.*, 24–25.

6. Wheeler and Sillanpää (1997), 167.

7. *Ibid.*, 168.

8. Ronald K. Mitchell, Bradley R. Agle, and Donna J. Wood, "Toward a Theory of Stakeholder Identification and Salience: Defining the Principle of Who and What Really Counts," *Academy of Management Review* (October 1997), 853–886.

9. Jim Carlton, "How Home Depot and Activists Joined to Cut Logging Abuse," *The Wall Street Journal* (September 26, 2000), A1.

10. Kenneth E. Goodpaster, "Business Ethics and Stakeholder Analysis," *Business Ethics Quarterly* (Vol. 1, No. 1, January 1991), 53–73.

11. *Ibid.*

12. Thomas Donaldson and Lee Preston, "The Stakeholder Theory of the Corporation: Concepts, Evidence, Implications," *Academy of Management Review* (Vol. 20, No. 1, 1995), 65–91.

13. *Ibid.*

14. Similar questions are posed by Ian C. MacMillan and Patricia E. Jones, *Strategy Formulation: Power and Politics* (St. Paul, MN: West, 1986), 66.

15. "Animal Rights Group Aims Ad Attack at McDonald's," *The Wall Street Journal* (August 30, 1999), p. B7.

16. Marcia Yablon, "Happy Hen, Happy Meal: McDonald's Chick Fix," *U.S. News & World Report* (September 4, 2000), 46.

17. *Ibid.*, 46.

18. "News Release: Chicken and Friends Have Bone to Pick with New Burger King CEO." People for the Ethical Treatment of Animals (PETA) Web page: http://www.peta-online.org/news/0301/0301miamibk.html.

19. "Does It Pay to Be Ethical? *Business Ethics* (March/April 1997), 14. See also "Activists Hang Banner at CITIGROUP Headquarters: 'Hey Citi, Not with My Money,'" http://www.ran.org/news/newsitem.php?id=97&area=finance.

20. Grant T. Savage, Timothy W. Nix, Carlton J. Whitehead, and John D. Blair, "Strategies for Assessing and Managing Organizational Stakeholders," *Academy of Management Executive* (Vol. V, No. 2, May 1991), 61–75.

21. MacMillan and Jones, 66-70.

22. Savage, Nix, Whitehead, and Blair, 65.

23. *Ibid.*, 72.

3

STRATEGIC MANAGEMENT IN A STAKEHOLDER CONTEXT

CHAPTER OBJECTIVES

After studying this chapter, you should be able to:

1   Explain the concept of corporate public policy and relate it to strategic management.

2   Articulate the four major strategy levels and explain enterprise-level strategy.

3   Enumerate and briefly describe how a concern for social and ethical issues fits into the strategic management process.

4   Identify and briefly explain the stages in the issues management process.

5   Discuss the challenges of crisis management.

The impact of the stakeholder environment on business organizations is becoming more pronounced each year. It is an understatement to suggest that this multifaceted environment has become tumultuous, and brief reminders of a few actual cases point out the validity of this claim quite dramatically. There are many examples in which social issues have had major impacts on firms at the general management level. Exxon's catastrophic *Valdez* oil spill and the tobacco industry's battles with the government over the dangers of its product are all examples of the impacts of top-level decisions that entail ethical ramifications. More recently, Coca-Cola's disastrous and massive recall of soft drinks in Belgium and France and Bridgestone-Firestone's tire tread separations in a number of countries provide examples of ethical issues that have dramatic implications for top executive decision makers. What kinds of strategies does a business generate to ensure its success and avoid major fiascos? How do organizations respond to, or, entirely avoid, a major crisis?

What started as an awareness of social issues and social responsibility matured into a focus on the management of social responsiveness and performance. Today, the trend reflects a preoccupation with ethics, stakeholders, and corporate citizenship as we navigate the first decade of the new millennium. The term *corporate public policy* is an outgrowth of an earlier term, *corporate social policy*, which had been in general usage for over 20 years. The two concepts have essentially the same meaning, but we will use "corporate public policy" because it is more in keeping with terminology more recently used in business. Much of what takes place under the banner of corporate public policy is also referred to as corporate citizenship by businesses today.

In this chapter, we more closely examine how management has responded and should respond, in a managerial sense, to the kinds of social, ethical, and stakeholder issues developed in this book. We provide a broad overview of how social, ethical, and public issues fit into the general **strategic management processes** of the organization. We introduce the term *corporate public policy* to describe that component part of management decision making that embraces these issues. The overriding goal of this chapter is to focus on planning for the turbulent social/ethical stakeholder environment, and this encompasses the strategic management process.

THE CONCEPT OF CORPORATE PUBLIC POLICY

What is meant by corporate public policy? **Corporate public policy** is a firm's posture, stance, strategy, or position regarding the public, social, and ethical aspects of stakeholders and corporate functioning. Later in the chapter we will discuss how businesses formalize this concern under the rubric of corporate public affairs, or public affairs management. Businesses encounter many situations in their daily operations that involve highly visible public and ethical issues. Some of these issues are subject to intensive public debate for specific periods of time before they become institutionalized. Examples of such issues include sexual harassment, employment equity, product safety, and employee privacy. Other issues are more basic, more enduring, and more philosophical. These issues might include the broad role of business in society, the corporate governance question, and the relative balance of business versus government direction that is best for our society.

The idea behind corporate public policy is that a firm must give specific attention to issues in which basic questions of right, wrong, justice, fairness, or public policy reside. The dynamic stakeholder environment of the past 40 years has necessitated that management apply a policy perspective to these issues. At one time, the social environment was thought to be a relatively constant backdrop against which the real work of business took place. Today these issues are centre stage, and managers at all levels must address them. Corporate public policy is the process by which management addresses these significant concerns.

CORPORATE PUBLIC POLICY AS PART OF STRATEGIC MANAGEMENT

Where does corporate public policy fit into strategic management? First, let us briefly discuss strategic management. **Strategic management** refers to the overall management process that focuses on positioning a firm relative to its environment. A basic way in which the firm relates to its environment is through the products and services it produces and the markets it chooses to address. Strategic management is also thought of as a kind of overall or comprehensive organizational management by the firm's top-level executives. In this sense, it represents the overall executive leadership function in which the sense of direction of the organization is decided upon and implemented.

Top management teams must address many issues as a firm is positioning itself relative to its environment. The more traditional issues involve product/market decisions—the principal decision thrust of most organizations. Other decisions relate to marketing, finance, accounting, information systems, human resources, operations, research and development, competition, and so on. Corporate public policy is that part of the overall strategic management of the organization that focuses specifically on the public, ethical, and stakeholder issues that are embedded in the functioning and decision processes of the firm. Therefore, just as a firm needs to develop policy on human resources, operations, marketing, or finance, it also must develop corporate public policy to proactively address the host of issues we have been discussing and will discuss throughout this book.

FOUR KEY STRATEGY LEVELS

Because organizations are hierarchical, it is not surprising to find that strategic management is hierarchical, too. That is, there are several different levels in the firm at which strategic decisions are made or the strategy process occurs. These levels range from the broadest or highest levels (where missions, visions, goals, decisions, and policies entail higher risks and are characterized by longer time horizons, more subjective values, and greater uncertainty) to the lowest levels (where planning is done for specific functional areas, where time horizons are shorter, where information needs are less complex, and where there is less uncertainty). Four key strategy levels have been recognized and are important to consider: **enterprise-level strategy**, **corporate-level strategy**, **business-level strategy**, and **functional-level strategy**.

THE FOUR STRATEGY LEVELS

The broadest level of strategic management is known as societal-level strategy or enterprise-level strategy, as it has come to be known. **Enterprise-level strategy** is the overarching strategy level that poses the basic questions, "What is the role of the organization in society?" and "What do we stand for?" Enterprise-level strategy, as we will discuss in more detail later, encompasses the development and articulation of corporate public policy. It may be considered the first and most important level at which ethics and strategy are linked. Until fairly recently, corporate-level strategy was thought to be the broadest strategy level. In a limited, traditional sense, this is true, because **corporate-level strategy** addresses what is often posed as the most defining question for a firm, "What business(es) are we in or should we be in?" It is easy to see how **business-level strategy** is a natural follow-on because this strategy level is concerned with the question, "How should we compete in a given business or industry?"

Thus, a company whose products or services take it into many different businesses or industries might need a business-level strategy to define its competitive posture in each of them. A competitive strategy might be based on low cost or a differentiated product. Finally, **functional-level strategy** addresses the question, "How should a firm integrate its various subfunctional activities and how should these activities be related to changes taking place in the various functional areas (finance, marketing, operations)?"[1]

The purpose of identifying the four strategy levels is to clarify that corporate public policy is primarily a part of enterprise-level strategy, which, in turn, is but one level of strategic decision making that occurs in organizations. Figure 3–1 illustrates that enterprise-level strategy is the broadest level and that the other levels are narrower concepts that cascade from it.

Figure 3-1

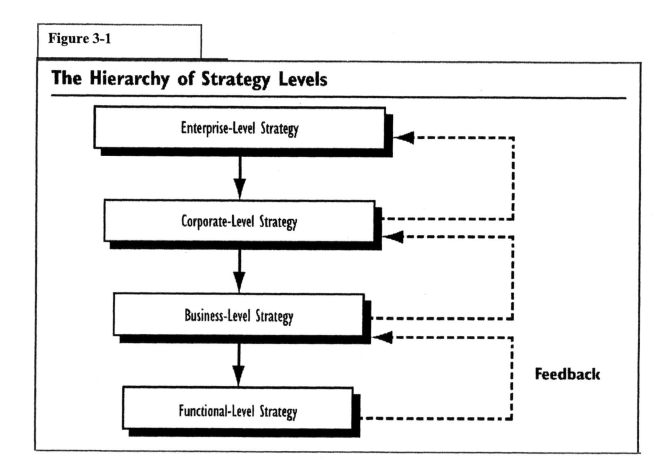

The Hierarchy of Strategy Levels

Enterprise-Level Strategy

Corporate-Level Strategy

Business-Level Strategy

Functional-Level Strategy

Feedback

EMPHASIS ON ENTERPRISE-LEVEL STRATEGY

The terms *enterprise-level strategy* and *societal-level strategy* may be used interchangeably. Many organizations today convey this enterprise or societal strategy in their missions, vision, or values statements. Others embed their enterprise strategies in codes of conduct. Igor Ansoff visualized the enterprise strategy level as one in which the legitimacy of the organization is addressed.[2]

According to Ed Freeman, enterprise-level strategy needs to be thought of in such a way that it more closely aligns "social and ethical concerns" with traditional "business concerns."[3] In setting the direction for a firm, a manager needs to understand the impact of changes in business strategy on the underlying values of the firm and the new stakeholder relations that will emerge and take shape as a result. Freeman proposes that enterprise-level strategy needs to address the overriding question, "What do we stand for?"[4]

Thus, at the enterprise level the task of setting strategic direction involves understanding the role in society of a particular firm as a whole and its relationships to other social institutions. Important questions then become:

- What is the role of our organization in society?

- How is our organization perceived by our stakeholders?

- What principles or values does our organization represent?

- What obligations do we have to society at large?

- What are the implications for our current mix of business and allocation of resources?

Many firms have addressed some of these questions—perhaps only in part, perhaps only in an ad hoc way. The point of enterprise-level strategy, however, is that the firm needs to address these questions intentionally, specifically, and cohesively in such a way that a corporate public policy is articulated.

How have business firms addressed these questions? What are the manifestations of enterprise-level thinking and corporate public policy? The manifestations show up in a variety of ways in different companies—for example, how a firm responds when faced with public crises. Does it respond to its stakeholders in a positive, constructive, and sensitive way or in a negative, defensive, and insensitive way? Corporate actions reveal the presence or absence of soundly developed enterprise-level strategy. Companies also demonstrate the degree of thinking that has gone into public issues by the presence or absence and use or nonuse of codes of ethics, codes of conduct, mission statements, values statements, corporate creeds, vision statements, or other such policy-oriented codes and statements.

One company that has addressed these concerns is the Canadian multinational corporation Nortel Networks. In a document entitled "Living the Values: A Guide to Ethical Business Practices at Nortel Networks," questions posed and then answered include:

- What kind of company are we anyway?

- What does Nortel stand for?

- What do we believe?

Figure 3–2 presents "The Integrity Value: Our Cornerstone," a portion of the larger document produced by Nortel that clearly manifests enterprise-level strategy and corporate public policy.

Figure 3-2

Nortel's Integrity Value

Integrity Means ...

We Strive to Do the Right Thing for Individuals, Organizations and Society in General.
Companies have obligations that extend well beyond the payment of taxes, employment of people, and provision of goods and services. As a global company, we face a special challenge: to uphold consistent corporate standards of ethical business conduct, while respecting the culture and varying business customs of every community and country in which we operate.

Our commitment means:

- **We consider communities in business decisions.**
  The long-term interests of the community influence such business decisions as the selection of sites for new facilities. We encourage the recruitment of qualified local personnel and local purchasing of materials and services where practical. We do not use forced labor or child labor.

- **We get involved.**
  Directly and through our employees, officers, and members of the board of directors, we contribute to the general well-being and improvement of the towns, cities, and regions where we operate. Many of our people are passionate about making a difference, and contribute time, financial resources, and experience to address the needs of their communities. In many locations, Nortel Networks provides support to community programs in such areas as social welfare, health, and education. For many years, we have focused our efforts on math, science, and technology education, with support given to universities, schools, students, and educators in communities across the globe. By sharing financial resources, equipment and expertise, Nortel Networks helps create innovative solutions to community challenges through the thoughtful application of communication technology.

- **We believe in environmental protection and enhancement.**
  Nortel Networks is committed to being environmentally responsible in all its endeavors. We take the initiative to develop innovative solutions to environmental issues before they arise. And we take responsibility for the environmental impacts of our products throughout their lifecycle—from design to final disposition. We work with customers, suppliers, industry associations, educational institutions, public interest groups, and governments throughout the world to promote the development and dissemination of innovative solutions to industry-related environmental impacts.

- **We support the international scientific community.**
  Where knowledge of product and manufacturing technology can be shared without harming our competitive position in the marketplace (or contravening national restrictions on the transfer of technology), we engage in technology cooperation projects with industry, institutions of higher education, and industry associations around the world.

- **We participate appropriately in the political process.**
  Nortel Networks does not use inappropriate measures to influence public issues—nor do we become involved in unethical or unlawful political activity. As a company, we express views on local and national issues that affect our business and our industry. We support and participate in the political process in accordance with applicable laws and regulations.

Other manifestations of enterprise-level strategic thinking in corporations include the extent to which firms have established board or senior management committees. Such committees might include the following: public policy/issues committees, ethics committees, social audit committees, corporate philanthropy committees, and ad hoc committees to address specific public issues. The firm's public affairs function can also indicate enterprise-level thinking. Does the firm have an established public affairs office? To whom does the director of corporate public affairs report? What role does public affairs play in corporate-level decision making? Do public affairs managers play a formal role in the firm's strategic planning?

Another major indicator of enterprise-level strategic thinking is the extent to which the firm attempts to identify social or public issues, analyze them, and integrate them into its strategic management processes. We will now discuss how corporate public policy is integrated into the strategic management process.

THE STRATEGIC MANAGEMENT PROCESS

To understand how corporate public policy is but one part of the larger system of management decision making, it is useful to provide an overview of the major steps that make up the strategic management process. There are several acceptable ways to conceptualize this process, but we will use the six-step process identified by Hofer and Schendel. These six steps are (1) **goal formulation**, (2) **strategy formulation**, (3) **strategy evaluation**, (4) **strategy implementation**, (5) **strategic control**, and (6) **environmental analysis**.[5] Figure 3–3 graphically portrays an expanded view of this process. Note that the environmental analysis component collects information on trends, events, and issues that are occurring in the stakeholder environment and that this information is then fed into the other steps of the process. Note also that, although the tasks or steps are discussed sequentially in this chapter, they are in fact interactive and do not always occur in a neatly ordered pattern or sequence. First, we will discuss the first five steps, and then consider environmental analysis, which links the stakeholder environment with the organizational environment.

Figure 3-3

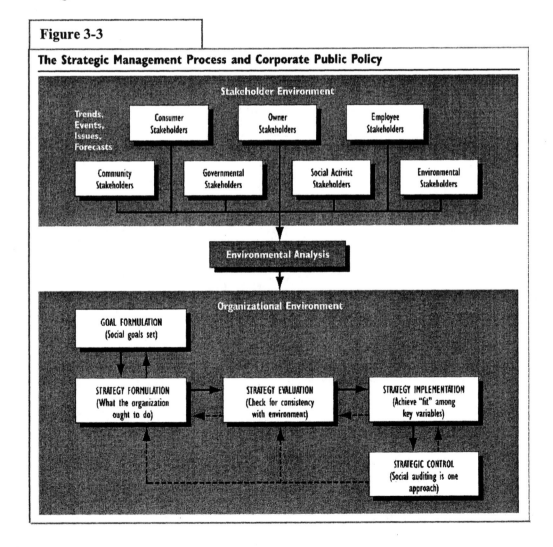

The Strategic Management Process and Corporate Public Policy

1) GOAL FORMULATION

The goal formulation process in an organization is a complex task. It involves both the establishment of goals and the setting of priorities among goals. Often a politically charged process, goal formulation integrates the personal values, perceptions, attitudes, and power of the managers and owners involved in the process. Economic or financial goals typically dominate the goal formulation process. It is being increasingly recognized, however, that goal setting as it pertains to the public, social, and ethical domains of the firm is in dire need of more attention.[6] Typical areas in which public policy goals might be set include employment equity, consumer product safety, occupational safety and health, corporate philanthropy, and environmental protection. Furthermore, it has become clear that economic and social goals are not at odds with each other and that the two can be integrated in such a way that the firm's best interests, as well as the best interests of the stakeholders, are simultaneously served.[7]

2) STRATEGY FORMULATION

Once goals have been established, the strategy formulation process becomes important. It is difficult to neatly factor out the formulation, evaluation, implementation, and control aspects of the process, because in real life they are intimately related and interdependent. For purposes of discussion, however, we will treat them as though they were distinct steps.

As shown in Figure 3–4, Andrews suggests that there are four major components of the strategy formulation decision: (1) identification and appraisal of the firm's *strengths and weaknesses*, (2) identification and appraisal of *opportunities and threats* in the environment, (3) identification and appraisal of *personal values and aspirations of management*, and (4) identification and appraisal of *acknowledged obligations* to society.[8]

Figure 3-4

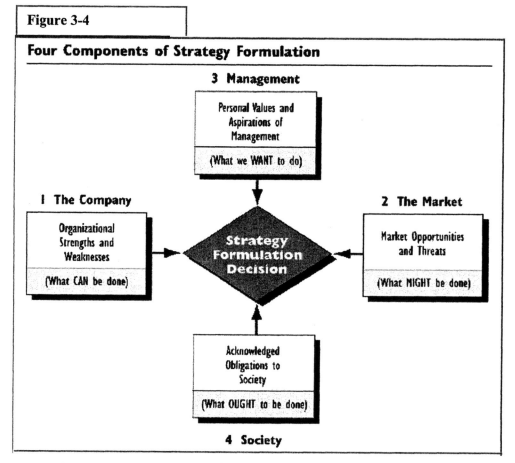

Part of the goal setting and strategy formulation stages is the creation of mission statements or vision statements. Many organizations today articulate their enterprise strategy by way of these statements.

Several writers have argued that the most successful companies in the future will be those who state "a noble purpose." They point to some of the most admired companies today that are striving to be examples of greatness. Examples include Merck & Co., Inc., whose "business is preserving and improving human life"; and British Petroleum, which recently announced a brand-name change to "Beyond Petroleum," signalling its leadership role in moving civilization out of the fossil-fuel era.[9]

3) STRATEGY EVALUATION

In some conceptualizations of the strategic management process, strategy evaluation occurs in conjunction with strategic control, after implementation has taken place. We are treating it as the third step in the strategic management process because, in an ongoing organization, it can also be viewed as an integrative process that takes place in conjunction with goal formulation and strategy formulation. In an ongoing organization that already has a strategy, strategy evaluation entails a continuing assessment of the firm's current goals and strategy relative to proposed goals and strategic alternatives.

Perhaps the most important evaluation criterion in terms of corporate public policy is the strategy's consistency with the environment. The stakeholder environment is complex and dynamic, and a strategy that was once successful may no longer be so. Careful attention to this criterion, then, should be the hallmark of successful public policy.

4) STRATEGY IMPLEMENTATION

No strategy design, however grand, will benefit an organization if it is left on the drawing board. In its simplest form, strategy implementation means putting the plans (goals, missions, strategies) that have been developed and evaluated into effect. It means working the plan with the aim of achieving the desired results. At a more complex level, implementation means that many different organizational processes must be activated and coordinated in such a way that the implementation is successful.

The **McKinsey 7S framework** is useful as a straightforward identification of seven key variables that must be skillfully coordinated in order for successful strategy implementation to occur. These seven variables are **strategy, structure, systems, style, staff, skills, and shared values.**[10]

The 7S framework was originally conceived as a way of broadly thinking about the problems of effective organizing, but it also provides an excellent vehicle for thinking about the elements that must be successfully coordinated in strategy implementation. Of particular note in terms of corporate public policy is the "shared values" element. Although these shared values did not refer to shared ethical or social responsiveness values in the original 7S framework, we can readily see how they should be expanded to embrace more than "corporate culture" as it has most typically been conceived. Much research, for example, has pointed to the significance of an organization's ethical culture.

The key to the successful use of the 7S framework is achieving "fit," or congruence, among all of the elements. Fit is a process, as well as a state, in which there is a dynamic quest that seeks to align an organization with its environment and to arrange internal resources in such a way that the alignment is supported. It is argued that a "minimal fit" is essential for survival in a competitive environment and that a "tight fit" is needed for long-term effectiveness.[11]

5) STRATEGIC CONTROL (VIA SOCIAL AUDITING)

As a management function, strategic control seeks to ensure that the organization stays on track and achieves its goals, missions, and strategies. The first three elements we have discussed so far in this section—goal formulation, strategy formulation, and strategy evaluation—are parts of the overall planning that is essential if firms are to succeed. Planning is not complete without control, however, because control strives to keep management activities in conformance with plans.

Management control subsumes three essential steps: (1) *setting standards* against which performance may be compared, (2) *comparing* actual performance with what was planned (the standard), and (3) *taking corrective action* to bring the two into alignment, if needed.[12] It has been argued that a planning system will not achieve its full potential unless at the same time it monitors and assesses the firm's progress along key strategic dimensions. Furthermore, there is a need to monitor and control the "strategic momentum" by focusing on a particular strategic direction while at the same time coping with environmental turbulence and change.[13]

In the context of corporate social performance or corporate public policy, the idea of a **social audit**, or social performance report, as a technique for providing control has been experimented with for a number of years. Although the term *social audit* has been used to describe a wide variety of activities embracing various forms of social performance reporting, in this discussion we define it as follows:

> The social audit is a systematic attempt to identify, measure, monitor, and evaluate an organization's performance with respect to its social efforts, goals, and programs.

The components of the social audit include identification, measurement, monitoring, and evaluation. The identification function is included as a part of the definition because experience has shown that companies often are not completely aware of all that they are doing in the public, social, or ethics arena. Any serious effort to determine what a company is doing requires the development of measures by which performance can be reported, analyzed, and compared. Monitoring and evaluation stress that the effort is continuous and aimed at achieving certain standards or goals the company may have in mind. Increasingly, communicating the results of corporate social performance reports is also becoming an important issue. There is a desire today for companies to be "transparent" about their social records, and good arguments can be made for companies releasing such information on a regular basis.

6) ENVIRONMENTAL ANALYSIS

The environment of business can be visualized in terms of three levels: (1) the *task environment*, which is that set of customers, suppliers, competitors, and others with which a firm interacts on an almost daily basis; (2) the *competitive or industry environment*, which comprises those firms functioning in the same markets or industry; and (3) the general environment, or *macroenvironment*, which includes everything else "out there" that influences the organization.[14]

Environmental analysis is the linking pin between the organization, which is the managerial setting for the strategic management process, and the stakeholder environment, from which information is gathered. As a basis or resource for information gathering, we should also observe that this environment is composed of trends, events, issues, expectations, and forecasts that may have a bearing on the strategic management process and the development of corporate public policy.

Narayanan and Fahey's conceptualization of the environmental analysis stage in the strategic management process is useful. They suggest that the process consists of four analytical stages:

1. *scanning* the environment to detect warning signals. The **environmental scanning stage** focuses on identification of precursors or indicators of potential environmental changes and issues. The purpose of this stage is to alert management to potentially significant events, issues, developments, or trends before they have fully formed or crystallized.[15]
2. *monitoring* specific environmental trends. Whereas environmental scanning entails an open-ended viewing of the environment to identify early signals, the **environmental monitoring stage** focuses on the tracking of specific trends and events with an eye toward confirming or disconfirming trends or patterns.
3. *forecasting* the future directions of environmental changes. Scanning and monitoring are restricted to the past and the present. Firms also need to obtain information concerning the likely future states of events, trends, or issues.
4. *assessing* current and future environmental changes for their organizational implications.[16] The *assessment stage* of environmental analysis shifts the attention away from gathering and projecting and toward the task of understanding what the information means to management. The central question becomes, "What are the implications of our analysis of the environment for our organization?"[17]

CORPORATE PUBLIC AFFAIRS AND ISSUES MANAGEMENT

A firm engages in strategic management, part of which includes the development of enterprise-level strategy, which poses the question, "What do we stand for?" The answers to this question should help the organization to form a corporate public policy, which is a more specific posture on the public, social, or stakeholder environment or specific issues within this environment. Some firms call this a **public affairs strategy.**

Corporate public affairs and **public affairs management** are umbrella terms used by companies to describe the management processes that focus on the formalization and institutionalization of corporate public policy. The public affairs function is a logical and increasingly prevalent component of the overall strategic management process, which we discussed earlier. Two important planning approaches in corporate public policy are **issues management** and, often, **crisis management**

ISSUES MANAGEMENT

Issues management is a process by which organizations identify issues in the stakeholder environment, analyze and prioritize those issues in terms of their relevance to the organization, plan responses to the issues, and then evaluate and monitor the results. It is helpful to think of issues management in connection with concepts introduced in the preceding chapter, such as the strategic management process, enterprise-level strategy, corporate public policy, and environmental analysis. The process of strategic management and environmental analysis requires an overall way of managerial thinking that includes economic, technological, social, and political issues. Enterprise-level strategy and corporate public policy, on the other hand, focus on public or ethical issues. Issues management, then, devolves from these broader concepts.

ISSUE DEFINITION AND THE ISSUES MANAGEMENT PROCESS

Before describing the issues management process, we should briefly discuss what constitutes an issue and what assumptions we are making about issues management. An **issue** may be thought of as a matter that is in dispute between two or more parties. The dispute typically evokes debate, controversy, or differences of opinion that need to be resolved. At some point, the organization needs to make a decision on the unresolved matter, but such a decision does not mean that the issue is resolved. Once an issue becomes public and subject to public debate and high-profile media exposure, its resolution becomes increasingly difficult. One of the features of issues, particularly those arising in the social or ethical realm, is that they are ongoing and therefore require ongoing responses.

John Mahon has described how complicated the question of issue definition can be in his observation about the multiple viewpoints that come into play when an issue is considered. He has noted that there are multiple stakeholders and motivations in any given management situation. Personal stakes frequently can be important factors but often are ignored or not taken into consideration. For example, some of the participants may be interested in the issue from a deep personal perspective and will not compromise or give up their positions even in the face of concrete evidence that clearly refutes them.[18] Thus, we can see that the resolution of issues in organizations is not easy.

MODEL OF THE ISSUES MANAGEMENT PROCESS

Like the strategic management process that entails a multitude of sequential and interrelated steps or stages, the issues management process has been conceptualized by many different authorities in a variety of ways. Conceptualizations of issues management have been developed by companies, academics, consultants, and associations.

Figure 3–5 presents a model of the issues management process as we will discuss it. It contains planning aspects (identification, analysis, ranking/prioritization of issues, and formulation of responses) and implementation aspects (implementation of responses and evaluation, monitoring, and control of results). Although we will discuss the stages in the issues management process as though they were discrete, we should recognize that in reality they may be interrelated and overlap one another.

Figure 3-5

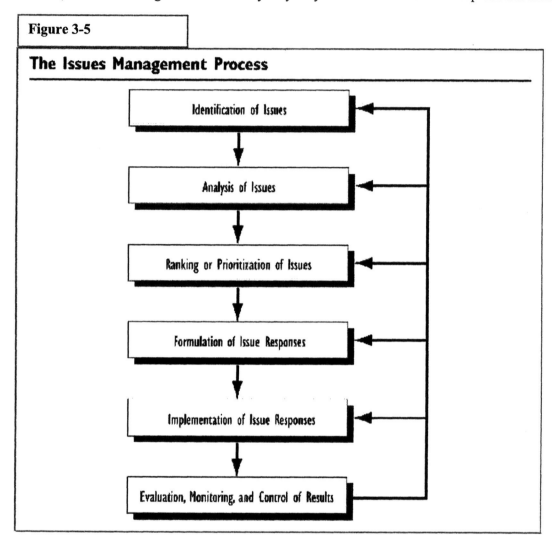

The Issues Management Process

Identification of Issues

Analysis of Issues

Ranking or Prioritization of Issues

Formulation of Issue Responses

Implementation of Issue Responses

Evaluation, Monitoring, and Control of Results

IDENTIFICATION OF ISSUES

Many names have been given to the process of issue identification. At various times, the terms *social forecasting*, *futures research*, *environmental scanning*, and *public issues scanning* have been used. Similarly, many techniques have been employed. All of these approaches/techniques are similar, but each has its own unique characteristics. Common to all of them, however, is the need to scan the environment and to identify emerging issues or trends that might later be determined to have some relevance to or impact on the organization.

Issue identification, in its most rudimentary form, involves the assignment to some individual in the organization the tasks of continuously scanning a variety of publications—newspapers, magazines, specialty publications, the World Wide Web—and developing a comprehensive list of issues. Often this same person, or group, is instructed to review public documents, records of parliamentary hearings, and other such sources of information. One result of this scanning is an internal report or a newsletter that is circulated throughout the organization. The next step in this evolution may be for the company to subscribe to a trend information service or newsletter that is prepared and published by a private individual or consulting firm that specializes in environmental or issue scanning.[19]

Writer and consultant T. Graham Molitor proposed that there are leading forces as predictors of social change:[20]

- Leading events
- Leading authorities/advocates
- Leading literature
- Leading organizations
- Leading political jurisdictions

If these five forces are monitored closely, impending social change can be identified and, in some cases, predicted. Figure 3–5 presents a number of Molitor's forces, as well as examples that might be thought to illustrate his points.

Figure 3-6

Examples of Forces Leading Social Change

Leading Forces	Examples	Public Issue Realm
Events	Three Mile Island/Chernobyl nuclear plant explosions	Nuclear plant safety
	Bhopal explosion	Plant safety
	Earth Day	Environment
	Tylenol poisonings	Product tampering
	Love Canal	Toxic waste—environment
	Firestone Tires	Product safety
	Martha Stewart scandal	Insider trading abuses
	Thomas hearings	Sexual harassment
	Valdez oil spill	Environment
Authorities/Advocates	Ralph Nader	Consumerism
	David Suzuki	Environment
	Rev. Martin Luther King	Civil rights
	Craig Kielburger	Children's rights
Literature	*Silent Spring* (Rachel Carson)	Pesticides—environment
	Unsafe at Any Speed (Ralph Nader)	Automobile safety
	Boom, Bust & Echo (David K. Foot & Daniel Stoffman)	Issues identification
Organizations	Friends of the Earth	Environment
	Free the Children	Children's welfare
	Mothers Against Drunk Driving (MADD)	Highway safety/alcohol abuse

ANALYSIS OF ISSUES

The next two steps (analysis and ranking of issues) are closely related. To analyze an issue means to carefully study, dissect, break down, group, or engage in any specific process that helps you better understand the nature or characteristics of the issue. An analysis requires that you look beyond the obvious manifestations of the issue and strive to learn more of its history, development, current nature, and potential for future relevance to the organization. William King proposed a series of key questions that focus on stakeholder groups in attempting to analyze issues:[21]

- Who (which stakeholders) are affected by the issue?
- Who has an interest in the issue?
- Who is in a position to exert influence on the issue?
- Who has expressed opinions on the issue?
- Who ought to care about the issue?

In addition to these questions, a consulting firm—Human Resources Network—proposed the following key questions to help with issue analysis:[22]

- Who started the ball rolling? (Historical view)
- Who is now involved? (Contemporary view)
- Who will get involved? (Future view)

Answers to these questions place management in a better position to rank or prioritize the issues so that it will have a better sense of the urgency with which the issues need to be addressed.

RANKING OR PRIORITIZATION OF ISSUES

Once issues have been carefully analyzed and are well understood, it is necessary to rank them in some form of a hierarchy of importance or relevance to the organization. We should note that some issues management systems place this step before analysis. This is done especially when it is desired to screen out those issues that are obviously not relevant and deserving of further analysis.

The analysis and ranking stages could be done by an individual, but more often the company has moved up to a next stage of formalization. This next stage involves assignment of the issues management function to a team, often as part of a public affairs department, which begins to specialize in the issues management function. This group of specialists can provide a wide range of issues management activities, depending on the commitment of the company to the process. A number of companies have created issues management units to alert management to emerging trends and controversies and to help mobilize the companies' resources to deal with them. Firms such as Monsanto, and Sears are among those that have used such units. At Monsanto, an issues manager organized a committee of middle managers to help do the work.

FORMULATION AND IMPLEMENTATION OF RESPONSES

For the sake of brevity in our discussion, these two steps in the issues management process are combined here. Formulation in this case refers to the response design process. Based on the analysis conducted, companies can then identify options that might be pursued in dealing with the issues, in making decisions, and in implementing those decisions. Strategy formulation refers not only to the formulation of the actions that the firm intends to take but also to the creation of the overall strategy, or degree of aggressiveness, employed in carrying out those actions. Options might include aggressive pursuit, gradual pursuit, or selective pursuit of goals, plans, processes, or programs.[23] All of these more detailed plans are part of the strategy formulation process.

Once plans for dealing with issues have been formulated, implementation becomes the focus. There are many organizational aspects that need to be addressed in the implementation process. Some of these include the clarity of the plan itself, resources needed to implement the plan, top management support, organizational structure, technical competence, and timing.[24]

EVALUATION, MONITORING, AND CONTROL

These recognizable steps in the issues management process were also treated as steps in the strategic management process. In the present context, they mean that companies should continually evaluate the results of their responses to the issues and ensure that these actions are kept on track. In particular, this stage requires careful monitoring of stakeholders' opinions. A form of stakeholder audit—something derivative of the social audit—might be used. The information that is gathered during this final stage in the issues management process is then fed back to the earlier stages in the process so that changes or adjustments might be made as needed. Evaluation information may be useful at each stage in the process.

We have presented the issues management process as a complete system. In actual practice, companies apply the stages in various degrees of formality or informality as needed or desired. For example, because issues management is more important in some situations than in others, some stages of the process may be truncated to meet the needs of different firms in different industries. In addition, some firms are more committed to issues management than others.

ISSUES MANAGEMENT IS A BRIDGE TO CRISIS MANAGEMENT

Ideally, firms use issues management to assist them in planning for and preventing crises that then require crisis management. Issues management represents careful planning that may head off impending crises. This is because many crises are embedded in issues or erupt from issues that could have been anticipated and studied in carefully designed issues management processes. Issues management can be seen as a form of pre-crisis planning. It is intended to help organizations anticipate and plan for possible crisis eruptions. Not all crises can be planned for, of course, but many can be anticipated through effective issues management programs. It has been suggested by Kate Miller that one of the most effective ways for keeping a crisis plan "living" is issues management.[25] Thus, we can see how issues and crisis management are different, but related.

CRISIS MANAGEMENT

Crisis management as a management term is largely a product of the past two decades. This has been the era of the mega-crisis: Union Carbide's Bhopal disaster, which killed over 2000 people in India; Johnson & Johnson's Tylenol poisonings, which resulted in numerous deaths; and Procter & Gamble's Rely tampon crisis, in which that product was associated with toxic shock syndrome; the terrifying attacks on the World Trade Center in New York, which resulted in the deaths of approximately 3000 people. In Canada, the recent battle with SARS has raised many concerns about the ability of hospitals to deal with such outbreaks and the ability of cities like Toronto to cope with the fallout of this illness. As *The Financial Post* reported:

> Memories of the SARS crisis are already starting to fade in Canada and around the world, but the virulent respiratory disease is still giving some in the airline industry a lot to worry about. Merrill Lynch aerospace analyst Byron Callan issued a report on the industry yesterday, and said that SARS remains the number one threat to the commercial airline industry. The spread of the SARS virus has been halted for now, and researchers are trying to develop treatments for the illness that claimed 44 lives in Ontario alone this year. But information about how the SARS situation has been handled in China has been scarce, and many worry that the illness could erupt again.[26]

Another significant blow to Canada and Canadian business in recent years was Mad Cow Disease. In May 2003 Canada's cattle industry was shaken by the discovery of bovine spongiform encephalopathy (BSE) in a northern Alberta Black Angus breeder cow. Subsequently, over 30 countries closed their borders to Canadian beef at that time. By October 2003, the crisis had cost Canadian exporters alone more than $1 billion in lost revenue. Producers were also hard hit after the price of animals collapsed and the market largely dried up at that time.[27]

Prior to these more recent disasters, those living in Walkerton, Ontario, were also forced to cope with life-and-death situations. Seven people died and 2300 others became severely ill after this small town's water system was besieged with the E. coli bacteria in May of 2000. Upon investigation of the source for this tragedy, it was uncovered that individual incompetence and fraudulent behaviour played a central role. Stan and Frank Koebel, who worked for the Walkerton Public Utilities, failed to maintain the water system in a satisfactory manner, including ensuring adequate levels of chlorination, and they consistently reported false chlorination levels. Ultimately, had the Koebel brothers admitted to their incompetence and deception earlier, the tragedy may have been averted.

Other significant crises have included the following:

- Dow Corning was targeted in a silicone breast implant probe. By 1999 the company had paid out approximately $40 million in damages to Canadian women. In 2001, a number of class action lawsuits were directed at Health Canada for their failure to recall implants from the market, despite having evidence they were harmful.

- Perrier Water's benzene incident led to product recalls.

- Coca-Cola experienced a crisis when its soft drinks were associated with illnesses in Belgium and France.

- Firestone and Ford were implicated in massive tire recalls due to faulty tires causing tread separations and deaths.

It has been said by a number of observers, including Ian Mitroff, author of *Managing Crises Before They Happen*, that the Tylenol poisonings in 1982 was the case that put crisis management "on the map." That is, it was the case that marked the beginning of the new corporate discipline known as crisis management because Johnson & Johnson's voluntary recall of some 31 million bottles of Tylenol was the first important example of an organization assuming responsibility for its products without being forced to do so.[28] Thus, the field of crisis management is just over 20 years old.

It should be apparent from this list of crises that there is a major distinction between issues management, discussed in the preceding section, and crisis management, the subject of this section. Issues typically evolve gradually over a period of time. Issues management is a process of identifying and preparing to respond to potential issues. Crises, on the other hand, occur abruptly. They cannot always be anticipated or forecast. Some crises occur within an issue category considered; many do not. Issues and crisis management are related, however, in that they both are concerned about organizations becoming prepared for uncertainty in the stakeholder environment.

THE NATURE OF CRISES

There are many kinds of crises. Those we have just mentioned have all been associated with major stakeholder groups and have achieved high-visibility status. Hurt or killed customers, hurt employees, injured stockholders, and unfair practices are the concerns of modern crisis management. Not all crises involve such public or ethical issues, but these kinds of crises almost always ensure front-page status. Major companies can be seriously damaged by such episodes, especially if the episodes are poorly handled.

What is a crisis? From a managerial point of view, a line needs to be drawn between a problem and a crisis. Problems, of course, are common in business. A crisis, however, is not as common. A useful way to think about a **crisis** is with a definition set forth by Laurence Barton:

> A crisis is a major, unpredictable event that has potentially negative results. The event and its aftermath may significantly damage an organization and its employees, products, services, financial condition, and reputation.[29]

Another definition set forth by Pearson and Clair is also helpful in understanding the critical aspects of a crisis:

> An organizational crisis is a low-probability, high-impact event that threatens the viability of the organization and is characterized by ambiguity of cause, effect, and means of resolution, as well as by a belief that decisions must be made swiftly.[30]

TYPES OF CRISES

Situations in which the executives surveyed by Fink felt they were vulnerable to crises included industrial accidents, environmental problems, union problems/strikes, product recalls, investor relations, hostile takeovers, proxy fights, rumours/media leaks, government regulatory problems, acts of terrorism, and embezzlement.[31] Other common crises include product tampering, executive kidnapping, work-related homicides, malicious rumours, and natural disasters that destroy corporate offices or information bases.[32] Since September 11, 2001, we have had to add terrorism to this list.

Mitroff and Anagnos (2001) have suggested that crises may be categorized according to the following types of crises:[33]

- *Economic*—labour strikes, market crashes, major declines in earnings
- *Informational*—loss of proprietary information, false information, tampering with computer records
- *Human resource*—loss of key executives, personnel or workplace violence
- *Reputational*—slander, tampering with corporate logos
- *Psychopathic*—product tampering, kidnapping, hostage taking
- *Natural*—earthquakes, fire, tornadoes

Of the major crises that have recently occurred, the majority of the companies reported the following outcomes: The crises escalated in intensity, were subjected to media and government scrutiny, interfered with normal business operations, and damaged the company's bottom line. As a result of the horrific attacks on the World Trade Center, companies have experienced major power shifts among executives as some bosses fumbled with their responsibilities and didn't handle the crisis well. Those bosses who handled the crisis well have garnered more responsibility while others have lost responsibilities.[34]

CRISIS COMMUNICATIONS

An illustration of crisis management without effective communications occurred during the Jack in the Box hamburger disaster of 1993. There was an outbreak of E. coli bacteria in the Pacific Northwest area, resulting in the deaths of four children. Following this crisis, the parent company, San Diego–based Foodmaker, entered a downward spiral after lawsuits by the families of victims enraged the public and franchisees. Foodmaker did most of the right things and did them quickly. The company immediately suspended hamburger sales, recalled suspect meat from its distribution system, increased cooking time for all foods, pledged to pay for all the medical costs related to the disaster, and hired a food safety expert to design a new food-handling system. But, it forgot to do one thing: communicate with the public, including its own employees.[35]

The company's **crisis communications** efforts were inept. It waited a week before accepting any responsibility for the tragedy, preferring to point fingers at its meat supplier and even the Washington state health officials for not explaining the state's new guidelines for cooking hamburgers at higher temperatures. The media pounced on the company. The company was blasted for years even though within the company it was taking the proper steps to correct the problem. The company suffered severe financial losses, and it took at least six years before the company really felt it was on the road to recovery. "The crisis," as it is still called around company headquarters, taught the firm an important lesson. CEO Robert Nugent was quoted as saying in 1999, "Nobody wants to deal with their worst nightmare, but we should have recognized you've got to communicate."[36]

Virtually all crisis management plans call for effective crisis communications. There are a number of different stakeholder groups with whom effective communications are critical, especially the media and those immediately affected by the crisis. Many companies have failed to successfully manage their crises because of inadequate or failed communications with key stakeholder groups.

Mitroff and Anagnos have stressed the importance of "telling the truth" in effective crisis communications. They argue that there are no secrets in today's society and that eventually the truth will get out. Therefore, from a practical point of view, the question is not whether the truth will be revealed but rather when that truth will become public and under what circumstances.[37] From both an ethical and a practical perspective, truth-telling is an important facet of crisis communications.

SUMMARY

Corporate public policy is a firm's posture or stance regarding the public, social, or ethical aspects of stakeholders and corporate functioning. It is a part of strategic management, particularly enterprise-level strategy. Enterprise-level strategy is the broadest, overarching level of strategy, and its focus is on the role of the organization in society. The other strategy levels include the corporate, business, and functional levels.

The strategic management process entails six stages, and a concern for social, ethical, and public issues may be seen at each stage. The stage at which public issues are most addressed for planning purposes is the environmental analysis stage. Vital components of environmental analysis include scanning, monitoring, forecasting, and assessing. In the overall environmental analysis process, social, ethical, and public issues are considered along with economic, political, and technological factors.

Public affairs might be described as the management function that is responsible for monitoring and interpreting a corporation's noncommercial environment and managing its response to that environment. Issues management and crisis management are two key approaches by which companies may plan for the turbulent stakeholder environment. Issues management is a process by which an organization identifies issues in the stakeholder environment, analyzes and prioritizes those issues in terms of their relevance to the organization, plans responses to the issues, and then evaluates and monitors the results. Crisis management, like issues management, is not a panacea for organizations. In spite of well-intended efforts by management, not all crises will be resolved in the company's favour. Nevertheless, being prepared for the inevitable makes sense, especially in today's world of instantaneous global communications and obsessive media coverage. Crisis communications is critical for successful crisis management. When used in tandem, issues and crisis management can help managers fulfill their economic, legal, ethical, and philanthropic responsibilities to stakeholders.

KEY TERMS

business-level strategy (page 39)

corporate-level strategy (page 39)

corporate public affaires (page 47)

corporate public policy (page 38)

crisis (page 53)

crisis communications (page 54)

crisis management (page 47)

enterprise-level strategy (page 39

environmental analysis (pages 43)

environmental scanning stage (page 46)

environmental monitoring stage (page 46)

functional-level strategy (page 39)

goal formulation (page 43)

issue (page 47)

issues management (page 47)

McKinsey 7S framework (page 45)

public affairs management (page 47)

public affairs strategy (page 47)

strategic control (page 43)

strategic management (page 39)

strategic management processes (page 38)

strategy evaluation (page 43)

strategy formulation (page 43)

strategy implementation (page 43)

DISCUSSION QUESTIONS

1. Explain the relationship between corporate public policy and strategic management.

2. Which of the four strategy levels is most concerned with social, ethical, or public issues? Discuss the characteristics of this level.

3. Identify the steps involved in the strategic management process. In which step is a concern for social issues planning most evident? Explain.

4. Which of the major stages in the issues management process do you think is the most important? Why?

ENDNOTES

1. Charles W. Hofer, Edwin A. Murray, Jr., Ram Charan, and Robert A. Pitts, *Strategic Management: A Casebook in Policy and Planning*, 2d ed. (St. Paul, MN: West Publishing Co., 1984), 27–29. Also see Gary Hamel and C. K. Prahalad, *Competing for the Future* (Boston: Harvard Business School Press, 1994).

2. H. Igor Ansoff, "The Changing Shape of the Strategic Problem," Paper presented at a Special Conference on Business Policy and Planning Research: The State of the Art (Pittsburgh, May 1977).

3. R. Edward Freeman, *Strategic Management: A Stakeholder Approach* (Boston: Pitman, 1984), 90.

4. *Ibid.*, 90–91. For further discussion, see Martin B. Meznar, James J. Chrisman, and Archie B. Carroll, "Social Responsibility and Strategic Management: Toward an Enterprise Strategy Classification," *Business & Professional Ethics Journal* (Vol. 10, No. 1, Spring 1991), 47–66. Also see William Q. Judge, Jr., and Hema Krishnan, "An Empirical Examination of the Scope of a Firm's Enterprise Strategy," *Business & Society* (Vol. 33, No. 2, August 1994), 167–190.

5. C. W. Hofer and D. E. Schendel, *Strategy Formulation: Analytical Concepts* (St. Paul: West, 1978), 52–55. Also see J. David Hunger and Thomas L. Wheelen, *Essentials of Strategic Management* (Reading, MA: Addison-Wesley, 2000).

6. Archie B. Carroll, "Setting Operational Goals for Corporate Social Responsibility," *Long Range Planning* (April 1978), 35. Also see Joseph A. Petrick and John F. Quinn, *Management Ethics: Integrity at Work* (Thousand Oaks, CA: Sage Publications, 1997), 129–165.

7. James J. Chrisman and Archie B. Carroll, "Corporate Responsibility: Reconciling Economic and Social Goals," *Sloan Management Review* (Winter 1984), 59–65.

8. Kenneth R. Andrews, *The Concept of Corporate Strategy*, 3d ed. (Homewood, IL: Irwin, 1987), 18–20.

9. Art Kleiner, George Roth, and Nina Kruschwitz, "Should a Company Have a Noble Purpose?" *Across the Board* (January 2001), 18–24.

10. Robert H. Waterman, Jr., Thomas J. Peters, and Julien R. Phillips, "Structure Is Not Organization," *Business Horizons* (June 1980), 14–26.

11. R. Miles and C. Snow, *Environmental Strategy and Organization Structure* (New York: McGraw-Hill, 1978), 1. Also see Hamel and Prahalad, 160–161.

12. Archie B. Carroll, *Business and Society: Managing Corporate Social Performance* (Boston: Little, Brown, 1981), 381.

13. Peter Lorange, Michael F. Scott Morton, and Sumantra Ghoshal, *Strategic Control Systems* (St. Paul, MN: West, 1986), 1, 10. Also see Hunger and Wheelen, 161–162.

14. Liam Fahey and V. K. Narayanan, *Macroenvironmental Analysis for Strategic Management* (St. Paul, MN: West, 1986), 25.

15. V. K. Narayanan and Liam Fahey, "Environmental Analysis for Strategy Formulation," in William R. King and David I. Cleland (eds.) *Strategic Planning and Management Handbook* (New York: Van Nostrand Reinhold, 1987), 156.Also see John D. Stoffels, *Strategic Issues Management: A Comprehensive Guide to Environmental Scanning* (New York: Pergamon Press, 1994).

16. *Ibid.*

17. Narayanan and Fahey, 162. Also see Frank Vanclay and Daniel Bronstein (eds.) *Environmental and Social Impact Assessment* (Brisbane: Chichester, John Wiley, 1995).

18. John Mahon, "Issues Management: The Issue of Definition," *Strategic Planning Management* (November 1986), 81–82. For further discussion on what constitutes an issue, see Steven L. Wartick and John F. Mahon, "Toward a Substantive Definition of the Corporate Issue Construct," *Business & Society* (Vol. 33, No. 3, December 1994), 293–311.

19. Joseph F. Coates, Vary T. Coates, Jennifer Jarratt, and Lisa Heinz, *Issues Management* (Mt. Airy, MD: Lomond Publications, 1986), 32.

20. T. Graham Molitor, "How to Anticipate Public Policy Changes," *SAM Advanced Management Journal* (Vol. 42, No. 3, Summer 1977), 4.

21. King, 259.

22. James K. Brown, *This Business of Issues: Coping with the Company's Environment* (New York: The Conference Board, 1979), 45.

23. I. C. MacMillan and P. E. Jones, "Designing Organizations to Compete," *Journal of Business Strategy* (Vol. 4, No. 4, Spring 1984), 13.

24. Roy Wernham, "Implementation: The Things That Matter," in King and Cleland, 453.

25. Kate Miller, "Issues Management: The Link Between Organization Reality and Public Perception," *Public Relations Quarterly* (Vol. 44, No. 2, Summer 1999), 5–11.

26. Steve Maich, *Financial Post* (October 8, 2003), http://www.nationalpost.com/financialpost/index.html.

27. Canadian Press, "Cattle Ban Not likely to Be Lifted," *Globe & Mail* (October 21, 2003), http://www.globeandmail.ca/.

28. Ian Mitroff, with Gus Anagnos, *Managing Crises Before They Happen: What Every Executive and Manager Needs to Know about Crisis Management* (New York: Amacom, 2001), Chapter 2.

29. Laurence Barton, *Crisis in Organizations: Managing and Communicating in the Heat of Chaos* (Cincinnati: South-Western Publishing Co., 1993), 2.

30. Christine M. Pearson and Judith Clair, "Reframing Crisis Management," *Academy of Management Review* (Vol. 23, No. 1, 1998), 60.

31. *Ibid.*, 68. For further discussion of types of crises, see Ian Mitroff, "Crisis Management and Environmentalism: A Natural Fit," *California Management Review* (Winter 1994), 101–113.

32. Pearson and Clair, 60.

33. Mitroff and Anagnos, 2001, Chapter 3.

34. Fink, 69. Also see Sharon H. Garrison, *The Financial Impact of Corporate Events on Corporate Stakeholders* (New York: Quorem Books, 1990); and Joe Marconi, *Crisis Marketing: When Bad Things Happen to Good Companies* (Chicago: NTC Business Books, 1997). See also, Carol Hymowitz, "Companies Experience Major Power Shifts as Crises Continue," *The Wall Street Journal* (October 9, 2001), B1 and Sue Shellenbarger, "Some Bosses, Fumbling in Crisis, Have Bruised Loyalty of Employees," *The Wall Street Journal* (October 17, 2001), B1.

35. Robert Goff, "Coming Clean," *Forbes* (May 17, 1999), 156–160.

36. *Ibid.*

37. Mitroff and Anagnos, 2001.

4

THE EMPLOYEE STAKEHOLDER

CHAPTER OBJECTIVES

After studying this chapter, you should be able to:

1 Outline the characteristics of the new social contract between employers and employees.

2 Describe and discuss the notion of just cause.

3 Explain the notion of discrimination and the legal bases for protection against discrimination in Canada.

4 Provide two different meanings of discrimination and give examples of how each might be committed.

5 Identify the purpose and functions of employment and pay equity.

The development of employee stakeholder rights has been a direct outgrowth of the kinds of social changes that have brought other societal issues into focus. The history of work has been one of steadily improving conditions for employees. Today's issues are quite unlike the old bread-and-butter concerns of higher pay, shorter hours, more job security, and better working conditions. These expectations still exist, but they have given way to other, more complex workplace trends and issues.

In the new millennium, two major themes or trends seem to be characterizing the modern relationship between employees and their employers. First, we will discuss the dramatic changes that have been occurring in the workplace. Prominent here will be our discussion of a newly evolving social contract between organizations and workers that is quite different from any such contract of the past. This new social contract is being driven by global competition. Second, we will consider a continuation of a trend toward more expansive employee rights. Many of the issues we treat in this chapter have grown out of the general notion that employees have certain workplace rights that ought to be protected. Employment discrimination is clearly an issue with both legal and ethical implications. We will consider the issue of discrimination and the obligations that employers have with regard to ensuring workplace equity for all groups.

THE NEW SOCIAL CONTRACT

Thirty years ago, employees stayed in the same job at the same company for years, and those companies rewarded that loyalty by offering job stability, a decent wage, and good benefits.[1] Today's typical worker has had nine jobs by the age of 30.[2] The work force of today is more mobile, less loyal, and more diverse. Their trust in their employers has eroded over the past 20 years. Recent studies indicate that fewer and fewer employees feel that their employer is committed to them.[3]

Today's employees aren't looking for a promise of lifetime employment. Instead, they are seeking competitive pay and benefits coupled with opportunities for professional growth. They want employers who provide them with opportunities, recognize their accomplishments, and communicate openly and honestly.[4] These work force changes have contributed to a newly emerging social contract between employers and employees. This new **social contract**—or set of reciprocal understandings and expectations regarding each party's role and responsibilities—represents a "revolution" in the workplace.[5] The revolution is basically this: The get-along-to-get-ahead culture of the past has been displaced by a high-risk environment in which North Americans are being asked to give up the employment security they once took for granted for opportunities that are no longer clearly defined or guaranteed.[6]

As *Business Week* appropriately observed, there are "no villains at work, just the inexorable forces of economic and technological change." But if there are no villains, there are certainly victims. Workers have been impacted as companies have had to reorganize, slim down, "re-engineer," and "reinvent" themselves. Downsizing and restructuring have significantly altered pay compensation systems. Pay based on longevity and status has been replaced with rewards based on performance, contributions, and value added.[7]

The new social contract places on employees more responsibility for their own success and prosperity in the employment relationship. Job security, compensation, and advancement depend more on what the employee is contributing to the organization's mission. The notion of "adding value" to the organization has become a crucial factor. In exchange, companies are expected to provide learning opportunities, meaningful work, and honest communication.[8] Figure 4–1 presents some of the characteristics of the old and new social contracts. An outline of the features of the new social contract between employers and employees has been provided by Chilton and Weidenbaum. This outline is presented in Figure 4–2.

Figure 4-1

The Changing Social Contract Between Employers and Employees

Old Social Contract	New Social Contract
Job security, long, stable career and employment relationships	Few tenure arrangements; jobs constantly "at risk"; employment as long as you "add value" to the organization.
Life careers with one employer	Fewer life careers; employer changes common; careers more dynamic
Stable positions/job assignments	Temporary project assignments
Loyalty to employer; identification with employer	Loyalty to self and profession; diminished identification with employer
Paternalism; family-type relationships	Relationships far less warm and familiar; no more parent–child relationships
Employee sense of entitlement	Personal responsibility for one's own career/job future
Stable, rising income	Pay that reflects contributions; pay for "value added"
Job-related skills training	Learning opportunities; employees in charge of their own education and updating
Focus on individual job accomplishments	Focus on team building and projects

Figure 4-2

One View of the New Social Contract Between Employers and Employees

Outline for a New Social Contract

Employer Expectations of Employees	Employee Expectations of Employers
• Performance to the best of one's ability	• "Fair" pay and benefits proportionate to contribution to company success
• Commitment to the objectives of the firm	• Security tied to fortunes of the company and ability to perform
• Participation (suggestions)	• Respect, recognition, and participation
• Willingness to take training to improve	• Opportunities for growth productivity
• Ethical and honest behaviour	• Access to timely information and openness by candid leaders
	• Safe and healthy workplace

Joint Expectations

- Partnering replaces paternalism
- Employees are value-adding resources, not merely costs to be cut
- Employee and employer must focus on customer needs and desires

Source: Kenneth Chilton and Murray Weidenbaum, *A New Social Contract for the American Workplace: From Paternalism to Partnering* (St. Louis: Center for the Study of American Business, Washington University, 1994), 43. Used with permission.

It is challenging to say whether the new social contract will be bad or good. More than anything else, it represents an adaptation to the changing world and changing business circumstances. In some respects, workers may prefer the new model. Whatever turns out to be the case, it is clear that employee stakeholders' expectations of fair treatment will continue to rise. We will continue to see the employee rights movement that has characterized business for decades, but it will grow in the new environment.

THE MEANING OF EMPLOYEE RIGHTS

Before we consider specific employee rights issues, it is useful to discuss briefly what the term **employee rights** means. A lawyer might look at employee rights as claims that may be enforced in a court of law. To many economists as well, rights are only creations of the law. More generally, however, employee rights might refer to legitimate and enforceable claims or privileges obtained by workers through group membership that entitle or protect them in specific ways from the prevailing system of governance. This latter perspective is the meaning that we adopt here. That is, employee rights represent guarantees of fair treatment in the workplace granted by the courts, legislatures or by employers.[9] In this light, employee rights are seen as individuals' legitimate and enforceable claims to some desired treatment, situation, or resource.[10] Richard Edwards has argued that employee or workplace rights serve to provide workers with either (1) desired outcomes or (2) protection from unwanted outcomes.

In Canada, two central employee rights are statutory rights and employer promises or contractual rights. Rights provided by law are called **statutory rights**. These rights include, for example, protection from discrimination on the basis of age, sex, and race under employment equity legislation. Pay equity legislation is aimed at addressing inequities in the compensation between men and women. Occupational health and safety legislation focuses on protecting employee rights for a safe and healthful work environment. These rights will be discussed in more detail in the following two chapters. The right to form and belong to unions and to negotiate for improvements in working conditions are rights provided by labour relations legislation.

Contractual rights are rights that derive from contracts that can be based on oral or written statements. Such contracts are legally binding statements. Formal, written contracts are not typically arranged between employers and full-time employees; rather, the "unwritten employment contract" governs much of this arrangement. An **implied contract** involves an employer's promise of some kind of job security. The legal system tends to judge both explicit and implicit promises of job security as binding.

The importance of employer promises is reflected in the case of *Wallace v. United Grain Growers*. This case involved the claim of an implicit contract or employer promise regarding job security. The claimant (Wallace) left his present employer in order to join a Winnipeg printing firm owned by United Grain Growers with a promise of job security. However, shortly after being hired, Wallace was dismissed by his new employer. The Supreme Court of Canada awarded Wallace damages after finding the employer acted in bad faith. The court based the salary and benefits award on what they felt would constitute a reasonable notice for dismissal (24 months) and the ruling also asserted that it is the responsibility of employers to ensure that the information about a job is accurate. This case and others caution employers to avoid making unsupportable claims of job security.[11]

THE RIGHT NOT TO BE FIRED WITHOUT CAUSE

Although Canadian employees may have reason to view their jobs as an established right, the law does not guarantee permanent or continuous employment. Employers weigh employee rights against the employer's responsibility to provide a safe workplace for all employees, and safe goods and services of high quality to consumers. Consequently, there may be grounds for terminating an individual's employment under the notion of **just cause**.

As lawyer Janice Payne observes, there are many activities that can constitute just cause for dismissal, and each case depends on numerous factors. However, in broad terms, the following are activities that *may* constitute just cause, depending on the specifics of the situation:[12]

1. *Serious misconduct.* Activities that may be included in this category are theft, dishonesty, and assault. On the other hand, absenteeism, lateness, and poor performance might only be considered serious misconduct if there has been some form of progressive discipline.

2. *Habitual neglect of duty or incompetence.* This involves failure to improve over a period of time, even though the job requirements are reasonable, the employee understands them, and has been given some assistance to correct the problems that were brought to the employee's attention.

3. *Conduct incompatible with the employee's responsibilities.* This may include activities that interfere with employment obligations or that compete with the employer's business.

4. *Willful disobedience.* This may involve an employee challenging or disobeying a manager's instructions.

When employers aim to terminate on the basis of just cause, it is their responsibility to prove the existence of just cause "beyond the balance of probabilities." For example, actual misconduct must exist rather than concern for a potential misconduct. If the employer cannot demonstrate the existence of just cause, the employee would be entitled to damages for wrongful dismissal.[13]

It is interesting to note that the there appears to be a rise in employee lawsuits against former employers for "wrongful or unjust dismissal." A recent review of such lawsuits indicated the highest success rate (65 percent) for employers in such lawsuits involved claims of incompatible conduct/conflicts of interest on the part of the employee. In cases involving claims of employee disobedience or insubordination, employers were successful 54 percent the time. Employers had a 40 percent success rate when charges involved employee dishonesty, theft, substance abuse, or abusive behaviour. Employers were least likely to be successful (25 percent) for claims of poor employee performance.[14] Figure 4-3 presents an interesting case.

Figure 4-3

Is Employee Dishonesty Just Cause for Dismissal?

Does a dishonest employee deserve to be fired? That was the question posed in a 2001 case before the Supreme Court of Canada (SCC).

Martin McKinley had worked as Controller, Treasurer & Assistant Secretary for BC Tel company. In 1994, after about 17 years of service, he was fired while he was on sick leave for high blood pressure. Subsequently, he sued BC Tel for unjust dismissal.

At the trial, BC Tel claimed that Mr. McKinley was fired for just cause because he was dishonest about his medical condition and the treatments that were available for it. Specifically, it was alleged that Mr. McKinley did not disclose to BC Tel that he was medically able to resume work and, if necessary, he could have used beta blockers to control his blood pressure.

What was the verdict? The SCC acknowledged that Mr. McKinley may not have provided full disclosure of all significant facts concerning his medical condition to BC Tel. However, the SCC upheld the ruling of the lower court: BC Tel did not have just cause to terminate Mr. McKinley's employment. The British Columbia jury awarded Mr. McKinley 22 months' notice of termination, plus four additional months' notice for bad-faith termination.

So when is dishonesty just cause for dismissal? According to the SCC, just cause for termination exists where dishonesty violates the essential condition of the employment contract, breaches the faith inherent in the work relationship, or is fundamentally or directly inconsistent with the employee's obligations to his or her employer.

Whether or not an act of dishonesty amounts to just cause requires an analysis of the specific circumstances, its level of seriousness, and the degree to which it affected the employment relationship.

Employers can insert a specific penalty clause in a written employment contract. For example, if an employer considers dishonesty in connection with sick leave to warrant termination, it can include a clause in the standard employment contract which states that the employee agrees that if he or she claims sick leave when he or she is not sick, then the employer has just cause to terminate his or her employment without notice.

Source: Doug MacLeod, barrister & solicitor and employment law expert, Fulcrum Search Sciences Inc., http://www.fulcrumsearchscience.com/Client/Articles/JustCauseTerminations.htm.

In addition to unfair dismissal, some employers have been found guilty of engaging in **constructive dismissal**. Constructive dismissal occurs when an employer, without the consent of the employee, changes the fundamental terms of employment in a manner that adversely impacts the employee. Specifically it involves altering the employee's working conditions in a way that reduces compensation, status, or prestige. Such actions result in the employee quitting the job because of the employer's wrongful actions. Claims for constructive dismissal most often result when an employer changes the employee's working conditions, job description and responsibilities (including a demotion), salary and benefits, or location of work (e.g., a transfer to another city).

REASONABLE NOTICE VERSUS JUST CAUSE

When an employer has grounds for dismissal (just cause), the employee can be fired without notice, and the termination can take effect immediately. However, in most cases, employers are required to provide "reasonable notice" to the employee for a termination. Why? Largely because "just cause" exists typically in relatively restricted situations. Recall that dismissals for cause require that an employee has engaged in significant misconduct in some way. As discussed above, it is difficult to claim just cause and, consequently, organizations seeking to dismiss an employee for any variety of reasons will more commonly employ reasonable notice.

The Labour Standards Code, which governs employment relationships within provincial jurisdictions, and the Canada Labour Code, which is applied in the federal jurisdiction, indicate the minimal notice periods and standards that must be provided (in the absence of just cause). There are also common-law standards regarding reasonable notice. Before terminating an employee, an employer should determine what constitutes reasonable notice, given that reasonable notice can depend on a number of factors. For example, length of employment, performance record, age of the employee, and the time the employee will require to become re-employed are among the factors that may need to be taken into account.

While some employers retain the employee during the notice period, more commonly, employers will pay a salary or compensation to the employee instead of providing reasonable notice. Why is this typically done? Employers view this compensation approach or "severance package" as preferable because of the belief that office morale or performance may be adversely affected during the notice period.[15]

PROTECTING EMPLOYEE RIGHTS AND DESIGNATED GROUPS

A significant portion of our valued labour pool is derived from members of **designated groups** whose participation in the workplace contributes to the success of an organization. With regard to past discrimination, there are four groups in Canada that traditionally have not received equitable treatment in employment: women, Aboriginal peoples, visible minorities, and people with disabilities. Figure 4–4 identifies their relative presence in the population and the labour pool. Ironically, while these groups represent 60 percent of the total work force, they have historically been denied fair treatment at work. These designated groups have faced significant obstacles related to their status in the labour force, including high unemployment, occupational segregation, pay inequities, and limited opportunities for career advancement. We have come to expect that organizations will help address the challenges faced by these groups.

Figure 4-4		
Representation of Designated Groups in the Labour Force		
	Representation in the Canadian Population	Representation in the Work Force
Women	50.85%	44.8%
Aboriginal people	3.3	1.6
People with disabilities	12.4	2.3
Members of visible minorities	13.4	11.7

Source: Statistics Canada, http://www.statcan.ca/english/Pgdb/labor20a.htm, table 282-0002.

LEGAL PROTECTION AGAINST DISCRIMINATION

The Department of Justice defines discrimination as occurring "when a law, program or policy—expressly or by effect—creates a distinction between groups of individuals which disadvantages one group based on shared personal characteristics of members of that group in a manner inconsistent with human dignity."[16]

There are a number of legal sources aimed at protecting individuals against discrimination, including the Charter of Rights and Freedoms and the federal Canadian Human Rights Act. In this section we will also consider employment equity legislation.

CANADIAN CHARTER OF RIGHTS AND FREEDOMS

A central principle behind human rights legislation in Canada is to balance individual and collective rights. Consequently, courts have traditionally upheld restrictions to individual rights in order to protect vulnerable groups in society. For example, while individuals have a right to free speech, there are also laws that place limits on this freedom if such speech threatens other groups.

The Constitution Act of 1982, which contains the Canadian Charter of Rights and Freedoms, is the central legislation governing human rights in Canada. It protects the fundamental rights of all Canadians, including:

- Fundamental freedoms that comprise the standard rights of freedom of speech, press, assembly, association, and religion

- Democratic rights

- Mobility rights regarding the right to move freely from province to province for the purposes of residence or employment

- Legal rights, which provide standard procedural rights in criminal proceedings

- Equality rights, which guarantee no discrimination by law on grounds of race, ethnic origin, colour, religion, sex, age, or mental and physical ability

- Language rights[17]

The Charter only applies to activities and institutions controlled by the government and, consequently, it does not protect individual rights against private businesses or individuals. Therefore, rights are additionally protected via other federal and provincial human rights legislation, as discussed below. With the increasing number of cases of alleged human rights violations perpetrated by employers, it is critical that management understand their responsibilities under the legislation, and consider that damages can be awarded for bad faith if there is noncompliance with the law.

THE CANADIAN HUMAN RIGHTS ACT

In 1977, Parliament passed the Canadian Human Rights Act. This act is aimed at ensuring equality of opportunity and freedom from discrimination in the federal jurisdiction. The spirit of the act reflects the view that individuals should not be disadvantaged or discriminated against simply because of their membership in any of the following categories: Race, Colour, National or ethnic origin, Religion, Age, Sex (including pregnancy and childbearing), Marital status, Family status, Physical or mental disability (including dependence on alcohol or drugs), Pardoned criminal conviction, Sexual orientation.

The act protects the rights of Canadians but applies to a specific class of organizations: all federal government departments and agencies; Crown corporations; and other businesses and industries under federal jurisdiction, such as banks, airlines, railway companies, and insurance and communications companies. An organization that doesn't fall into one of these categories will be governed by one or more of the provincial or territorial human rights acts or codes. Therefore, organizations not covered under the federal jurisdiction will be covered under provincial human rights laws. For example, if a company has offices in Nova Scotia and Alberta, then the codes from both of those provinces will apply.

The Canadian Human Rights Act and each of the provincial human rights codes govern human rights issues and provide detailed procedures for investigation and resolution. Provincial laws are similar to federal laws, and the provisions of most provincial codes are largely identical. For example, each provincial jurisdiction or territory has a human rights act or code. In addition, all codes contain a blanket provision that outlaws discrimination based on disability and provisions that specifically relate to discrimination in employment.

THE CANADIAN HUMAN RIGHTS COMMISSION

At the federal level, the Canadian Human Rights Commission (CHRC) is granted authority under the Canadian Human Rights Act to prohibit employment discrimination in federally regulated businesses, including such areas as race, religion, sex, age, national or ethnic origin, physical handicap, and marital status. Each of the provincial human rights codes also enforces fundamental freedoms and governs human rights issues.

The role of the CHRC is to examine allegations of discrimination (addressed by the Canadian Human Rights Act) and to assist in the establishment of greater equality of opportunity. The CHRC describes its mandate as follows:

- To provide effective and timely means for resolving individual complaints.

- To promote knowledge of human rights in Canada and to encourage people to follow principles of equality.

- To help reduce barriers to equality in employment and access to services.[18]

Individuals have a right to file a complaint if they feel they have been the target of discrimination. The complainant is first required to complete a written report describing the discriminatory action. A CHRC representative assesses the facts and determines whether the claim is legitimate. After a complaint has been accepted by the CHRC, an investigator is assigned the task of gathering more facts, and a report is subsequently submitted to the CHRC recommending a finding of either substantiation or nonsubstantiation of the allegation. Once a claim is substantiated, the parties may choose to attempt to settle the matter in the course of the investigation. However, if the parties cannot reach an agreement, a human rights tribunal may be appointed to further investigate. The tribunal has the power to seek damages for the victim, in the event that the accused is found guilty of a discriminatory practice. The enforcement of human rights through commissions can occur at both the federal and provincial levels.

In a recent article in the *Canadian HR Reporter*, Natalie McDonald made the following observation:

> With the growing number of cases alleging human rights violations in the courts, it is critical that all employees at the management level understand the legislation under which they are governed and the duty to comply with the legislation, particularly given the damages which can be awarded for bad faith if there is non-compliance.[19]

EMPLOYMENT DISCRIMINATION

Over time, it has become apparent that two specific kinds of discrimination have been identified. These two kinds can be viewed as (1) direct discrimination or disparate treatment and (2) indirect discrimination, also referred to as adverse effect or disparate impact.

DIRECT DISCRIMINATION OR DISPARATE TREATMENT

Initially, the word *discrimination* meant the use of race, colour, sex, and so on, as a basis for treating people differently or unequally. This direct form of discrimination became known as unequal treatment, or **disparate treatment**. The Department of Justice defines **direct discrimination** as involving "a law, rule or practice which on its face creates harmful differential treatment on the basis of particular group characteristics."[20]

Examples of direct discrimination or disparate treatment might include refusing to consider Aboriginals for a job, paying women less than men for the same work, or supporting any decision rule with a racial or sexual premise or cause.[21] A famous example of direct discrimination involved the U.S.-based Texaco corporation. In 1994, six Texaco employees filed a class-action lawsuit charging racial discrimination in hiring practices and workplace treatment. In 1996, when a tape of Texaco executives surfaced containing racial slurs directed at employees, as well as evidence that the executives were planning to shred incriminating documents and withhold information from the plaintiff's lawyers, they settled the suit for US$115 million.[22] When news of the tape became public, an activist friend called New York State Comptroller Carl McCall, the first African-American to be elected to statewide office in New York, and asked him to join a picket line at the company's headquarters. McCall replied, "When you own 1 million shares of stock, you don't have to picket." McCall oversaw a public pension fund that is one of the largest in the United States and one of the few that is managed by an individual rather than by a committee. He simply called Texaco Chairman Peter Bijur to express his concern. Since then, Bijur has continued to update McCall regularly on the progress of Texaco's diversity plan.[23]

INDIRECT DISCRIMINATION: ADVERSE EFFECT OR DISPARATE IMPACT

As discussed above, disparate treatment may include such direct discrimination as including in a job posting the statement that "no women need apply" or "foreigners not allowed." One method to combat such direct discrimination, was to permit the employer to impose any employment criteria so long as they were imposed on all groups alike.[24] This view of discrimination equated nondiscrimination with colour-blind decision making. In other words, to avoid this kind of discrimination, it meant that all groups or individuals had to be treated equally, without regard for colour, sex, or other characteristics.[25]

However, more subtle forms of discrimination also exist. For example, an individual may believe that he or she has somehow been treated differently, such as failing to be hired for a job simply because of that person's age, race, gender, and so on. Sometimes, the only feasible way to determine if discrimination exists in such cases is to assess the effects at an aggregate or group level. How many women who work in that company have high-level positions? Does the company hire any Aboriginals who have applied for jobs there? If a company appears to be treating members of such groups in certain ways, we can question whether the reasons are legitimate or discriminatory.

The government's intent in prohibiting discrimination was to eliminate practices that contributed to economic inequality. What it found was that, although companies could adhere to the disparate treatment definition of discrimination, this did not eliminate all of the economic inequalities it was intended to address. For example, a company could use two neutral criteria for selection, whereby men and women could be treated the same under the criteria. However, a problem can arise when it becomes apparent that the policy of equal treatment results in unequal consequences for men and women.

According to the Department of Justice, adverse effect discrimination "occurs when the application of an apparently neutral law or policy has a disproportionate and harmful impact on individuals on the basis of particular group characteristics. It is also referred to as 'indirect' discrimination or 'disparate (unequal) impact' discrimination."[26]

Employers may be justified in maintaining such discriminatory policies or practices if they are based on a bona fide occupational qualification (BFOQ) or BFOR (bona fide occupational requirement). Any policy or practice viewed as discriminatory must pass three criteria in order to support the claim that it is a bona fide occupational requirement:[27]

- It must be rationally related to the requirements of job performance.

- It must be created in good faith.

- It must be reasonably necessary in order to accomplish a valid purpose. That is, no other standard could be employed that it could not use a different standard without undue hardship, such as compromising safety.

In other words, a BFOQ or BFOR is permissible if the employer can prove that this "discrimination" is necessary for business operations (e.g., for safety or effectiveness reasons). In other words, disparate treatment and disparate impact are not discrimination if there is a legitimate or justifiable reason (this was not proven in the *Duke Power* case). In Canada, this issue was clearly brought to the public's attention in a Supreme Court decision regarding a female firefighter who lost her job following an employment test.

In 1994, a 33-year-old woman, Tawney Meiorin, was dismissed by her employer, the B.C. Ministry of Forests, because she took 49.4 seconds too long to complete a 2.5-kilometre run, a component of the provincial firefighting test. Because the test standards did not account for the differing physiology of men and women, the test largely excluded women (i.e., 65 to 70 percent of men who took the test passed on their initial attempt, but only 35 percent of female applicants passed on their initial attempt). This was a form of indirect discrimination—the test standards resulted in a disparate impact. Consequently, when the case appeared before the Supreme Court, it was necessary for the employer to prove that the test standards were based on a bona fide occupational qualification (BFOQ) or BFOR (bona fide occupational requirement).

The employer (B.C. Ministry of Forests) proved two of the three requirements necessary to support the claim that the testing was a bona fide occupational requirement (the test was rationally related to the job and it was created in good faith). However, the court deemed that the employer failed to show that the additional difficulty of the standard for women was necessary in order to achieve the standard's purpose—the physical tests for British Columbia forest firefighters were not considered to be bone fide occupational requirements. Consequently, the test's adverse effect on women could not be justified as a BFOQ/BFOR.

In 1999, five years after Meiorin lost her job, the Supreme Court of Canada reinstated the woman's position as a firefighter and ordered the B.C Ministry of Forests to compensate her for lost wages and benefits.[28]

Cases such as this one underscore the obligations of employers to assess whether their workplace rules and standards exclude any individuals—and, if so, the employer must be prepared to justify such exclusion. Prior to this case, a policy or test that had a disparate impact simply required that employers find a way to accommodate the individual facing adverse discrimination. However, subsequent to this case, any discriminatory effect must be scrutinized as to whether or not it is a bona fide occupational requirement. The rationale behind this change is: Why maintain any rule with discriminatory effects if it is not required by the workplace?

SYSTEMIC DISCRIMINATION

The potential for indirect discrimination exists in many organizational policies and processes and, consequently, a lack of scrutiny on the part of the employer may unwittingly contribute to the development of systemic discrimination. According to the Department of Justice, **systemic discrimination** "occurs when problems of discrimination are embedded in institutional policies and practices. Although the institution's policies or practices might apply to everyone, they create a distinction between groups of individuals which disadvantage one group based on shared personal characteristics of members of that group in a manner inconsistent with human dignity."[29]

A recent U.S. lawsuit faced by Coca-Cola Co. underscores the need for vigilance against systemic discrimination. The class-action racial discrimination lawsuit alleged that Coke's pay policies, promotions, and performance evaluations discriminated against black employees. The company was forced to compensate 2000 black employees and former employees (between 1995 and 2000) an average of US$40 000 each. The company also agreed to pay out an estimated US$43.5 million over ten years in order to eliminate pay disparities between white and black employees. An additional US$36 million was to be spent in order to implement an employment equity plan that will ensure that most of the company's personnel policies and practices (i.e., pay, promotions, and performance evaluation) be reviewed by an independent committee.[30]

The threat of systemic discrimination demands that organizations closely examine their employment policies and practices in such areas as job classifications and descriptions, recruitment processes, training and development, performance evaluation systems, promotions, compensation, termination policies, discipline procedures, and facilities (e.g., building design, barrier-free access). The traditional test for assessing whether organizational policies harbour systemic barriers includes the following criteria:

- Is it job-related?

- Is it valid? (i.e., does it have a direct relationship to job performance?)

- Is it consistently applied?

- Does it have a disparate impact? (i.e., does it impact members of certain groups more than those of other groups?)

- Is it a business requirement?

- Does it conform to human rights and employment standards legislation?[31]

The concepts of systemic discrimination and disparate impact are quite significant because they run counter to so many traditional employment practices. There are many examples. The minimum height and weight requirements of some police departments have unequal impact and have been struck down by courts because they tend to disproportionately screen out women and certain ethnic groups.[32]

Systemic discrimination is also reflected in the perpetuation of a homogenous workplace due to recruitment strategies that are unintentionally exclusive. Imagine a company that recruits new employees by posting job vacancies only within the company or by word of mouth among the employees. This recruitment strategy may be deemed to be discriminatory given that it encourages only those candidates similar to those in the current work force to apply, to the exclusion of other groups of potential candidates from the broader labour pool.

Other examples of indirect and systemic discrimination can include the following:

- A workplace environment that does not expressly discourage sexual or racial harassment.

- Job descriptions and job evaluation systems that undervalue the work of positions traditionally held by women.

- Physical access that restricts those who are mobility impaired (e.g., no ramps, heavy doors, narrow passageways).[33]

With at least two different ways in which to commit discrimination, managers have to be extremely careful, because many actions they take could possibly have discriminatory effects. Figure 4–5 summarizes the characteristics of indirect and direct discrimination.

Figure 4-5

Two Kinds of Employment Discrimination

Definition 1 Direct Discrimination	Definition 2 Indirect Discrimination
Disparate treatment	Adverse effect/disparate impact
Unequal treatment	Unequal consequences or results
Decision rules with a racial/sexual premise or cause	Decision rules with racial/sexual consequences or results
Intentional discrimination	Unintentional discrimination
Prejudiced actions	Neutral, colour-blind actions
Different standards for different groups	Same standards, but different consequences for different groups

Sources: James Ledvinka and Vida G. Scarpello, *Federal Regulation of Personnel and Human Resources Management,* 2d ed. (Boston: PWS-Kent, 1991), 48; Department of Justice Canada, 2003.

EMPLOYMENT EQUITY

The Department of Justice Canada defines equity as focusing on "treating people fairly by recognizing that different individuals and groups require different measures to ensure fair and comparable results."[34] In layperson's terms, the notion of equity is equated with fairness and impartiality. **Employment equity** refers to the treatment of employees in a fair and nonbiased manner. This term was developed by Judge Rosalie Silberman Abella, Commissioner of the Royal Commission on Equality in Employment (1984) to reflect a distinct Canadian process for achieving equality in all areas of employment. In addition, the term was intended to distinguish the process from the U.S. notion of "affirmative action," as well as to move beyond the "equal opportunity" measures that were available in Canada at that time.

Under the authority of the Commission, a process was developed to deal with systemic discrimination in the workplace. According to the Commission, "systemic discrimination" was responsible for most of the inequality found in employment. Employment equity was designed as an ongoing planning process used by an employer to accomplish a number of objectives, including:

- Eliminating employment barriers for the four designated groups identified in the Employment Equity Act—women, persons with disabilities, Aboriginal people, and members of visible minorities.

- Redressing past discrimination in employment opportunities and preventing future barriers.

- Improving access for the designated groups and increasing their distribution throughout all occupations and at all levels.

- Fostering a climate of equity in the organization.

- Implementing positive policies and practices to ensure the effects of systemic barriers are eliminated.[35]

Employment equity is an issue for all individuals regardless of their sex, religion, age, national origin, colour, or position in an organization. Consequently, managers must understand the issue of fairness and how personal biases can influence the employee–employer relationship. They should also be aware that both direct discrimination and indirect discrimination are forbidden by employment law.

Employment equity is a desirable aim beyond the ethical and legal reasons. By extending the base of qualified individuals for employment, training, and promotions, it can help organizations improve effectiveness. By ensuring fair treatment across the board, it reduces the risk of losing valued members due to discontent with the work environment. It can also help build employee moral and commitment by sending out a clear message that the company cares about the treatment of its employees. In addition, such treatment can reflect positively on the organization's image and reputation.[36]

THE LEGAL BASIS OF EMPLOYMENT EQUITY ACT

The notion of employment equity is derived from the wording of federal and provincial employment standards legislation, human rights codes, and the Canadian Charter of Rights and Freedoms. Employment equity encompasses a number of activities, including identifying and removing systemic barriers to employment opportunities that adversely affect the four designated groups and implementing special measures to remove any barriers and provide reasonable accommodation.

The Employment Equity Act was passed in 1986. Its purpose includes the following mandate:

> … to achieve equality in the workplace so that no person shall be denied employment opportunities or benefits for reasons unrelated to ability and, in the fulfillment of the goals, to correct the conditions of disadvantage in employment experienced by women, Aboriginal peoples, persons with disabilities, and visible minority people by giving effect to the principle that employment equity means more than treating persons in the same way but also requires special measures and the accommodation of differences."[37]

The second Employment Equity Act received royal assent in 1995 and came into force on October 24, 1996. It built upon the earlier legislation and clarifies and enforces employer obligations as outlined in the act. The act governs private sector employers under federal jurisdiction as well as almost all employees of the federal government.[38] Figure 17–6 offers a brief outline of the history leading up to the development of the Employment Equity Act.

The Employment Equity Act (1995) requires employers and Crown corporations that have 100 employees or more and that are regulated under the Canada Labour Code to implement employment equity and report on their results. Under the act, the employer must:

- Distribute to employees a questionnaire that allows them to indicate whether they belong to one of the four designated groups.

- Identify jobs in which the percentage of members of designated groups is below their relative representation in the labour market.

- Disseminate information on employment equity to employees, and consult with employee representatives.

- Scrutinize the current employment system in order to assess whether any barriers exist which may limit the employment opportunities of members of designated groups.

- Generate an employment equity plan directed at promoting an equitable workplace.

- Endeavour to implement the employment equity plan.

- Monitor, assess, and revise the plan in a timely fashion.

- Complete an annual report on the company's employment equity status and activities.

More and more businesses have begun to recognize that employment equity is "good for business," and Canada continues to strengthen its programs in order to exploit the strength of an increasingly diverse workforce. Among the numerous organizations that focus on employee equity is the Bank of Montreal Group of Companies (BMO). BMO recently received accolades from the Conference Board of Canada for their employment equity and diversity initiatives, including its employee-led diversity action teams, internal employee assistance program, and its recently launched project to help identify workplace barriers among persons with disabilities. Figure 4–6 lists other business who have modelled employment equity practices.

Figure 4-6

Employment Equity Awards

Vision Awards: IBM Canada, Markham, Ontario

- Diversity presentations are given to all new employees with an emphasis on the importance of equity and a discrimination-free workplace. Additional training opportunities are available focusing on cultural differences, misconceptions, and stereotypes.

- In 2003, IBM launched the Canadian Women's Leadership Council, involving the participation of women executives and senior leaders to become active in the development of high-potential women in IBM Canada. This program mirrors the goals of a similar body created in 2002 to increase development of visible minorities.

- For the past five years, IBM Canada's visually impaired employees have mentored students at the Canadian National Institute for the Blind's Summer Camp to acquaint them with technology.

- The company's Black Network Group delivers technology workshops at community-based organizations with donated equipment to assist with program delivery and training. Members of the Aboriginal work force and Native students also participate in company-sponsored workshops and outreach programs.

Certificates of Merit: Shell Canada Limited, Calgary, Alberta

- Shell Canada provides diversity awareness training to all employees, including management, and has implemented an Ombuds office to facilitate fair and equitable resolution of workplace issues.

- In 2001, the company completed a review of their progress related to diversity and implemented various initiatives, including hiring a full-time diversity advisor and developing a diversity gap analysis to help identify priority areas of action.

- The company offers a disability management program to assist ill or injured employees.

- Shell Canada supports the recruitment and retention of Aboriginal employees through participation in Aboriginal community outreach programs, funding of educational initiatives, and offering scholarships through the National Aboriginal Achievement Foundation.

Source: Government of Canada, http://www.sdc.gc.ca/en/lp/lo/lswe/we/programs/epp/index-we.shtml.

PAY EQUITY

Pay equity refers to two different issues—the legislation and the principles behind it. On the one hand, pay equity is entrenched in legislation and can be referred to in its legal sense. Pay equity came into law as the result of an amendment to the Canadian Human Rights Act in 1978 that made it illegal for employers to discriminate against individuals on the basis of job content. There are legislated programs that attempt to achieve equity in pay. The objective of pay equity legislation is to eliminate the historical wage gap that has existed between men and women and to ensure that salary ranges reflect the value of the work performed.

Three kinds of laws offer provisions governing equal pay: human rights legislation, employment standards legislation, and pay equity legislation. Human rights laws and employment standards laws typically target the more blatant kinds of discrimination—the wage gap between men and women who hold the same, or similar, job. Some of these laws apply to both government and private sectors, while in some jurisdictions they apply only to the government sector.

Aside from its legal meaning, the notion of pay equity refers to two important principles: (1) equal pay for equal work and (2) equal pay for work of equal value or comparable worth.[39] That is, pay equity can be approached from two directions: equal pay and comparable worth. Each of these principles has a different implication with regard to how comparisons are made in the wage gaps between men and women.

Equal pay argues that workers doing the same job should receive the same pay, irrespective of gender. All else being equal, men and women should receive the same pay for the same job. Implementing this principle involves a direct comparison of jobs filled by men and women where the job is the same or essentially the same. Violations of the principle of "equal pay for equal work" potentially constitute blatant wage discrimination on the basis of gender.

Although many believe that the gap between men's and women's incomes has closed since the human rights activism of the 1960s, a recent study by the Economic Policy Institute says otherwise. The report shows that, in recent times, women continue to earn only about three-fourths of the income earned by men.[40] This is relatively unchanged from the wage differentials throughout the 1990s.[41] In 2002, women aged 15 and over who had employment income made 79.3 cents for every dollar earned by their male counterparts (however, the gap was smaller for younger women).[42] Some have tried to explain the discrepancy by arguing that these statistics include women who lost both time and experience through extended maternity leave. A recent study from the Economic Policy Institute evaluated this issue by studying highly accomplished new media workers. They found that female Internet workers were earning, on average, $10 000 less per year than comparable male workers. According to Rosemary Batt, a co-author of the study, "Along gender lines, the new economy doesn't seem to be very different from the old economy."[43]

The second principle behind pay equity, equal pay for work of equal value, underscores the need to eliminate wage gaps between men and women that may exist in jobs of a different nature that are considered "male" or "female" jobs. In other words, male and female workers must be paid the same wage rate for jobs of a similar nature even though they may have different titles (e.g., "nurse's aide" and "orderly"). This principle of comparable worth presents a more controversial solution: Workers doing different jobs should receive the same pay if those different jobs have equal inherent worth (i.e., contribute equally to the firm's performance). While pay equity legislation requires that people holding equal positions receive equal compensation, the pay of men and women remains disparate, due largely to the wage effects of labour market segregation, whereby jobs traditionally held by women pay less than their requirements or contributions might indicate. The persistent disparity between men's and women's median incomes has led some legal scholars and women's advocates to recommend comparable worth.[44] Opponents counter that it is not pragmatic to apply comparable worth[45] given that inherent job worth is a subject that is difficult to measure reliably and accurately.[46]

Advocates of comparable worth argue that differences in seniority and education cannot explain the fact that women generally earn only about three-fourths of what men do. They argue that certain jobs are paid less just because they are traditionally held by women. Consider the case of clerical work. Clerical work was a male-dominated occupation for most of the nineteenth century. However, subsequent to the invention of the typewriter, clerical work became routinized, and it no longer provided entry into the organization's internal labour market. Consequently, clerical work was *re-gendered* as female work, given that women could be hired to perform it for less pay, while men were able to obtain higher-paying work with greater opportunities for advancement.[47]

Achieving the directives of pay equity first requires a comparison of the work of female-dominated job classes with the value of work performed by males. Such comparisons require the use of a gender-neutral, unbiased comparison system to evaluate the jobs in an organization.[48] Comparisons are based on the amount and type of skill, effort, and responsibility needed to perform the job as well as on the working conditions. The comparison may include a fair valuation of job characteristics that have traditionally been associated with male and female work. For example, the valuation must be conducted in a manner that is equitable in its valuation of the characteristics of "male" jobs, such as heavy lifting and "dirty" working conditions, in comparison to the characteristics of "female" jobs, such as manual dexterity and caring for others.[49]

Among the most prominent companies embroiled in pay equity disputes in recent years has been Bell Canada. Its battle over pay equity started when seven human rights complaints were filed against Bell Canada between 1990 and 1994, alleging that female employees were being paid lower wages than male employees for performing work of equal value. In addition, a complaint was filed with the Canadian Human Rights Commission in 1995. The Bell workers had claimed that they were owed raises of as much as 20 percent going back to 1992. The demand for salary adjustments was based on a study of the work performed in such positions as telephone operators, clerical staff, and sales associates, most of these employees being women. Their salaries were compared with other job functions that were dominated by men. In 2002, Bell Canada tentatively settled the pay equity dispute with thousands of its largely female staff for $178 million. More than two-thirds of the settlement, $128 million, was set aside as a cash payout. The other $50 million was allocated for pension improvements. The agreement was reached between representatives of Bell Canada and the Canadian Telecommunications Employees' Association (CTEA), the union representing 96 percent of the employees involved in the dispute.[50]

SUMMARY

Employee stakeholders today are more sensitive about employee rights issues for a variety of reasons. Underlying this new concern are changes in the social contract between employers and employees. Central among the growing employee rights issues that are treated in this chapter are the right not to be fired without just cause. Society's concept of what represents fair treatment to employees is also changing.

Organizations need to take a closer look at their policies and practices in order to combat and prevent both direct and indirect discrimination. Employment equity was one of the government's answers to the problem of systemic discrimination. While some controversy has surrounded the question of how far employment equity should go, it seems clear that corporate Canada cannot ignore the needs of an increasingly diverse labour force. Corporations have undertaken employment equity by building their human resource management policies on employment equity principles, and they will likely continue these practices in the future. Sound stakeholder management requires that companies continue to be fair in their employment practices.

KEY TERMS

constructive dismissal (page 64)

contractual rights (page 62)

Canadian Charter of Rights and Freedoms (page 66)

designated groups (page 65)

direct discrimination (page 68)

disparate treatment (page 68)

employment equity (page 71)

employee rights (page 62)

implied contract (page 62)

indirect discrimination (page 68)

just cause (page 63)

pay equity (page 74)

social contract (page 60)

statutory rights (page 62)

systemic discrimination (page 69)

DISCUSSION QUESTIONS

1. Do you think that the criteria for "just cause" are fair and reasonable? Explain.

2. List the major legislation protecting against discrimination and indicate what they prohibit. Which agency is primarily responsible for enforcing these laws?

3. Give two different definitions of discrimination, and provide an example of each.

4. What effect do you think employee equity programs have in the Canadian workplace? Explain your answer.

5. To whom do you think preferential treatment should be given in university admissions? Explain your answer.

ENDNOTES

1. Diane Lewis, "Out in the Field: Workplace Want Loyal Workers? Then Help Them Grow," *Boston Globe* (July 15, 2001), H2.

2. Michelle Conlin, "Job Security, No. Tall Latte, Yes," *Business Week* (April 2, 2001), 62–64.

3. Lewis, H2.

4. Lewis, H2.

5. "Revolution in America's Workplace," *Business Week* (October 17, 1994), 252.

6. *Ibid.*

7. *Ibid.*

8. Hal Lancaster, "A New Social Contract to Benefit Employer and Employee," *The Wall Street Journal* (November 29, 1994), B1.

9. Alfred G. Felio, *Primer on Individual Employee Rights* (Washington, DC: Bureau of National Affairs, 1996).

10. Richard Edwards, *Rights at Work* (Washington, DC: The Brookings Institution, 1993), 25–26.

11. K. Makin, "Insensitive Firings Not Tolerated: Supreme Court Decision Will Aid Future Victims of Wrongful Dismissal, Lawyers Say," *The Globe and Mail* (October 31, 1997), A4; D. Johnston, "Promises, Promises: the Case of Queen versus Cognos," *Law Now* (Vol. 22, No. 3, December 1997/January 1998), 16–18.

12. Janice B. Payne, "Termination for Cause Update: A Briefing for Human Resource Professionals," http://www.nelligan.ca/e/PDF/terminationforcause.pdf 2001.

13. *Ibid.*

14. T. Wagar, "Wrongful Dismissal: Perception vs. Reality," *Human Resources Professional* (Vol. 8, No. 10, 1996).

15. Kathryn A. Raymond, Boyne Clarke Law Practice (2003), http://www.boyneclarke.ns.ca/Law_Letters/fired.html.

16. Department of Justice, http://canada.justice.gc.ca/en/dept/pub/guide/appendix_C.htm.

17. *Ibid.*

18. Canadian Human Rights Commission, http://www.chrc-ccdp.ca/.

19. Natalie C MacDonald, "Training Staff on Human Rights," *Canadian HR Reporter* (Vol. 16, No. 20, November 17, 2003), G5.

20. Department of Justice, http://canada.justice.gc.ca/en/dept/pub/guide/appendix_C.htm.

21. James Ledvinka, *Federal Regulation of Personnel and Human Resource Management* (Boston: Kent 1982), 37. Also see W. N. Outten, R. J. Rabin, and L. R. Lipman, *The Rights of Employees and Union Members* (Carbondale, IL: Southern Illinois University Press, 1994), chapter VIII, 154–156.

22. Roy S. Johnson, "The New Black Power," *Fortune* (August 4, 1997), 47.

23. Eileen P. Gunn, "The Money Men," *Fortune* (August 4, 1997), 75.

24. William F. Glueck and James Ledvinka, "Equal Employment Opportunity Programs," in William F. Glueck, *Personnel: A Diagnostic Approach*, rev. ed. (Dallas, TX: Business Publications, 1978), 304.

25. Ledvinka, 37–38.

26. Department of Justice, http://canada.justice.gc.ca/en/dept/pub/guide/appendix_C.htm.

27. A.P. Aggarwal, *Sex Discrimination: Employment Law and Practices* (Toronto: Butterworths Canada 1994).

28. Lesley Young, "Employers Need to Scrutinize All Job Testing for Human Rights Violations, Supreme Court Rules," *Canadian HR Reporter* (Vol. 12, No. 17, October 4, 1999), 3.

29. Department of Justice, http://canada.justice.gc.ca/en/dept/pub/guide/appendix_C.htm.

30. David Brown, "Employers Ignoring Systemic Discrimination," *Canadian HR Reporter* (Vol. 13, No. 22, December 18, 2000), 1, 3.

31. Employment and Immigration Canada, *Employment Equity: A Guide for Employers*, Cat. No. LM-143-5-91 (May 1991), 9.

32. Christine L. Taylor, "Dimensions of Diversity in Canadian Business: Building a Business Case for Valuing Ethnocultural Diversity," *Conference Board of Canada Report 143-95* (April 1995), 1.

33. Employment and Immigration Canada.

34. Department of Justice, http://canada.justice.gc.ca/en/dept/pub/guide/appendix_C.htm.

35. Human Resources Development Canada, http://info.load-otea.hrdc-drhc.gc.ca/workplace_equity/information/what.shtml.

36. (*Employment Equity: A Guide for Employers*, Employment and Immigration Canada, Cat. No. LM-143-5-91, May 1991: 9).

37. *Ibid.*

38. *Ibid.*

39. Russel J. G. Juriansz, *Equal Pay Legislation and Ontario's New Pay Equity Act* (Toronto: Blake, Cassels & Graydon, 1995), 3–5.

40. Victor D. Infante, "Why Woman Still Earn Less Than Men," *WorkForce* (April 2001), 31.

41. Rochelle Sharpe, "Women Make Strides, But Men Stay Firmly in Top Company Jobs," *The Wall Street Journal* (March 29, 1994), A1.

42. Human Resources Development Canada, *Annual Report, Employment Equity Act, 2001,* Labour Standards and Workplace Equity, Cat. No. LT-020-12-01.

43. Rosemary Batt, Susan Christopherson, Ned Rightor, and Danielle Van Jaarsveld, "Net Working: Work Patterns and Workforce Policies for the New Media Industry," *Economic Policy Institute* (February 2001), 1–57. Quoted in Infante.

44. Laura Pincus and Bill Shaw, "Comparable Worth: An Economic and Ethical Analysis," *Journal of Business Ethics* (April 1998), 455–470.

45. Cathy Trost, "Pay Equity, Born in Public Sector, Emerges as an Issue in Private Firms," *The Wall Street Journal* (July 8, 1985), 15.

46. E. Jane Arnault, Louis Gordon, Douglas H. Jones, and G. Michael Phillips. "An Experimental Study of Job Evaluation and Comparable Worth," *Industrial and Labor Relations Review* (July 2001), 806–815.

47. S. Cohn, *The Process of Occupational Sex-Typing: The Feminization of Clerical Labor In Great Britain* (Philadelphia: Temple University Press, 1985).

48. Susan Riggs, "Comparing Apples and Oranges: Job Evaluations," *Worklife* (Vol., 8, No. 1, 1991), 7–10.

49. "Achieving Pay Equity First Goal, But through Co-operation: Commissioner," *Pay Equity Commission Report* 1, no. 1 (March 1988), 6.

50. *CBC Online,* http://cbc.ca/storyview/CBC/2002/09/04/bell020904.

5

OWNER STAKEHOLDERS AND CORPORATE GOVERNANCE

CHAPTER OBJECTIVES

After studying this chapter, you should be able to:

1   Link the issue of legitimacy to corporate governance.

2   Discuss the components of corporate governance and the challenges to "good governance."

3   Describe the general obstacles to achieving properly functioning boards of directors.

4   Explain the major changes required to improve corporate governance.

5   Identify the principal ways in which shareholder activism can help improve governance.

We seem to have been plagued by massive corporate scandal in recent years. For example, it was WorldCom that grabbed the headlines in 2002, when the U.S. telecommunications giant admitted to perpetrating one of the largest accounting frauds in history. The company had inflated its profits by US$3.8 billion between January 2001 and March 2002. Adelphia Communications Corp. founder John Rigas, also made headlines, along with his two sons, when they were arrested in 2002 and faced charges of improperly taking US$1 billion from the cable-television giant.[1] Tyco, Parmalat, Merrill Lynch, and Global Crossing were among the other high-profile cases of corporate misdeeds and fraudulent acts in recent years. And, of course, among the most prominent corporate scandals in recent memory was Enron. This energy and trading company was once the U.S.'s seventh largest corporation, with 21 000 employees, and the largest marketer of electricity and natural gas. Enron's downward spiral in 2001 began when the company revealed that it falsified accounting records, including keeping hundreds of millions of dollars of losses off the accounting records. In the third quarter of 2001 alone, Enron had incurred a US$600 million loss, and its bankruptcy (declared on December 2, 2001) was among the largest in U.S. corporate history. In addition to the massive lay-offs, employees lost much of their retirement money since their pension accounts were built around Enron stock—stock that once sold for US$85 a share became worthless.

Why have so many organizations crashed and burned over such a short period of time? Where are our corporate leaders? Indeed, corporate leadership or governance is, in many ways, at the heart of much of the turmoil that we have witnessed in recent years. Like their U.S. counterparts, many Canadian corporate scandals, including Hollinger Inc., Bre-X Minerals Ltd., YBM Magnex International, Livent Inc., and Cinar Corporation "violated the basic tenets of good governance by staffing their boards with insiders, rubber-stamping rich compensation packages and interest-free loans for executives and failing to disclose company financial dealings to investors."[2]

News of the latest unfolding debacles seems to only confirm the lack of credibility of the governance of many businesses. These scandals have caused shareholder groups to become increasingly critical of how management groups and boards of directors run their firms. There is outrage over management's lack of accountability, ineffective and complacent boards, excessive managerial compensation, and a general lack of focus on the importance of shareholders relative to management.

In this chapter, we will explore corporate governance and the ways in which it has evolved. First, we will examine the concept of legitimacy and the role that corporate governance plays in establishing the legitimacy of the firm. We will explore how good corporate governance can mitigate the problems created by the separation of ownership and control and examine some of the specific challenges facing board members today.

THE ISSUE OF CORPORATE GOVERNANCE

Talcott Parsons's argued that "organizations are legitimate to the extent that their activities are congruent with the goals and values of the social system within which they function."[3] From this definition, we may see legitimacy as a condition that prevails when there is a congruence between the organization's activities and society's expectations. Thus, whereas legitimacy is a condition, **legitimation** is a dynamic process by which business seeks to perpetuate its acceptance. The dynamic process aspect should be emphasized, because society's norms and values change, and business must change if its legitimacy is to continue.

The issue of corporate governance is a direct outgrowth of the question of legitimacy. For business to be legitimate and to maintain its legitimacy in the eyes of the public, its governance must correspond to the will of the people.

Corporate governance refers to the method by which a firm is being governed, directed, administered, or controlled and to the goals for which it is being governed. Corporate governance is concerned with the relative roles, rights, and accountability of such stakeholder groups as owners, boards of directors, managers, employees, and others who assert to be stakeholders.

COMPONENTS OF CORPORATE GOVERNANCE

To appreciate fully the legitimacy and corporate governance issues, it is important that we understand the major groups that make up the corporate form of business organization, because it is only by so doing that we can appreciate how the system has failed to work according to its intended design.

ROLES OF FOUR MAJOR GROUPS

The four major groups we need to mention in setting the stage are the shareholders (owners/stakeholders), the board of directors, the managers, and the employees. Overarching these groups is the legal **charter**, giving the corporation the right to exist and stipulating the basic terms of its existence. Figure 5–1 presents these four groups, along with the charter, in a hierarchy of corporate governance authority.

Figure 5-1

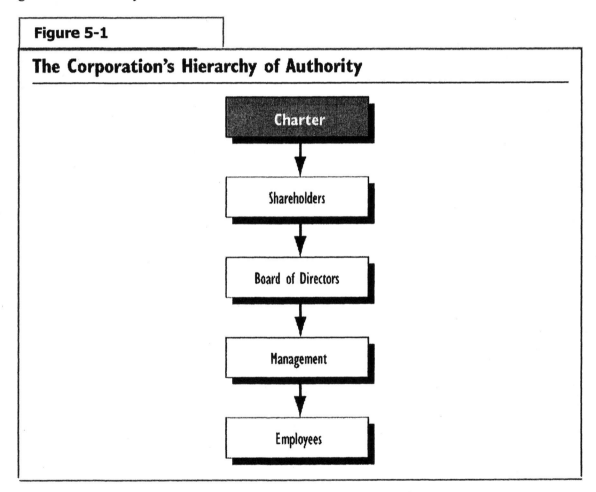

The Corporation's Hierarchy of Authority

Charter
↓
Shareholders
↓
Board of Directors
↓
Management
↓
Employees

Under corporate law, **shareholders** are the owners of a corporation. As owners, they should have ultimate control over the corporation. This control is manifested primarily in the right to select the board of directors of the company. Generally, the degree of each shareholder's right is determined by the number of shares of stock owned. The individual who owns 100 shares of Apple Computer, for example, has 100 "votes" when electing the board of directors. By contrast, the large public pension fund that owns 10 million shares has 10 million "votes."

Because large organizations may have hundreds of thousands of shareholders, they elect a smaller group, known as the **board of directors**, to govern and oversee the management of the business. The board is responsible for ascertaining that the manager puts the interests of the owners (i.e., shareholders) first. The third major group in the authority hierarchy is **management**—the group of individuals hired by the board to run the company and manage it on a daily basis. Along with the board, top management establishes overall policy. Middle- and lower-level managers carry out this policy and conduct the daily supervision of the operative employees. **Employees** are those hired by the company to perform the actual operational work. Managers are employees, too, but in this discussion we use the term *employees* to refer to nonmanagerial employees.

SEPARATION OF OWNERSHIP FROM CONTROL

The social and ethical issues that have evolved in recent years focus on the *intended* versus *actual* roles, rights, responsibilities, and accountability of these four major groups. The major condition embedded in the structure of modern corporations that has contributed to the corporate governance problem has been the **separation of ownership from control**. In the precorporate period, owners were typically the managers themselves. Thus, the system worked the way it was intended; the owners also controlled the business. Even when firms grew larger and managers were hired, the owners often were on the scene to hold the management group accountable. For example, if a company got in trouble, the Carnegies or Mellons or Morgans were always there to fire the president.[4]

As the public corporation grew and stock ownership became widely dispersed, a separation of ownership from control became the prevalent condition. Figure 5–2 illustrates the precorporate and corporate periods. The dispersion of ownership into hundreds of thousands or millions of shares meant that essentially no one or no one group owned enough shares to exercise control. This being the case, the most effective control that owners could exercise was the election of the board of directors to serve as their representative and watch over management.

Figure 5-2

Precorporate Versus Corporate Ownership and Control

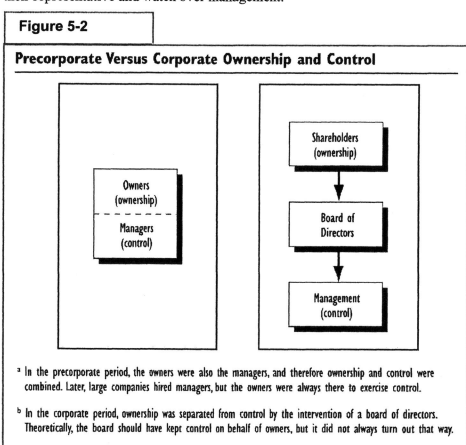

a In the precorporate period, the owners were also the managers, and therefore ownership and control were combined. Later, large companies hired managers, but the owners were always there to exercise control.

b In the corporate period, ownership was separated from control by the intervention of a board of directors. Theoretically, the board should have kept control on behalf of owners, but it did not always turn out that way.

The problem with this evolution was that authority, power, and control rested with the group that had the most concentrated interest at stake—management. The corporation did not function according to its designed plan with effective authority, power, and control flowing downward from the owners. The shareholders were owners in a technical sense, but most of them perceived themselves as investors rather than owners. If you owned 100 shares of Walt Disney Co. and there were 10 million shares outstanding, you likely would see yourself as an investor rather than an owner. With just a telephone call issuing a sell order to your stockbroker, your "ownership" stake could be gone. Furthermore, with stock ownership so dispersed, no conscious, intended supervision of corporate boards was possible.

The other factors that added to management's power were the corporate laws and traditions that gave the management group control over the **proxy process**—the method by which the shareholders elected boards of directors. Over time, it was not difficult for management groups to create boards of directors of like-minded executives who would simply collect their fees and defer to management on whatever it wanted. The result of this process was that power, authority, and control began to flow upward from management rather than downward from the shareholders (owners). **Agency problems** developed when the interests of the shareholders were not aligned with the interests of the manager, and the manager (who is simply a hired *agent* with the responsibility of representing the owner's best interest) began to pursue self-interest instead.

THE ROLE OF THE BOARD OF DIRECTORS

All democratic societies endeavour to develop legal frameworks for safeguarding the operations of corporations. Legal statutes require that boards be appointed by the owners of corporations to hold corporations accountable. Boards are intended to connect owners' interests with the operation of the corporation, and consequently should provide for corporate legitimacy, accountability, and responsible ownership.[5] As indicated earlier, a potential governance problem is built into the corporate system because of the separation of ownership from control. It is equally clear that the board of directors is intended to oversee management on behalf of the shareholders. However, this is where the system has broken down. For corporate governance to function as it was originally intended, the board of directors must be an effective, potent body carrying out its roles and responsibilities in ascertaining that management pursue the shareholders' best interests.

Are boards doing what they are supposed to be doing? Many observers suggest that boards have been largely irrelevant to the operations of many organizations. In an article for *Corporate Knights*, Caroline Oliver made the following comments:

> Given that boards are so essential to the operation of corporations within a citizen-democracy and essential to the operation of owner-democracy within a corporation, how do they come to be so irrelevant in practice? Why do boards only cross our screens when there is a crisis—is democracy merely an insurance policy for when things go awry or is it a permanent commitment to making all human endeavors work? I believe that a large part of the reason why boards are considered irrelevant is not that this democracy does not matter but that their job, as currently constructed, is impossible. Boards may sound important in theory but if in practice they can't deliver it is not surprising that they are ignored.[6]

Enron's demise was closely linked not just to management but also to its board of directors. The agency problem is traditionally viewed as a consequence of the separation of the management of the company from the owners of the company. That is, top managers cannot be trusted to necessarily act in the best interest of the owners—the shareholders. Boards of directors were initially viewed as offering an answer to the agency problem because they have a legal responsibility to protect and serve the shareholders. However, the case of such scandals as Enron illustrates that boards may also have incentives not to act in the best interest of shareholders.[7] Enron and the other corporate wrongdoers that followed all share one common characteristic—they represent business failures that were a consequence of failures in corporate governance.

Board deficiencies have been painfully evident in many other recent corporate scandals. In 2002, the U.S. Security and Exchange Commission (SEC) filed a civil suit against Xerox for misstating four years' worth of profits, resulting in an overstatement of close to US$3 billion. In the settlement of the lawsuit, Xerox agreed to pay a US$10 million fine and restate four years' worth of financial statements. *Business Week* characterized Xerox as possessing a board that was "asleep at the wheel" with a "host of governance problems."[8] In the case of Xerox, the board was flawed in such ways as having too many members with ties to the firm, having board members who sat on too many other boards, and having directors who owned little equity in the firm.[9] Many of the firms recently embroiled in legal battles share much in common with these board characteristics.

A recent KPMG survey of 116 board directors in 75 large Canadian companies found that almost half of these directors believed that they may be sitting on a board that could likely fall prey to financial manipulation and corporate misconduct in the near future. These findings were viewed as a "stunning admission about the state of corporate governance in Canada and one that will do very little to boost investor confidence," according to J. Richard Finlay, chairman of the Centre for Corporate and Public Governance. Interestingly, only 28 percent of the respondents viewed the board of directors as ultimately responsible for ensuring against financial manipulation and fraud. In addition, 72 percent of the respondents indicated that they largely rely on the company's external auditor to inform them of attempts at manipulation. Ironically, representatives of major auditing firms suggest that this is a misguided belief—external auditors cannot compensate for a lack of internal controls that would bring to light any financial wrongdoing, since external auditors don't look for fraud, and they have signed agreements that defer those responsibilities to the company's management or directors.[10]

THE NEED FOR BOARD INDEPENDENCE

Board independence from management is a crucial aspect of good governance. It is here that the difference between **inside directors** and **outside directors** becomes most pronounced. Outside directors are independent from the firm and its top managers. In contrast, inside directors have some sort of ties to the firm. Sometimes they are top managers in the firm; other times, insiders are family members or others with close ties to the CEO. To varying degrees, each of these parties is "beholden" to the CEO and, therefore, might be hesitant to speak out when necessary. As Professor Bujaki of the University of Ottawa comments:

> Boards of directors need to adhere to, or exceed, principles of good governance, and need to represent the interests of all shareholders. To do this effectively, boards need to be able to function independently from management and be sufficiently well-versed in accounting and finance to be able to effectively challenge management's accounting and reporting practices.[11]

The importance of board independence was starkly addressed in the recent scandal involving Canadian media baron Conrad Black. In 2003 Conrad Black was forced to step down as chief executive of Hollinger International, the newspaper publisher. The resignation followed accusations that he and other senior Hollinger executives and parent company Hollinger Inc. received millions in unauthorized payments. Allegedly, $32.15 million in payments were made that were not authorized by either the audit committee or the full board of directors of Hollinger. According to many observers, a salient feature of this case was the complicity of the company's board of directors in all this activity and its lack of independence from the CEO.[12]

Lack of board independence also played a central role in the downfall of Parmalat Finanziaria, the Italian dairy and food giant. This company filed for bankruptcy protection in Italy on December 27, 2003, following discovery that huge assets, estimated from US$8–$12 billion were unaccounted for. The alleged financial fraud at Parmalat spans more than a decade. Founder, chairman, and chief executive Calisto Tanzi was fired from the company and board and placed under arrest in 2003. Interestingly, at the time the scandal broke, Parmalat had a particularly poor rating on Institutional Shareholder Service's Global Corporate Governance Quotient, which measures corporations' governance practices against a set of 61 criteria. Parmalat ranked at the bottom of all 69 Italian companies that were rated. Why did Parmalat receive such poor corporate governance scores? As Michael Gray observed, Parmalat shared many of the same weaknesses in corporate governance structure and practices as those found in other family-controlled companies. However, the combination of shortcomings across numerous areas drove Parmalat's poor rating, including the following deficiencies:

- *Lack of board independence.* The board was composed of nine insiders, one affiliated outsider, and just three independent directors. The company was family-owned and went public in 1990.

- *Deficiencies in key board committees.* Insiders sat on each key board committee. Members of the audit and remuneration committee also served on the executive committee with founder and boss Tanzi. The executive committee, which consists of company executives, proposes actions for board approval and then implements them.

- *Deficiencies in disclosure.* There was a lack of timely disclosure of executive and director compensation and directors' stock ownership.[13]

Courtney Brown, an experienced director who served on many boards, said that he never saw a subordinate officer serving on a board dissent from the position taken by the CEO.[14] Insiders might also be professionals such as lawyers under contract to the firm or bankers whose bank does business with the firm: This can create conflict-of-interest situations.[15] For example, a commercial banker/director may expect the company on whose board she or he is serving to restrict itself to using the services of her or his own firm and be willing to support the CEO in return for the business provided.

Another problem is **managerial control** of the board processes. CEOs often can control board perks such as director compensation and committee assignments. Board members who rock the boat may find they are left out in the cold. As one corporate board member told *Fortune*, under conditions of anonymity, "This stuff is wrong.... What people understand they have to do is go along with management, because if they don't they won't be part of the club.... What it comes down to is that directors aren't really independent. CEOs don't want independent directors.[16] Shortly following the announcements of a workers' severance-pay agreement, it was disclosed that Enron had paid more than US$800 million in the previous year to 152 executives and senior managers.

Unfortunately, a recent glimpse into the composition of many Canadian companies presents a disturbing picture of board independence. A recent study, conducted by *The Globe and Mail*'s *Report on Business*, assessed the quality of boards and the governance practices of 270 companies that comprised Canada's benchmark Standard and Poor's/Toronto Exchange Index. The results indicated that many of Canada's largest corporations did not score well with regard to board member independence.

In the study, boards considered to be "independent" typically would separate the roles of the chairman and CEO, and the board's audit, compensation, and nominating committees would have complete autonomy from management. The study's standards defined as "related" any directors who are immediate family members of management, who provide professional services to the company (typically lawyers, accountants, bankers, and consultants), who are former executives of the company, or who are executives of a parent company. The results indicated that 29 percent of companies scored lower than 10 out of 26 possible marks for independence of boards and key committees, meaning they lack most of the features of independent boards.[17]

Based on data from 2002, the results exposed a number of inconsistencies in terms of the objective of board member independence. For example, though grocery store chain Sobeys Inc. claimed its board is composed of a majority of independent directors, "the Sobeys board of directors includes five people with the surname 'Sobey,' plus two lawyers whose firm acts as the company's primary external legal counsel, as well as the head of a frozen food company that sells to Sobeys, and a partner in a consulting firm that also does work for Sobeys.... [while] Barrick Gold Corp., for example, admits that it does not have an independent board, noting that it only has five unrelated directors out of 13."[18]

There are many additional challenges to achieving board independence. For example, another question raised in the post-Enron environment is the issue of share ownership among board members. Is it better or worse for board members to own shares of a company? While one popular view is that board members should own shares if they are to represent the shareholders, the implication of the Enron-type debacles is that when board members own shares, there may also be a disincentive to fully scrutinize corporate behaviour for fear that such scrutiny and criticism could reduce share values.[19] Figure 5–3 lists some of the best and worst boards according to a recent *Business Week* survey.

Figure 5-3

Business Week's Winners and Losers: The Best and Worst Boards

The Best Boards	The Worst Boards
3M With just one insider on its nine-member board, the company gets high marks for independence. Outside directors include the CEOs of Lockheed-Martin, Allstate, and Amgen. Audit-committee chairman is the former CFO at Sears. No directors have business ties to the company.	**Apple** Founder Steve Jobs owns just two shares in the company. Recently departed director Larry Ellison had none and had missed more than 25 percent of meetings in the past five years. The CEO of Micro Warehouse, which accounted for nearly 2.9 percent of Apple's net sales in 2001, sits on the compensation committee. Since 2000, the board has awarded Jobs 27.5 million stock options and a US$90 million jet. There is an interlocking directorship—with Gap CEO Mickey Drexler and Jobs sitting on each other's boards.
General Electric This talent-packed board, with an unrivalled record of creating shareholder value, remains a favourite with governance experts, although there have been recent revelations of lavish retirement perks for former CEO Jack Welch. The company is improving board independence; it recently added Ralph Larsen, former CEO of Johnson & Johnson and a long-time champion of good governance.	**Gap** Self-dealing includes contracts with the chairman's brother to build and remodel stores and a consulting deal with the chairman's wife. Slow to replace outgoing CEO Mickey Drexler as performance declined. Interlocking directorship with Drexler sitting on the Apple board, while Apple's Steve Jobs sits on Gap's. Two other directors sit on the Charles Schwab board, while Chuck Schwab sits on Gap's.
Home Depot With the departure of co-founder Bernard Marcus, the 12-member board now has only two insiders. Independent directors meet regularly without management. Directors are required to visit 20 stores a year.	**Tyson Foods** Out of 15 board members, 10 have ties to the company, including seven who have extensive business dealings. CEO John Tyson got a US$2.1 million bonus for negotiating the acquisition of meatpacker IBP—which Tyson Foods tried unsuccessfully to back out of—in a year when net income fell 42 percent.
Intel One of the few boards that has a lead director. No insiders sit on the audit, compensation, or nominating committees. The board conducts an annual self-evaluation. Directors have big stakes in the company.	**Xerox** The bungled succession of Paul Allaire, accusations of funny accounting, billions in shareholder wealth up in smoke, and a decades-long failure to keep up with changing technology add up to an ineffectual board. With departures of Allaire and CFO Barry Romeril, the board is far more independent. But too many directors sit on too many boards. Director Vernon Jordan's law firm provides legal services. Two audit committee members had attendance problems in 2001.
Pfizer The board was second only to GE in overall approval by governance experts. Independent directors meet without the CEO. No Pfizer executives sit on the audit, nominating, or compensation committees. Stock transactions for directors and executives are posted on the company Web site.	

Source: "The Best and Worst Boards," *Business Week* (cover story, October 7, 2002), http://www.businessweek.com/magazine/content/02_40/b3802001.htm.

IMPROVING CORPORATE GOVERNANCE

In light of the long string of corporate scandals and the increased public and government scrutiny, organizations need to take a much more serious approach to the role and functions of their boards of directors. In a recent annual report on the "Best and Worst Corporate Boards in America," *Business Week* suggested that boards are becoming much more accountable than in the past and "in the face of shareholder dissatisfaction they are more likely to demand change."[20] However, the corporate governance war is far from over. In addition to the need for significant improvements in the large corporations, mid-size and smaller companies, and overseas boards, also have a long way to go in terms of adopting strict guidelines for good governance. Dot-coms in particular have tended to have boards dominated by insiders, a combination of current management and others with connections to the company.[21] Europe too is just entering the corporate governance battle. Mass stock ownership is a new phenomenon but investors who feel stung by steep price drops are taking action. European shareholders are going to court and showing up en masse at annual meetings.[22]

THE SARBANES-OXLEY ACT

Credit for the improvements in corporate governance goes to several sources. Information on executive and director compensation is much more clearly presented than it was in the 1980s and early 1990s.[23] However, the aftermath of the scandals in the early twenty-first century were the biggest impetus for change, which led to the enactment of such legislation as the 2002 Sarbanes-Oxley Act in the U.S. and the initiation of similar legislation in Canada.

The Sarbanes-Oxley Act was introduced in the United States following the flood of accounting scandals at companies such as Enron and WorldCom. The act was aimed at re-establishing corporate accountability and investor confidence. The central purpose of the act is to make public companies more accountable by increasing transparency in their financial reporting. This required additional regulations governing public company accounting, corporate responsibility, and investor protection. In order to accomplish this, increased requirements were also placed on CEOs, chief financial officers (CFOs), and the functions that they oversee.

The significant impact of the Sarbanes-Oxley Act is evident to many observers, such as Megan Barnett, who made the following comments:

> More than just a buzzword born in the depths of the corporate scandals, good governance has turned into a new way of life for some company gatekeepers.... Under the new rule regime, boards find themselves under intense scrutiny. They have fired members who have conflicts of interest, possess thin credentials, or are past their prime. They have hired new directors they believe are beyond reproach, with no skeletons and talents more suited to the job. They have more meetings, more conference calls, and more questions to ask of senior management. They face the challenge of simultaneously beefing up controls to meet new regulatory requirements while remaining active in shaping the company's strategy. They consult more with their lawyers.... Boards must now comprise mostly independent directors, which means the individuals must not have any material ties (à la Enron) to the company or its management.[24]

While the Sarbanes-Oxley Act itself is not directed at Canadian jurisdictions, it does affect Canadian companies that trade on U.S. stock exchanges, and it has served as an impetus for similar Canadian legislation. In 2004, the OSC presented 18 new corporate governance standards for boards of publicly traded companies that replaced the guidelines drafted by the Toronto Stock Exchange in 1994. The redeveloped guidelines add new, more stringent standards for Canadian boards.

The OSC's new corporate governance standards for boards of publicly traded companies included the following:

- Boards should be a majority of independent directors.

- Chairperson must be an independent director.

- Board satisfied as to integrity of CEO.

- Develop clear position descriptions for directors.

- Adopt a written code of conduct and ethics.

- Independent directors on compensation committees.[25]

Efforts to improve corporate governance may be classified into two major categories for discussion purposes. First, changes could be made in the composition, structure, and functioning of boards of directors. Second, shareholders—on their own initiative or on the initiative of management or the board—could assume a more active role in governance. Each of these possibilities deserves closer examination.

COMPOSITION, STRUCTURE AND FUNCTIONING OF BOARDS

In the past decade or so, changes have begun to be made in boards of directors. These changes have occurred because of the growing belief that CEOs and executive teams need to be made more accountable to shareholders and other stakeholders. Here we will discuss several of these changes and some other recommendations that have been set forth for improving board functioning.

COMPOSITION OF THE BOARD

The 2003 Canadian Spencer Stuart Board Index (CSSBI) was the eighth annual survey of board trends and practices of leading Canadian companies, conducted by Spencer Stuart in partnership with the University of Toronto's Rotman School of Management.[26] The CSSBI analysis was conducted from 100 leading public Canadian companies. Among the interesting findings are the following outlined below.

The average board size among the CSSBI 100 firms was about 12 members, which is about 17 percent larger than comparable U.S. firms. The presence of women in Canadian boards continues to rise. In addition, the survey suggests that that the gender gap between Canadian and U.S. boards has largely closed. Overall, 79 percent of Canadian firms report at least one women director, compared to 83.2 percent in the U.S. However, women still only represent 11.7 percent of all directors (12.8 percent in the U.S.).

While Canadian boards have traditionally trailed their U.S. counterparts in the representation of women as directors, these findings indicate that for Canadian public boards (of firms with revenues over $1 billion), the gender balance is close to those in similar-sized U.S. firms. On the other hand, the survey indicates that Canada still significantly lags behind the U.S. in the representation of visible minorities on boards. Directors who are also visible minorities account for only 1.7 percent of board directorships among the surveyed companies, compared to 13 percent in the U.S. In addition, only 19 percent of the firms had at least one minority director, while 76 percent of comparable U.S. firms had at least one minority director.

Canadian boards do make use of international directors—with 86 percent of the firms surveyed having at least one international director, while only 28 percent of comparable U.S. firms make use of international directors. In addition, over two-thirds of those international directors on Canadian boards are United States citizens. On the other hand, Canadian citizens account for only about 18 percent of international directors who sit on U.S. company boards.

The survey indicates that, for the most part, board independence is relatively high. One key indicator of board independence is the separation of the chair and CEO functions. Among the companies surveyed, 77 percent separated the role of the chair from that of the CEO. This reflects an increase of 15 percent over the past five years. On the other hand, only about 25 percent of comparable U.S. firms split the functions of the chair and the CEO. Among the 41 largest of the Canadian firms surveyed, almost 80 percent of the directors are unrelated. Figure 5–4 reports the average numbers of directors and related directors for the CSSBI 100 firms and their comparable U.S. counterparts.

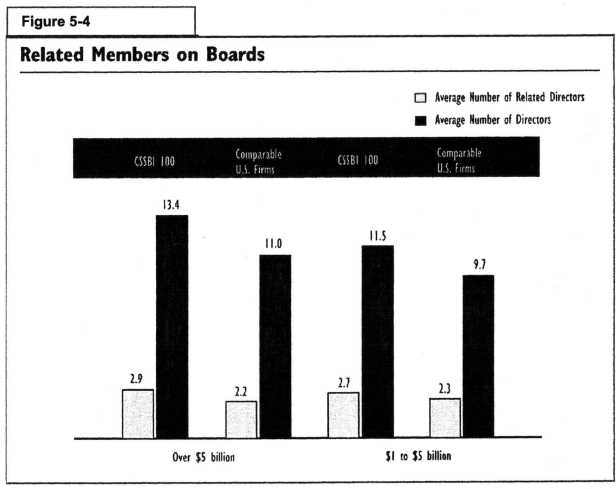

Figure 5-4

Related Members on Boards

☐ Average Number of Related Directors
■ Average Number of Directors

| CSSBI 100 | Comparable U.S. Firms | CSSBI 100 | Comparable U.S. Firms |

Over $5 billion: 13.4, 2.9, 11.0, 2.2
$1 to $5 billion: 11.5, 2.7, 9.7, 2.3

Source: The 2003 Canadian Spencer Stuart Board Index (CSSBI), conducted by Spencer Stuart in partnership with the University of Toronto's Rotman School of Management, http://www.rotman.utoronto.ca/news/boardindex.pdf.

Finally, the CSSBI survey noted that it is becoming increasingly difficult to find **qualified individuals** to serve on boards. It is estimated that up to 75 percent of directors will be retiring in the next decade, given that the average age of a director is 60, and most of these boards impose mandatory retirement between the ages of 65 and 72.[27] Among the companies surveyed, the other most common reasons for looking to add new directors in the coming year are to increase board diversity, to add directors with financial expertise, and to add more independent members.

Another part of the problem is an **increase in demand** for good independent directors. Institutional investors value good corporate governance so highly that they are willing to pay a premium for firms with outside directors. This increase in demand for outside directors is part of the reason they are in increasingly short supply. In 2004, the Ontario Securities Commission released new draft guidelines that force corporate boards to include a majority of independent directors. These rules also require a company's chairperson to be an independent director. Boards must be satisfied with the integrity of the CEO, and independent directors must sit on compensation committees.[28]

Another factor limiting the supply of directors is the **greater level of expectations** placed on board members. Board committees and subcommittees are now given more to do than ever before. Furthermore, the globalization of business has placed new demands on board members for travel. Last, firms realize the time demands placed on outside directors and so they limit the number of outside boards on which their own executives may sit. For example, former General Electric CEO Jack Welch would not allow his senior managers to sit on the boards of other companies.[29]

The difficulty in finding outside board members is exacerbated when searching for members of minority groups or women to bring **diversity** to the board. In the past, many candidates were excluded because they never had the title of CEO. A new trend in board recruitment, focusing more on experience than title, is helping to bring more independence and diversity to the boardroom. This broadens the pool of candidates available.[30]

Today, advocates of strong, independent, and diverse boards have largely succeeded in convincing corporations of the importance of board composition. The difficulty now is in putting those recommendations into effect.

USE OF BOARD COMMITTEES

Boards often have to make use of a variety of committees in order to keep them properly apprised of the company's situation. The committee structure of many Canadian boards differs from their U.S. counterparts. According to the CSSBI survey, 43 percent of Canadian boards have an environmental or health and safety committee, compared to only 5 percent of U.S. boards. The survey also revealed that 18 percent of Canadian boards have a risk committee, compared to only 2 percent of their U.S. counterparts. Figure 5–5 offers more information on the variety of committees employed by boards in Canada versus the U.S.

Figure 5-5

Board Committees

Committee	Percent of CSSBI 100 Firms with Committee	Percent of Comparable U.S. Firms with Committee
Audit	100%	100%
Compensation/Human Resources	95%	100%
Nominating Governance	92%	95%
Environment, Health and Safety	43%	5%
Investment/Pension	32%	7%
Executive	27%	46%
Risk	18%	2%
Finance	10%	30%
Conduct Review	8%	1%
Public Policy and Social Responsibility	7%	12%
Strategy and Planning	3%	3%
Stock Options and Retraction Price	2%	4%

Source: The 2003 Canadian Spencer Stuart Board Index (CSSBI), conducted by Spencer Stuart in partnership with the University of Toronto's Rotman School of Management, http://www.rotman.utoronto.ca/news/boardindex.pdf.

The **audit committee** is typically responsible for assessing the adequacy of internal control systems and the integrity of financial statements. Recent scandals underscore the importance of a strong audit committee. Commenting on such scandals, *The Wall Street Journal* recently opined, "Too many audit committees are turning out to be toothless tigers."[31] To lessen the occurrence of such scandals, the SEC and the OSC have placed much emphasis on audit committees. Recent legislation in Canada requires public companies to hire auditors who are members of the Canadian Public Accountability Board. Companies must also have "an independent and financially literate" audit committee.

Charles Anderson and Robert Anthony, authors of *The New Corporate Directors: Insights for Board Members and Executives*,[32] argue that the principal responsibilities of an audit committee are as follows:

1. To ensure that published financial statements are not misleading.

2. To ensure that internal controls are adequate.

3. To follow up on allegations of material, financial, ethical, and legal irregularities.

4. To ratify the selection of the external auditor.

According to Arjay Miller, a board member and former president of Ford Motor Company, there should be at least one meeting per year between the audit committee and the firm's internal auditor.[33] The internal auditor should be scheduled to meet alone with the committee and always be instructed to speak out whenever she or he believes something should be brought to the committee's attention. The committee should also meet with the outside auditor in a setting in which members of management are not present. Three major questions should be asked of the outside auditor by the audit committee:

1. Is there anything more that you think we should know?

2. What is your biggest area of concern?

3. In what area did you have the largest difference of opinion with company accounting personnel?

The **nominating committee**, which should be composed of outside directors, or at least a majority of outside directors, has the responsibility of ensuring that competent, objective board members are selected. Many observers have recommended that this committee be composed entirely of independent outside directors. The function of the nominating committee is to nominate candidates for the board and for senior management positions. In spite of the suggested role and responsibility of this committee, in most companies the CEO continues to exercise a powerful role in the selection of board members. As one observer commented:

> In the pre-Sarbox [Sarbanes-Oxley] world, new directors frequently materialized from a spin of the CEO's Rolodex and a handshake over lunch. Now nominating committees, mandated under the new rules, are playing a much more active role in attracting talent.[34]

The **compensation committee** has the responsibility of evaluating executive performance and recommending terms and conditions of employment. This committee should be composed of outside directors. Although most large companies have compensation committees, one might ask how objective these board members are when the CEO has played a significant role in their being elected to the board.

The CSSBI survey indicates that about 20 percent of Canadian firms still have related directors on their compensation committees, while only about 6 percent of U.S. boards reported related directors on their compensation committees. In light of the onslaught of recent corporate scandals, there is a concern over this presence of boards with related directors in compensation/human resources committees, given that "this is the group that is supposed to be evaluating the performance and pay of the senior executives with an unbiased perspective," as Professor David Beatty of the University of Toronto observed.[35]

Finally, each board has a **public issues committee**, or **public policy committee**. Although it is recognized that most management structures have some sort of formal mechanism for responding to public or social issues, this area is important enough to warrant a board committee that would become sensitive to these issues, provide policy leadership, and monitor management's performance on these issues. Most major companies today have public issues committees that typically deal with such issues as employment equity, environmental affairs, employee health and safety, consumer affairs, political action, and other areas in which public or ethical issues are present. Debate continues over the extent to which large firms really use such committees, but the fact that they have institutionalized such concerns by way of formal corporate committees is encouraging. It has been recommended that firms develop evaluation systems to help them monitor the social performance of their corporate executives, but the evidence does not show that companies are doing this.[36]

Other suggestions have been proposed for creating effective boards of directors and for improving board members' abilities to monitor executive teams to ensure that crises do not occur undetected. Figure 5–6 summarizes some of these recommendations.

Figure 5-6

Improving Boards and Board Members

Building a Better Board[a]

- Don't overload it with too many members.
- Don't think you need high-profile CEOs or famous academics.
- Keep directors on for at least five years.
- Encourage directors to buy large quantities of stock.

Sharpening the Board's Sensors[b]

- Insist that board members become educated about their company.
- Insist that information-gathering systems deliver quickly the right information from the bottom to the top.
- Insist that board members understand board decision-making processes and not operate by consensus.
- Insist that the company undergo periodic audits of corporate activities and results.

Board Actions[c]

- Directors should evaluate regularly the CEO's performance against established goals and strategies.
- Evaluations of the CEO should be done by "outside directors."
- Outside directors should meet alone at least once a year.
- Directors should set qualifications for board members and communicate these expectations to shareholders.
- Outside directors should screen and recommend board candidates who meet the established qualifications.

Keep Directors' Eyes on CEO[d]

- CEOs need written job descriptions and annual report cards.
- Boards should measure their own performance as well as assess individual members.
- Board nominating committees should exclude the company's major suppliers, officials of non-profit organizations that receive substantial donations from the corporation, and the CEO's close friends.
- A chief executive should hold only one outside board seat.

Sources: [a]Graef S. Crystal, "Do Directors Earn Their Keep?" *Fortune* (May 6, 1991), 79. [b]Richard O. Jacobs, "Why Boards Miss Black Holes," *Across the Board* (June 1991), 54. [c]The Working Group on Corporate Governance, "A New Compact for Owners and Directors," *Harvard Business Review* (July–August 1991), 142–143. [d]Joann S. Lublin "How to Keep Directors' Eyes on the CEO," *The Wall Street Journal* (July 20, 1994), B1.

INCREASED ROLE OF SHAREHOLDERS

Managing the demands of owner stakeholders has grown increasingly challenging in recent years. This challenge is partly a consequence of the growing need to manage the interests of two potentially different and broad types of shareholders. First, there are the **traditional shareholder** groups that are primarily interested in the firm's financial performance. Examples of such groups include the large institutional investors, such as pension funds. Second, there are growing numbers of **social activist shareholders**. These groups are may pressure firms to adopt their desired postures on social causes, such as Third World employment practices, animal testing, affirmative action, and environmental protection.

A major problem seems to be that both groups of shareholders feel like neglected constituencies, particularly in light of recent corporate abuses. Shareholders are attempting to rectify this condition through a variety of means. They are demanding effective power. They want to hold management groups accountable. They want to make changes, including changes in management if necessary. Like companies' earlier responses to other stakeholder activist groups, many organizations are resisting. The result is a battle between managers and shareholders for corporate control.[37]

A recent example of this battle between managers and shareholders is the effort by the Living Wage, an anti-sweatshop group, to use shareholder resolutions to raise wages for workers in Indonesia. A shareholder must own US$2000 of Nike stock for a minimum of one year to propose a resolution that would change company policy. Jim Keady and Leslie Kredu, directors of the group, are travelling the United States, speaking at colleges in an effort to find individuals and organizations to donate to their cause. Among other demands, the group wants Nike to disclose all factory locations, remove language that prohibits athletes who wear Nike gear from criticizing Nike, allow monitoring of factories by a worker rights consortium, and only work with factories that pay a wage sufficient to support a small family and still allow savings. Nike spokeswoman Vada Manager questions the group's claims and states that Nike has strict wage, labour, and environmental codes in its factories that are monitored and enforced.[38]

Shareholder activism motivated by a concern for social and environmental issues gained momentum during the mid-1970s and '80s in Canada. Collections of churches and religious groups united to form the Taskforce on Churches and Corporate Responsibility (TCCR). The initial aim was to pressure Canadian banks to stop making loans to the apartheid regime in South Africa. Later, this group attempted to persuade forest companies to adopt environmental codes of practice. This culminated in the creation of the Forest Stewardship Council. Other issues included convincing Noranda to improve its environmental reporting to shareholders.

More recently, a major success for the task force involved pressuring Calgary's Talisman Energy to divest its 25 percent ownership in an oil facility in Sudan, where a violent civil war had already accounted for millions of civilian deaths. The activists were outraged that money flowing from the project to the Sudanese government was used to build new factories for manufacturing ammunition and thereby fuelling continued war in the region.

A shareholder resolution filed in January 2000 outlined the risk of sanctions by investors and government if Talisman refused to cooperate. The resolution also demanded that the company file an independently verified report on its compliance with human rights standards and the International Code of Ethics for Canadian Business, ensuring that revenue from the Greater Nile Petroleum Operating Company wasn't being used to finance the government's war requirements. Failing these conditions, the resolution urged Talisman to leave the region. Following investor pressure, Talisman finally agreed to sell its interest in the Sudan facility to an Indian firm for $1.2 billion, citing public pressure. Following this news, Talisman shares rose almost 9 percent.[39]

While these examples sound encouraging for shareholders, Josef Fridman makes the following skeptical observations:

> Some successes of shareholder activists and the ability of shareholders to dominate or even disrupt annual meetings has created the belief that shareholders are winning back some control of a company from management. However, other than the expanding role of the institutional investor, with both the benefits and the challenges it brings, the notion that shareholder capitalism is gaining ground is mostly an illusion. Real power, for the most part, still rests in the hands of executives, a view a majority of those interviewed held and wished to perpetuate. In fact, for what they see as very practical reasons, most would not like to see shareholders given greater control as they believed it could lead to mismanagement.[40]

This skepticism might be somewhat tempered by recent additions to the shareholder movement in Canada—including the establishment of such relatively new institutions as the Canadian Coalition for Good Governance (CCGG). This organization represents a coalition among such institutional investors as the Ontario Teachers Pension Plan Board, the CPP Investment Board, Mackenzie Financial Corp. and UBS Global Asset Management. Together, they possess approximately $600 billion in assets under management. The mission of the CCGG is "to represent Canadian institutional shareholders through the promotion of best corporate governance practices and to align the interests of boards and management with those of the shareholder."[41] According to a recent *Globe and Mail* report, the CCGG reflects "a new form of shareholder activism. Institutional investors had long pursued issues on an individual basis but the coalition represented the first time they had banded together with the purpose of raising governance standards in Canada."[42]

Among CCGG's central objectives are to encourage the following corporate governance practices:

- All public corporations have highly qualified boards of directors who understand that they are accountable only to the shareholders in carrying out their fiduciary duties.

- Boards of directors insist on excellent and ethical management.

- Boards of directors supervise management proactively.

- All committees of the board of directors are independent from management and highly qualified.

- External auditors follow policies of transparent accounting, reporting directly to the audit committee, thereby ensuring independence from the management of the company.

- Compensation schemes reward employees for superior performance.[43]

SUMMARY

To remain legitimate, corporations must be governed according to the intended and legal pattern. Corporations are not always being governed the way they were intended to be, and the governance challenge has yet to be adequately addressed across the entire business sector. Among the challenges present is finding qualified and independent candidates to fill vacant board seats. According to many observers, the corporate governance picture is gradually improving. However, in light of recent scandals, it appears that continual vigilance must be maintained if corporate governance is to fully realize its promise—being responsive to the needs of the range of individuals and groups who have a stake in the firm.

KEY TERMS

agency problems (page 85)

audit committee (page 93)

board of directors (page 84)

charter (page 83)

compensation committee (page 94)

corporate governance (page 82)

inside directors (page 86)

legitimation (page 82)

nominating committee (page 94)

outside directors (page 86)

separation of ownership from control (page 84)

shareholder activism (page 96)

DISCUSSION QUESTIONS

1. Explain the evolution of corporate governance. What problems developed? What are the current trends?

2. What are the major criticisms of boards of directors? Which single criticism do you find to be the most important? Why?

3. Outline the major suggestions that have been set forth for improving corporate governance. In your opinion, which suggestions are most important? Why?

4. In what ways have companies taken the initiative in becoming more responsive to owners/stakeholders? Where would you like to see more improvement? Discuss.

ENDNOTES

1. Joseph McCafferty, "Adelphia Comes Clean," *CFO Magazine* (December 1, 2003).

2. Nadine Winter, "Fair Pay for Fair Play," *CA Magazine* (Vol. 136, No. 10, December 2003), 34.

3. Cited in Edwin M. Epstein and Dow Votaw (eds.) *Rationality, Legitimacy, Responsibility: Search for New Directions in Business and Society* (Santa Monica, CA: Goodyear Publishing Co., 1978), 72.

4. Carl Icahn, "What Ails Corporate America—And What Should Be Done," *Business Week* (October 17, 1986), 101.

5. Caroline Oliver, "Democracy in the Boardroom," *Corporate Knights*, http://www.corporateknights.ca/stories/democracy_in_the_boardroom.asp.

6. *Ibid.*

7. John Della Contrada, "Faculty Comment on Enron Debacle," *University of Buffalo Reporter* (Vol. 33, No. 15, January 31, 2002).

8. Louis Lavelle, "Shhh, You'll Wake the Board," *Business Week* (March 5, 2001), 92.

9. *Ibid.*

10. David Paddon, "Canadian Corporate Directors Bracing for More Scandals in 2004: KPMG," *Canadian Press* (February 10, 2004), http://www.canada.com/national/; KPMG, http://www.kpmg.ca/english/.

11. Christopher Guly, "Greed Will Trigger Capitalist Reformation: Professor," *The Ottawa Citizen* (June 29, 2002), http://www.crgq.com/press/06_29_2002/.

12. Seth Sutel, "Lawyers for Hollinger Lay Out Case Against Conrad Black in Delaware Court," *Canadian Press* (February 18, 2004), http://www.canada.com/search/story.html?id=d9ac2f5d-8e7c-48f7-a2e8-018c07cd6451.

13. Michael Gray, Carlotta Amaduzzi, and Stephen Deane, "Governance Lessons from Europe's Enron," http://www.issproxy.com/articles/2004archived/001.asp.

14. Murray L. Weidenbaum, *Strengthening the Corporate Board: A Constructive Response to Hostile Takeovers* (St. Louis: Washington University, Center for the Study of American Business, September 1985), 4–5.

15. Linda Himelstein, "Boardrooms: The Ties That Blind," *Business Week* (May 2, 1994), 112–114.

16. Carol J. Loomis, "This Stuff Is Wrong," *Fortune* (June 25, 2001), 72–84.

17. Janet McFarland, "Related Boards a Matter of Opinion," *Globe and Mail, Report on Business* (October 8, 2002), B1, http://www.globeandmail.com/series/boardgames/stories/20021008related.html.

18. *Ibid.*

19. Della Contrada, *op cit.*

20. John A. Byrne, "The Best and Worst Boards," *Business Week* (January 24, 2000), 142.

21. "The Fading Appeal of the Boardroom," *The Economist* (February 10, 2001), 67–69.

22. "Europe's Shareholders to the Barricades," *Business Week* (March 19, 2001).

23. Robert W. Lear and Boris Yavitz, "Boards on Trial," *Chief Executive* (October 2000), 40–48.

24. Megan Barnett, Margaret Mannix, and Tim Smart, "The New Regime; Corporate Reform Measures Are Forcing Boards of Directors to Clean Up Their Act," *U.S. News & World Report* (Vol. 136, No. 6, February 16, 2004), E.2.

25. Janet McFarland, "Guidelines Urge Ethics Codes New Standards Being Unveiled Today Get Tougher With Boards Of Directors," *Globe and Mail* (January 16, 2004), http://ctv2.theglobeandmail.com/servlet/story/LAC.20040116.ROSCRULES16/business/Business/Business/&id=LAC_20040116_ROSCRULES16.

26. Rotman School of Management, http://www.rotman.utoronto.ca/news/boardindex.pdf.

27. Rotman School of Management, http://www.rotman.utoronto.ca/news/newsrelease_021003.htm.

28. "CEOs, CFOs Will Have to Sign Off on Financial Statements," *CBC Online* (January 16, 2004), http://www.cbc.ca/storyview/CBC/2004/01/16/securitiesrules_040116.

29. "The Fading Appeal of the Boardroom," *The Economist* (February 10, 2001), 67.

30. Toddi Gutner, "Wanted: More Diverse Directors," *Business Week* (April 30, 2001), 134.

31. Joann S. Lublin and Elizabeth MacDonald, "Scandals Signal Laxity of Audit Panels," *The Wall Street Journal* (July 17, 1998), B1.

32. Charles A. Anderson and Robert N. Anthony, *The New Corporate Directors: Insights for Board Members and Executives* (New York: John Wiley & Sons, 1986), 141.

33. Arjay Miller, "A Director's Questions," *The Wall Street Journal* (August 18, 1980), 10.

34. Barnett et al., *op cit.*

35. Rotman School of Management, http://www.rotman.utoronto.ca/news/newsrelease_021003.htm; http://www.rotman.utoronto.ca/news/boardindex.pdf.

36. Donald E. Schwartz, "Corporate Governance," in Thorton Bradshaw and David Vogel (eds.) *Corporations and Their Critics* (New York: McGraw-Hill, 1981), 227–228.

37. Bruce Nussbaum and Judith Dobrzynski, "The Battle for Corporate Control," *Business Week* (May 18, 1987), 102–109.

38. Andy Dworkin, "Critic Aims to Change Nike from Within," *The Oregonian* (March 9, 2001).

39. Patricia Coppard, "Share and Share Alike," http://www.vancourier.com/021203/news/021203nn1.html.

40. Fridman, *op cit.*

41. Canadian Coalition for Good Governance, http://www.ccgg.ca/web/website.nsf/web/ccgghome.

42. Michael Ryval, "CCGG: Much Done, Much More Remains," Globe and Mail (October 9, 2003), http://www.globeinvestor.com/servlet/ArticleNews/story/GAM/20031009/CGCCGG09.

43. Canadian Coalition for Good Governance, http://www.ccgg.ca/web/website.nsf/web/ccggmandate.

6

STAKEHOLDERS IN THE GLOBAL BUSINESS ARENA

CHAPTER OBJECTIVES

After studying this chapter, you should be able to:

1   Identify and describe the concepts of internationalization and globalization of business.

2   Summarize the arguments for and against globalization.

3   Explain the evolving role of and problems with multinational corporations in the global environment.

4   Recognize the major ethical challenges of operating in the multinational environment.

5   Discuss strategies for improving global ethics.

Global or international business has been characterized as including such activities as importing, exporting, acting as licensor to a foreign company, establishing joint ventures outside the home country with foreign companies, and establishing or acquiring wholly owned businesses outside the home country.[1]

Given the rapid expansion of business activities across international boundaries, the phenomenon of **globalization** has come to refer to the "global economic integration of many formerly national economies into one global economy."[2] This is made possible by free trade, especially by free capital mobility, and by easy or uncontrolled migration. Globalization is the "effective erasure of national boundaries for economic purposes."[3] Obviously, true globalization is an extreme status that has not yet been achieved, but one that many hold as an ultimate aspiration.

According to *Business Week*, globalization today is a term that has come to encompass everything from "expanded trade" and "factories shifting around the world" to the "international bodies that set the rules for the global economy" (i.e., World Trade Organization, International Monetary Fund, and the World Bank).[4] For our purposes, *Business Week*'s broad concept of globalism or globalization probably fits best.

This chapter underscores the stakeholder challenges posed by the phenomenon of globalization. Among the challenges discussed are: global marketing practices, corruption, bribery, sweatshops, and the role of MNCs in Third World countries. We also consider recent efforts to grapple with these issues and address the concerns of stakeholders in the global marketplace. Given the nature and scope of the issues raised by globalization, it is easy to understand that business's greatest stakeholder challenges in the future will very likely occur at the global level.

BACKLASH AGAINST GLOBALIZATION

There has been an evident backlash against globalization that has been most apparent since the protests in Seattle in fall 1999 against the activities of the World Trade Organization (WTO). The protestors at the Seattle meeting have been described in various ways. They have been identified as a peculiar meld of extreme leftists and rightists, trade unionists, radical environmentalists, and self-appointed representatives of civil society insisting on saving the poor people of developing countries from economic development.[5] They have also been described as a visible coalition between labour and environmentalists— "teamsters and turtles"—as one sign said, as well as other key constituencies, such as human rights activists.[6] In short, they are special interest groups committed to halting the expansion of global capitalism and trade.

The backlash against globalization that began in Seattle has been perpetuated at a number of important global meetings since then. After Seattle came the meeting of the IMF and the World Bank in Washington, DC, in April 2000. These organizations were accused by environmental and anti-poverty groups of inflicting misery and poverty on developing nations. Next, came the European meeting of the IMF and World Bank in Prague in the fall of 2000, and a meeting of the heads of state of 34 nations in Quebec City in April 2001 to discuss a hemispheric free-trade zone.

The height of protest and destruction came in Genoa, Italy, in the summer of 2001 at the G8 Summit meeting of the eight wealthiest countries in the world. There were at least two days of violent riots that resulted in death and destruction. The violence at the G8 Summit shocked the world. One positive outcome of the Genoa meetings was an exposure of and split within the anti-globalization ranks between those who want to peacefully reform global capitalism and the anarchists who want to destroy it.

Many studies have been conducted to investigate the nature and consequences of globalization. A myriad of reports have been generated on the pros and cons of globalization. Numerous reports have observed that on one side we see the "globalists," who strongly advocate open markets with private firms moving freely across the globe. They believe that investors, consumers, employees, and environmentalists are better off due to globalization. On the other side are the "antiglobalists," who have taken to the streets to protest the expansion and greed of corporate global enterprises. They believe that globalization is responsible for the destruction of local environments and emerging economies, abuses of human rights, the undermining of local cultures, and the sovereignty of nation-states. The antiglobalists also decry the power of international bodies, notably the World Trade Organization, the International Monetary Fund, and the World Bank.[7] These opposing views were succinctly stated by Nicholas Stern in an article in the *Ivey Business Journal*:

> Is globalization making the rich, richer and the poor, poorer? ... Corporations are a driving force and important beneficiaries of global economic integration. They are also the ultimate targets of anti-globalization demonstrators, who blame multinational corporations for ills ranging from deforestation to child labor. If development efforts have failed and globalization is further impoverishing the world's poorest people, then corporations surely deserve part of the blame. If, on the other hand, global poverty is declining and global integration is helping people to escape poverty, then corporations are presumably part of the solution.[8]

Figure 6–1 summarizes some of these two groups' opposing views on globalization as it affects consumers, workers, the environment, developing nations, and human rights. It should be clear from these pros and cons that globalization has significant ethical issues embedded in it for stakeholders.

Figure 6-1

The Pros and Cons of Globalization

Impact On:		Globalists	Antiglobalists
	Consumers	Open markets allow for free trade of goods and services, lower costs, greater efficiency. Lower prices, greater variety of goods and services, rising living standards.	Benefits the wealthy and further impoverishes the poor. Widening wealth gap worldwide. Harmful to low-income consumers.
	Employees	Faster economic growth; higher wages; more employment; improved working conditions.	Globalism places profits above people—depressing wages, displacing workers, undermining workers' rights.
	Environment	Global capitalism means rapid economic growth, resources necessary to clean up environments, development of more efficient CO_2-reducing technologies, protection of ecosystems; pollution reduction.	Results in exploitation and destruction of ecosystems in name of corporate greed. Ignores adverse impacts on environments. More pollution, especially carbon dioxide. Exacerbated global warming.
	Developing Nations	Open markets, cross-border investments are keys to national economic development. Higher standards of living, better working conditions, cleaner environments.	Global capitalism, world trade bodies, world financial institutions conspire to keep developing nations in debt, destroys local economies, further impoverishes peoples.
	Human Rights	Free and open markets create cultures/institutions supporting rule of law and free expression. Spreads economic/political freedom to far corners of world (e.g., Taiwan and South Korea).	In blind pursuit of profits, global corporations ignore abuses of human rights, including political and religious oppression, false imprisonment, torture, free speech, and abuses of workers, especially women and children.

Source: Summarized from Robert Batterson and Murray Weidenbaum, *The Pros and Cons of Globalization* (St. Louis: Center for the Study of American Business, January 2001), 3–12.

MNCs: Global Stakes & Challenges

A global business is a business that engages directly in some form of international business activity, including such activities as exporting, importing, or international production. A business that has direct investments (whether in the form of marketing or manufacturing facilities) in at least two different countries is specifically referred to as a **multinational corporation (MNCs)**. In other words, multinational organizations, or MNCs, are business enterprises that control assets, factories, and so on, operated either as branch offices or affiliates in two or more countries. An MNC generates products or services through its affiliates in several countries, and it maintains control over the operations of those affiliates, and manages from a global perspective. MNCs may also be referred to as global companies when they operate in many countries around the world.

Underlying Challenges of Operating in a Multinational Environment

It has been argued that there are at least two underlying and related challenges or problems as firms attempt to operate in a multinational environment. One problem is *corporate legitimacy* as the MNC seeks a role in a foreign society. The other problem is the fundamentally *differing philosophies* that may exist between the firm's home country and the host country in which it seeks to operate.[9] These two challenges set the stage for understanding how ethical problems arise in the global environment.

Corporate Legitimacy

For an MNC to be perceived as legitimate in the eyes of a host country, it must fulfill its social responsibilities. As we discussed earlier, these include economic, legal, ethical, and philanthropic responsibilities. Larger firms, in particular, are seen as outsiders, and the expectations on them are greater than on smaller, less visible firms. Further, the similarities and differences between the cultures of the two countries affect the perceived legitimacy. For example, an American firm operating in Canada is not likely to experience major problems. An American or a Western firm operating in Iran, however, could be perceived as quite alien.[10] Differences between the values and lifestyles of managers who live in the two countries could pose serious legitimacy problems. If a host country finds the lifestyles or values repugnant—as many LDCs may well find the materialistic lifestyles and values of American managers— legitimacy may be difficult to achieve.

Another, perhaps more basic, barrier to achieving legitimacy is the inherent conflict that may exist between the interests of the MNC and those of the host country. The MNC is seeking to *optimize globally*, while host governments are seeking to *optimize locally*. This may pose little difficulty for an MNC operating in a developed country, where macroeconomic or regulatory policies are sophisticated and appropriate. But it may pose serious problems in the LDCs, where there is often the perception that MNCs are beyond the control of local governments. In these latter situations, especially, it is not uncommon to see the local government impose various control devices, such as indigenization laws requiring majority ownership by locals, exclusion of foreign firms from certain industries, restrictions on foreign personnel, or even expropriation.[11]

Part of the reason MNCs have difficulty achieving legitimacy is a reaction to the real or perceived conflicts between the interests of the firm and those of the host country or government that place the MNC in a "no-win" situation. If the MNC tries to bring in the latest labour-saving technology, this may conflict with the perceived need for labour-creating technology in high-unemployment-prone LDCs.

If the MNC repatriates large parts of its profits, this may be seen as depriving the local economy of new wealth. If the MNC reinvests the profits locally, this may be perceived as furthering its control over the economy. If the MNC pays market rate wages, this may be seen as exploiting labour with low wage rates. If the MNC pays a premium for labour, this may be seen as skimming the cream of the local labour supply and thus hurting local businesses that cannot afford to pay a premium. Consequently, whatever it does, the MNC is a convenient target for criticism from some faction or stakeholders. In this sometimes hostile environment, legitimacy can be both elusive and fleeting—difficult to get and even harder to keep.[12]

DIFFERING PHILOSOPHIES BETWEEN MNCS AND HOST COUNTRIES

Closely related to the legitimacy issue is the dilemma of MNCs that have quite different philosophical perspectives from those of their host countries. The philosophy of Western industrialized nations, and thus their MNCs, focuses on economic growth, efficiency, specialization, free trade, and comparative advantage. By contrast, LDCs, for example, have quite different priorities. Other important objectives for them might include a more equitable income distribution or increased economic self-determination. In this context, the industrialized nations may appear to be inherently exploitative in that their presence may perpetuate the dependency of the poorer nation.[13]

These philosophical differences build in an environment of tension that sometimes results in stringent actions being unilaterally taken by the host country. During the 1970s, for example, the environment for MNCs investing in LDCs became much more harsh. Some of these harsh actions initiated by the host countries included outright expropriation (as occurred in the oil industry) and creeping expropriation (as occurred in the manufacturing industries when foreign subsidiaries were required to take on some local partners). Other restrictions included limits on profits repatriation.[14] As a result of the dilemmas that the MNCs face, it is easy to understand why philosopher Richard DeGeorge has argued that "First World MNCs are both the hope of the Third World and the scourge of the Third World."[15]

Thus, MNCs increasingly find themselves in situations where their very legitimacy is in question and their philosophical perspective is radically different from that of their host countries. Added to this are the normal problems of operating in a foreign culture with different types of governments, different languages, different legal systems, diverse stakeholders, and different social values. One could well argue that ethical problems are built into this environment. MNCs are attempting to bridge the cultural gaps between two peoples; yet, as they attempt to adapt to local customs and business practices, they are assailed at home for not adhering to the standards, practices, laws, or ethics of their home country. Indeed, these pose ethical dilemmas for MNCs. Figure 6–2 portrays the dilemma of MNCs caught between the characteristics and expectations of their home country and those of one or more host countries.

Figure 6-2

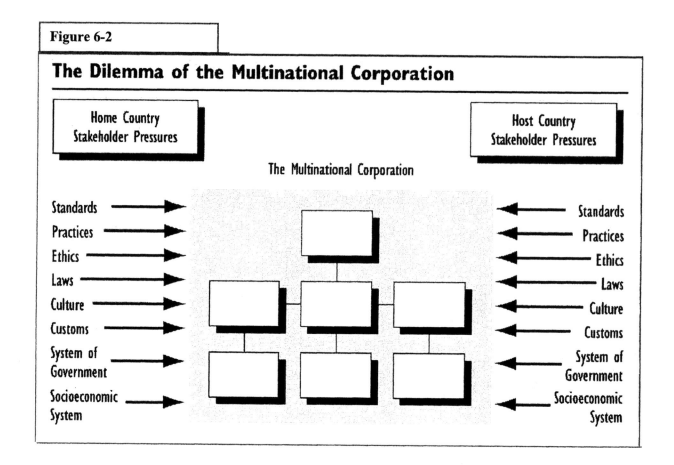

The Dilemma of the Multinational Corporation

Home Country Stakeholder Pressures

Host Country Stakeholder Pressures

The Multinational Corporation

Home Country	Host Country
Standards	Standards
Practices	Practices
Ethics	Ethics
Laws	Laws
Culture	Culture
Customs	Customs
System of Government	System of Government
Socioeconomic System	Socioeconomic System

ETHICAL ISSUES IN THE GLOBAL BUSINESS ENVIRONMENT

For many companies, most of the ethical problems that arise in the international environment are in the same categories as those that arise in their domestic environments. These ethical issues reside in all of the functional areas of business: production/operations, marketing, finance, and management. These issues concern the fair treatment of stakeholders—employees, customers, the community, and competitors. These issues involve product safety, plant safety, advertising practices, human resource management, environmental problems, and so on.

The ethical problems seem to be somewhat fewer in developed countries, but they exist there as well. The ethical difficulties seem to be worse in underdeveloped countries, LDCs, or developing countries because these countries are at earlier stages of economic development. This situation creates an environment in which there is a temptation to adhere to lower standards, or perhaps no standards, because few government regulations or activist groups exist to protect the stakeholders' interests. In the LDCs, the opportunities for business exploitation and the engagement in questionable (by developed countries' standards) practices are abundant.

QUESTIONABLE MARKETING: THE INFANT FORMULA CONTROVERSY

The **infant formula controversy** is a classic in illustrating the ethical questions that can arise while doing business abroad. We will briefly refer to James Post's observations about this now-classic case.[16] For decades, physicians working in tropical lands (many of which were LDCs) realized that there were severe health risks posed to infants from bottle feeding as opposed to breast feeding. Such countries typically had neither refrigeration nor sanitary conditions. Water supplies were not pure, and, therefore, infant formula mixed with this water contained bacteria that would likely lead to disease and diarrhea in the bottle-fed infant. Because these LDCs are typically poor, this condition encourages mothers to overdilute powdered formula, thus diminishing significantly the amount of nutrition the infant receives. Once a mother begins bottle-feeding, her capacity for breast-feeding quickly diminishes. Poverty also leads the mother to put in the bottle less expensive substitute products. These products, such as powdered whole milk and cornstarch, are not acceptable substitutes. They are nutritionally inadequate and unsatisfactory for the baby's digestive system.

By the late 1960s, it was apparent that in the LDCs there was increased bottle-feeding, decreased breast-feeding, and a dramatic increase in the numbers of malnourished and sick babies. Bottle-feeding was cited as one of the major reasons. The ethical debate began when it was noted that several of the infant formula companies, aware of the environment just described, were promoting their products and, therefore, promoting bottle-feeding in an intense way. Such marketing practices as mass advertising, billboards, radio jingles, and free samples became commonplace. These promotional devices typically portrayed the infants who used their products as healthy and robust, in sharp contrast with the reality that was brought about by the conditions mentioned.

One of the worst marketing practices entailed the use of "milk nurses"—women dressed in nurses' uniforms who walked the halls of maternity wards urging mothers to get their babies started on formula. In reality, these women were sales representatives employed by the companies on a commission basis. Once the infants began bottle-feeding, the mothers' capacity to breast-feed diminished.[17]

Although several companies were engaging in these questionable marketing practices, the Swiss conglomerate Nestlé was singled out by a Swiss social activist group in an article published in 1974 entitled "Nestlé Kills Babies." At about the same time, an article appeared in Great Britain entitled "The Baby Killers."[18] From this point on, a protracted controversy developed with Nestlé and other infant formula manufacturers on one side and a host of organizations on the other side filing shareholder resolutions and lawsuits against the company. Among the groups that were actively involved in the controversy were church groups such as the National Council of Churches and its Interfaith Center on Corporate Responsibility (ICCR), UNICEF, the World Health Organization (WHO), and the Infant Formula Action Coalition (INFACT). Nestlé was singled out because it had the largest share of the world market and because it aggressively pushed sales of its infant formula in developing countries, even after the World Health Organization developed a sales code to the contrary.[19]

In 1977, INFACT and ICCR organized and led a boycott against Nestlé that continued for almost seven years. More than 70 American organizations representing churches, doctors, nurses, teachers, and other professionals participated in the boycott. These groups mounted an international campaign aimed at changing these objectionable marketing practices in the LDCs.[20] In 1984, after spending tens of millions of dollars resisting the boycott, Nestlé finally reached an accord with the protesters. The company agreed to four changes in its business practices:

1. It would restrict the distribution of free samples.

2. It would use Nestlé labels to identify the benefits of breast-feeding and the hazards of bottle-feeding.

3. It promised to help ensure that hospitals would use its products in accordance with the WHO code.

4. It agreed to drop its policy of giving gifts to health professionals to encourage them to promote infant formula.

The protesters, in return, agreed to end their boycott but to continue monitoring Nestlé's performance.[21]
The infant formula controversy continued through the 1980s and well into the 1990s. In 1991, Nestlé (which controlled more than 40 percent of the worldwide market) and American Home Products (which controlled about 15 percent of the worldwide market) announced that after decades of boycotts and controversy, they planned to discontinue the practice of providing free and low-cost formula to developing countries.

With this action—its most aggressive ever—Nestlé attempted to quell the protracted criticism that it had defied WHO's marketing restrictions by dumping huge quantities of baby formula on Third World hospitals. The distribution of supply had been a lingering concern in the infant formula controversy. Until this announcement, Nestlé had supplied formula on a request basis but over the next several years planned to distribute formula only on a request basis to children "in need," as outlined in the WHO guidelines. The pledges by Nestlé and American Home Products, the world's two biggest infant formula makers, were regarded as a watershed in the bitter infant formula controversy.[22]

The infant formula controversy has been rich with examples of the actions and power of social activist groups and governments and the various strategies that might be employed by MNCs. For our purposes, however, it illustrates the character of questionable business practices by firms pursuing what might be called normal practices were it not for the fact that they were being pursued in foreign countries where local circumstances made them questionable.[23] The infant formula controversy also illustrates the endurance of certain ethical issues, particularly in the global arena.

A recent survey shows numerous Web sites that are still devoted to the infant formula controversy and that document how the Nestlé boycott continues still today (http://www.infactcanada.ca, http://www.wfn.org, http://www.essential.org/monitor).

SWEATSHOPS AND LABOUR ABUSES

No issue has been more prominent since the early 1990s in the global business ethics debate than MNCs' use and abuse of women and children in cheap-labour factories in developing countries. The major players in this controversy, large corporations, have highly recognizable names—Nike, Wal-Mart, Kmart, Reebok, J. C. Penney, and Disney—to name a few. The countries and regions of the world that have been involved are also recognizable—Southeast Asia, Pakistan, Indonesia, Honduras, Dominican Republic, Thailand, the Philippines, and Vietnam. Sweatshops have not been eliminated in the United States or Canada either.[24]

Though **sweatshops**, characterized by child labour, low pay, poor working conditions, worker abuse, and health and safety violations, have existed for decades, they have grown in number in the past few years as global competition has heated up and corporations have gone to the far reaches of the world to lower their costs and increase their productivity. A landmark event that brought the sweatshop issue into sharp focus was the 1996 revelation by labour rights activists that part of Wal-Mart's Kathie Lee Collection, a line of clothes endorsed by prominent U.S. talk-show host Kathie Lee Gifford, was made in Honduras by seamstresses slaving 20 hours a day for 31 cents an hour. The revelation helped turn Gifford, who was unaware of where the clothes were being made or under what conditions, into an anti-sweatshop activist.[25] The Nike Corporation has also become a lightning rod for social activists concerned about overseas manufacturing conditions, standards, and ethics. A major reason for this is the company's high visibility, extensive advertising, and expensive shoes, as well as the stark contrast between the tens of millions of dollars Nike icon Michael Jordan earned and the $2.23 daily wage rate the company's subcontractors paid their Indonesian workers.[26]

Former U.S. ambassador to the United Nations Andrew Young calls the recent debate over child labour "the world's next moral crusade."[27] Young likens the sweatshop issue with the civil rights movement, a crusade for freedom against the injustices done to helpless children and poor women. To support his argument, Young invoked a 1997 UNICEF publication, "The State of the World's Children 1997," which documented the high level of suffering that millions of child labourers are forced to endure. Referring to India, the UNICEF report disclosed:

> Thousands of children in the carpet industry are kidnapped or lured away or pledged by their parents for paltry sums of money. Most of them are kept in captivity, tortured, and made to work for 20 hours a day without a break. Little children are made to crouch on their toes, from dawn to dusk every day, severely stunting their growth during formative years.[28]

The International Labor Organization (ILO) reported that there are an unprecedented number of child labourers in the world—some 250 million. The ILO estimate, which is double previous estimates, documents almost 153 million child labourers in Asia, 80 million in Africa, and 17.5 million in Latin America. All these children are between ages five and fourteen, and nearly half work full-time.

Critics of MNC labour practices, including social activist groups and grassroots organizations, have been speaking out, criticizing business abusers and raising public awareness. These critics claim certain businesses are exploiting children and women by paying them poverty wages, working them to exhaustion, punishing them for minor violations, violating health and safety standards with them, and tearing apart their families. Many of these companies counter that they offer the children and women workers a superior alternative. They say that, although their wage rates are embarrassing by developed-world standards, those rates frequently equal or exceed local legal minimum wages, or average wages. They further say that, because so many workers in LDCs work in agriculture and farming, where they make less than the average wage, the low but legal minimums in many countries put sweatshop workers among the higher-paid workers in their areas.[29]

The sweatshop issue has been so prominent in the past few years that, to improve their situations or images, many criticized companies have begun working to improve working conditions, further joint initiatives, establish codes of conduct or standards for themselves and their subcontractors, conduct social or ethical audits, or take other steps. In 1996, U.S. President Clinton, with Kathie Lee Gifford, was instrumental in helping to establish the Fair Labor Association (FLA), an organization of clothing firms, unions, and human-rights groups focused on the worldwide elimination of sweatshops. Its members, which include L. L. Bean, Nike, Liz Claiborne, Nicole Miller, and Reebok, were encouraged by a survey showing that three-quarters of shoppers would pay higher prices for clothes and shoes bearing "No Sweat" labels.

In Canada, the Ethical Trading Action Group (ETAG) is an anti-sweatshop coalition, combining the forces of such parties as the Canadian Auto Workers, the Steelworkers' Humanity Fund, the church-based Kairos coalition, Oxfam Canada, and Students Against Sweatshops. A central focus is to lobby for stricter corporate codes of conduct in the apparel industry. ETAG has fought to establish a code that would require a company and its contractors to treat workers fairly by paying a living wage that meets workers' basic needs, stopping forced overtime, ensuring that workers have the right to form trade unions without harassment or firings and can engage in collective bargaining, and committing to not using child labour or prison labour.[30]

The labour movement is a major force behind the growing anti-sweatshop movement in Canada. For example, UNITE—the Union of Needletrades, Industrial and Textile Employees—has played a major role in fighting sweatshops, a central part of its mission which is described as follows:

> Our mission is to strengthen and improve working conditions for all UNITE members and to give a voice to the concerns of working people, particularly low-wage workers, women and immigrant workers whose voices are under-represented... to mobilize for a workers' agenda and to fight sweatshops through international solidarity.[31]

The Toronto-based **Maquila Solidarity Network (MSN)** is a major player in Canada's anti-sweatshop movement. Its members include such organizations as the BC Teachers Federation, Canadian Auto Workers, Canadian Catholic Organization for Development and Peace, the Communications, Energy and Paperworkers Union, the Canadian Labour Congress, and the Canadian Union of Public Employees. MSN facilitates communication with anti-sweatshop groups in Mexico, Central America, and Asia. This network targets specific companies such as Disney and Nike, lobbies for government intervention, and tries to educate the public. MSN has been pressuring the government to force companies to disclose where their clothes are made, using provisions under the Textile Labelling Act. The aim is to make companies accountable for the employee abuses that occur in the process of producing the merchandise that they distribute. In the absence of such information, the potential for poor working conditions increases. However, most companies have refused to provide such disclosure.[32] ETAG persuaded several universities and municipalities across Canada to adopt "no sweat" buying policies, which require companies that sell to those organizations provide evidence that their clothing is not made in sweatshops.[33]

Sweatshops and labour abuses sharply contrast the "haves" and the "have-nots" of the world's nations. Consumers in developed countries have benefited greatly by the lower prices made possible by cheap labour. It remains to be seen how supportive those consumers will be if prices rise because MNCs improve wage rates and conditions in LDCs. The MNCs face a new and volatile ethical issue that is not likely to go away. Their profits, public image, and reputations may hinge on how well they respond. The MNCs must handle a new dimension in their age-old quest to balance shareholder profits with the desires of expanded, global stakeholders who want better corporate social performance.

Recently, the Maquila Solidarity Network awarded the infamous title of "Sweatshop Retailer of the Year" to the Hudson's Bay Company and Wal-Mart. The Bay received this unwelcome award for its alleged acceptance of sweatshop abuses in three Lesotho factories. Wal-Mart was targeted for its alleged unethical treatment of its North American employees, such illegal intimidation and harassment of employees seeking union representation. In addition, Wal-Mart was cited for its use of over 20 factories in Lesotho, where poverty wages and employee abuse are rampant.[34]

CORRUPTION, BRIBERY, AND QUESTIONABLE PAYMENTS

Corruption, **bribes**, and questionable payments occurred for decades prior to the 1970s. It was in the mid-1970s, however, that evidence of widespread questionable corporate payments to foreign government officials, political parties, and other influential persons became widely known. Such major corporations as Lockheed, Gulf Oil, Northrop, Carnation, and Goodyear were among those firms admitting to such payments. Huge sums of money were involved. Gulf, for example, admitted paying US$4.2 million to the political party of Korean President Park. Gulf also created a subsidiary in the Bahamas that was then used as a conduit for unlawful political contributions. Lockheed acknowledged payments of US$22 million, mostly to officials in the Middle East.[35]

One of the most notorious cases was that of Lockheed giving US$12.5 million in bribes and commissions in connection with the sale of US$430 million worth of Tri-Star airplanes to All Nippon Airways. The president of Lockheed defended the payments, claiming that it was common practice and it was expected to give bribes in Japan. The news of the payments rocked Japan more than it did the United States, because Prime Minister Kakuei Tanaka and four others were forced to resign and stand trial. Another important point made about this case was that Lockheed did not offer a bribe, but rather the Japanese negotiator demanded it. This point raises the continuing question in matters of this kind: "Are those who accede to bribery equal in guilt to those who demand bribes?"[36]

In recent times, Canada has endured the embarrassing spotlight as home to a company convicted of bribing a government official in South Africa. In 2002, the Canadian engineering company Acres International was fined $15 million for the bribery of Masupho Sole, the former chief executive of the Lesotho Highlands Development Authority, in order to secure a contract on the construction of the Katse Dam. Sole was sentenced to 18 years in prison. In delivering his verdict, the judge said, "Corruption is of growing international and regional concern. Corruption has a particularly devastating impact on development and good governance in developing countries in Africa, because it undermines economic growth, discourages foreign investment and reduces the optimal utilisation of limited resources available for infrastructure, public services and antipoverty programmes."[37]

Corruption in international business continues to be a major problem. It starts with outright bribery of government officials and the giving of questionable political contributions. Beyond these there are many other activities that are corrupt: the misuse of company assets for political favours, kickbacks and protection money for police, free junkets for government officials, secret price-fixing agreements, and insider dealing, just to mention a few. All of these activities have one thing in common. They are attempts to influence the outcomes of decisions wherein the nature and extent of the influence are not made public. In essence, these activities are abuses of power.[38] Bribes, more than any other form of corruption, have been the subject of continuing debate, and they merit closer examination.

Arguments typically given in favour of permitting bribery include the following: (1) they are necessary for profits in order to do business; (2) everybody does it—it will happen anyway; (3) it is accepted practice in many countries—it is normal and expected; and (4) bribes are forms of commissions, taxes, or compensation for conducting business between cultures.

Arguments frequently cited against giving bribes include (1) bribes are inherently wrong and cannot be accepted under any circumstances; (2) bribes are illegal in North America and, therefore, unfair elsewhere; (3) one should not compromise her or his own beliefs; (4) managers should not deal with corrupt governments; (5) such demands, once started, never stop; (6) one should take a stand for honesty, morality, and ethics; (7) those receiving bribes are the only ones who benefit; (8) bribes create dependence on corrupt individuals and countries; and (9) bribes deceive shareholders and pass on costs to customers.[39]

The costs of bribes and other forms of corruption are seldom fully understood or described. Several studies suggest the economic costs of such corrupt activities. When government officials accept "speed" money or **"grease payments"** to issue licences, the economic cost is 3 to 10 percent above the licensing fee. When tax collectors permit underreporting of income in exchange for a bribe, income tax revenues may be reduced by up to 50 percent. When government officials take kickbacks, goods and services may be priced 20 to 100 percent higher to them. In addition to these direct economic costs, there are many indirect costs—demoralization and cynicism and moral revulsion against politicians and the political system. Due to bribery and corruption, politicians have been swept from office in Brazil, Italy, Japan, and Korea.[40]

IMPROVING GLOBAL BUSINESS ETHICS

The most obvious conclusion to extract from the discussion up to this point is that business ethics is more complex at the global level than at the domestic level. The complexity arises from the fact that a wide variety of value systems, stakeholders, cultures, forms of government, socioeconomic conditions, and standards of ethical behaviour exists throughout the world. Recognition of diverse standards of ethical behaviour is important, but if we assume that North American firms should operate in closer accordance with North American standards than with foreign standards, the strategy of ethical leadership in the world is indeed a challenging one. MNCs have a heavy responsibility, particularly in underdeveloped countries and LDCs. The power-responsibility equation also argues that MNCs have a serious ethical responsibility in global markets. That is, the larger sense of ethical behaviour and social responsiveness that should exist derives from the enormous amount of power that MNCs possess.

BALANCING AND RECONCILING THE BUSINESS ETHICS TRADITIONS OF HOME AND HOST COUNTRIES

Perhaps one of the greatest challenges that face businesses operating in foreign countries is achieving some kind of reconciliation and balance in honouring both the cultural and moral standards of their home and host countries. Should a business adhere to its home country's ethical standards for business practices or to the host country's ethical standards? There is no simple answer to this question. The diagram presented in Figure 6–3 frames the extreme decision choices businesses face when they consider operating globally.

Figure 6-3

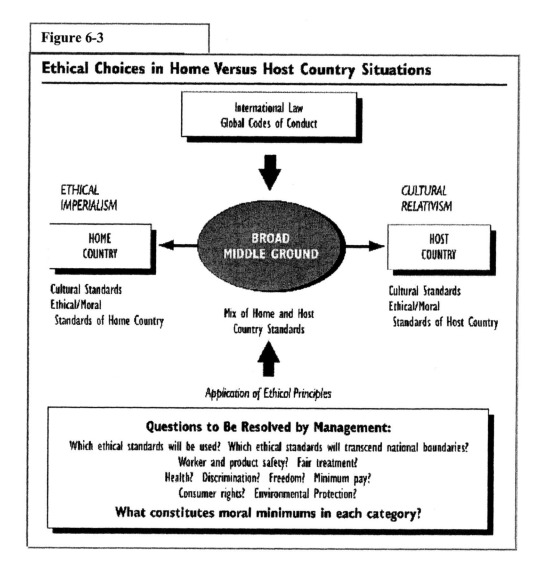

Ethical Choices in Home Versus Host Country Situations

International Law
Global Codes of Conduct

ETHICAL
IMPERIALISM

CULTURAL
RELATIVISM

HOME
COUNTRY

BROAD
MIDDLE GROUND

HOST
COUNTRY

Cultural Standards
Ethical/Moral
Standards of Home Country

Mix of Home and Host
Country Standards

Cultural Standards
Ethical/Moral
Standards of Host Country

Application of Ethical Principles

Questions to Be Resolved by Management:

Which ethical standards will be used? Which ethical standards will transcend national boundaries?
Worker and product safety? Fair treatment?
Health? Discrimination? Freedom? Minimum pay?
Consumer rights? Environmental Protection?

What constitutes moral minimums in each category?

At one extreme is a position some might call "ethical imperialism." This position argues that the MNC should continue to follow its home country's ethical standards even while operating in another country. Because North American standards for treating employees, consumers, and the natural environment are quite high relative to the standards in many other less-developed countries, it is easy to see how managers might find this posture appealing.

As reliance on foreign factories has soared in recent years and harsh conditions have been documented by the media, an increasing number of companies, such as Levi Strauss, Nordstrom, Wal-Mart, and Reebok, have espoused higher standards for foreign factories that cover such issues as wages, safety, and workers' rights to organize.[41] These standards more nearly approximate North American views on how such stakeholders ought to be treated than some host countries' views. Such higher standards could be seen by foreign countries, however, as North America and particularly the United States attempting to impose its standards on the host country—thus the name "ethical imperialism" for one end of the continuum.

At the other extreme in Figure 6–3 is a position often called **"cultural relativism."** This position is characterized by foreign direct investors such as MNCs following the host country's ethical standards. This is the posture reflected in the well-known saying, "When in Rome, do as the Romans." This position would argue that the investing MNC should set aside its home country's ethical standards and adopt the ethical standards of the host country. For example, if Saudi Arabia holds that it is illegal to hire women for most managerial positions, the investing MNC would accept and adopt this standard, even if it counters its home country's standards. Or, if the host country has no environmental protection laws, this position would argue that the MNC need not be sensitive to environmental standards.

As Tom Donaldson has argued, cultural relativism holds that no culture's ethics are better than any other's and that there are, therefore, no international rights or wrongs. If Thailand tolerates the bribery of government officials, then Thai tolerance is no worse than Japanese or German intolerance. If Switzerland does not find insider trading morally repugnant, then Swiss liberality is no worse than American restrictiveness.[42] Most ethicists find cultural relativism to be a case of moral or ethical relativism and, therefore, an unacceptable posture for MNCs to take.

ACTIONS FOR IMPROVING INTERNATIONAL BUSINESS ETHICS

Laczniak and Naor have set forth four actions, outlined below, that would help MNCs conduct international business while maintaining an ethical sensitivity in their practices and decision making.

GLOBAL CODES OF CONDUCT

There are two ways of thinking about **global codes of conduct**. First, there are specific corporate global codes that individual companies have developed. Second, there are global codes or guidelines that have been developed by various international organizations. Each of these deserves some consideration.

While operating in the global sphere, MNCs have been severely criticized for operating with divergent ethical standards in different countries, thus giving the impression that they are attempting to exploit local circumstances. A growing number of MNCs, such as Caterpillar Tractor, Allis Chalmers, Johnson's Wax, and Rexnord, have developed and used codes geared to worldwide operations.[42]

One of the first and most well known of the codes is that of Caterpillar Tractor Company, issued by the chairman of the board, entitled "A Code of Worldwide Business Conduct." The code goes into considerable detail and has major sections that cover the following vital areas: ownership and investment, corporate facilities, relationships with employees, product quality, sharing of technology, accounting and financial records, different business practices, competitive conduct, observance of local laws, business ethics, relationships with public officials, and international business.[43]

Other companies do not have comprehensive codes addressing their international operations but rather codes containing sections that address foreign practices. For example, in its "General Dynamics Standards of Business Ethics and Conduct," General Dynamics has a section entitled "International Business." One excerpt from this section is encouraging and illustrates the point we have been developing:

> Our policy is to comply with all laws which apply in the countries where we do business. In countries where common practices might indicate acceptance of standards of conduct lower than those to which we aspire, we will follow our own Standards as outlined in this booklet.[44]

An example of a global code of conduct aimed at improving workplace standards and workers' standards of living was implemented in the late 1990s by Mattel, Inc., the US$4.5 billion toy manufacturer. According to Jill E. Barad, then Mattel chairman and CEO, "We are as concerned with the safety and fair treatment of the men and women who manufacture our products as we are with the safety and quality of the products themselves, and our new Global Manufacturing Principles demonstrate our strong commitment to that philosophy."[45]

In addition to individual corporate codes, there are a number of international organizations that have developed global codes or standards that they aspire companies to adopt and follow. Some of these codes focus on one specific issue; many provide standards across a number of issue areas.

ETHICS AND GLOBAL STRATEGY

Strategic decisions that may be influenced by ethical considerations in the global sphere include, but are not limited to, product/service decisions, plant location, manufacturing policy, marketing policy and practices, and human resources management policies. A useful illustration of ethics being factored into strategic decision making is provided by Levi Strauss & Co. Because Levi Strauss operates in many countries and diverse cultures, it reasoned that it must take special care in selecting its contractors and the countries where its goods are produced in order to ensure that its products are being made in a manner consistent with its values and reputation. In the early 1990s, therefore, the company developed a set of *global sourcing guidelines* that established standards its contractors must meet. As examples, their guidelines banned the use of child and prison labour. They stipulated certain environmental standards. Wages must, at minimum, comply with the law and match prevailing local practice. By factoring these ethical considerations into its strategic decisions, Levi argued that it receives important short- and long-term commercial benefits.[46]

Another example of a company integrating ethical concerns into its corporate strategies is that of Starbucks Coffee Co., the Seattle-based firm. In an innovative pilot program announced in 1998, Starbucks plans to pay a premium above-market price for coffee, with the bonus going to improve the lives of coffee workers. The initial payments would be made to farms and mills in Guatemala and Costa Rica, which would cofund health-care centres, farm schools, and scholarships for farm workers' children. Starbucks' incentive program was part of a larger "Framework for Action," its plan for implementing its code of conduct, created in 1995.[47]

The major recommendation here is that the ethical dimensions of multinational corporate activity should be considered as significant inputs into top-level strategy formulation and implementation.[48] Carroll, Hoy, and Hall have argued even more broadly that corporate social policy should be integrated into strategic management.[49] At the top level of decision making in the firm, corporate strategy is established. At this level, commitments are made that will define the underlying character and identity that the organization will have. The overall moral tone of the organization and all decision making and behaviours are set at the strategic level, and management needs to ensure that social and ethical factors do not get lost in the preoccupation with market opportunities and competitive factors.

If ethics does not get factored in at the strategic formulation level, it is doubtful that ethics will be considered at the level of operations where strategy is being implemented. Unfortunately, much current practice has tended to treat ethics and social responsibility as residual factors. A more proactive stance is needed for dealing with ethical issues at the global level.

SUSPENSION OF ACTIVITIES

An MNC may sometimes encounter unbridgeable gaps between the ethical values of its home country and those of its host country. When this occurs, and reconciliation does not appear to be in sight, the MNC should consider suspending activities in the host country. For example, years ago IBM and Coca-Cola suspended their activities in India because of that country's position on the extent of national ownership and control.[50]

Also, Levi Strauss undertook a phased withdrawal from China, largely in response to human rights concerns, and suspended sourcing in Peru because of concerns about employee safety. It later lifted the suspension because conditions had improved.[51] More recently, companies have pulled out of Burma due to human rights violations.

Numerous Canadian MNCs have also faced the question of whether they should be conducting business with countries that have questionable human rights practices. Such was the case faced by Talisman Energy Inc., one of Canada's largest independent oil and gas producers. The company had operations in Sudan since 1998 and, with a 25 percent stake, was the lead partner in the Greater Nile Oil Project. The Sudanese government received about $1 million a day from Talisman and part of these funds were being used to fund a war effort against antigovernment rebels. Critics argued that the company was helping to finance a war that included slavery, scorched earth, and depopulation campaigns. Consequently, Talisman's business activity was heavily criticized by human rights groups and members of the investment community. In 2001, a U.S. human rights group filed a $1 billion lawsuit against Talisman claiming that its operations in Sudan contributed to an ethnic cleansing campaign against civilians. After mounting public pressure, Talisman sold its 25 percent stake in the Greater Nile Petroleum Operating Company to India's state-owned Oil and Natural Gas Corp for $1.2 billion in 2002.[52] This case underscores the need for multinationals to consider the role they play in the host country and their impact on all stakeholders.

Suspension of business in a foreign country is not a decision that can or should be taken precipitously, but it must be regarded as a viable option for those firms that desire to travel on the higher moral road. Each country is at liberty to have its own standards, but this does not mean that North American firms must do business in that country. What does ethical leadership mean if it is not backed up by a willingness and an ability to take a moral stand when the occasion merits?

ETHICAL IMPACT STATEMENTS

MNCs should be constantly aware of the impacts they are having on society, particularly foreign societies. One way to do this is to periodically assess the company's impacts. Companies have a variety of impacts on foreign cultures, and ethical impacts represent only a few of these. The impact statement idea probably derived, in part, from the practice of environmental impact statements that environmental protection legislation pioneered in the1970s and 1980s. These statements are similar to the corporate *social audit* or the "systematic attempt to identify, analyze, measure (if possible), evaluate, and monitor the effect of an organization's operations on society (that is, specific social groups) and on the public well-being."[53] **Ethical impact statements** would be an attempt to assess the underlying moral justifications for corporate actions and the consequent results of those actions. The information derived from these actions would permit the MNCs to modify or change their business practices if the impact statement suggested that such changes would be necessary or desirable.

One form of ethical impact assessment is a firm's attempt to monitor compliance with its global ethics codes. For example, Mattel developed an independent audit and monitoring system for its code. Mattel's monitoring program is headed by an independent panel of commissioners who select a percentage of the company's manufacturing facilities for annual audits. In one audit, for example, Mattel terminated its relationship with three contractor facilities—one in Indonesia for its inability to confirm the age of its employees and two in China for refusing to meet company-mandated safety procedures.[54] Such audits conducted for monitoring compliance are not as comprehensive as ethical impact statements, but they serve similar purposes.

SUMMARY

Ethical dilemmas pose difficulties, in general, for businesses, and those arising in connection with doing business in foreign lands are among the most complex. Marketing controversies, corruption, bribery, sweatshops, and the exploits of MNCs in Third World countries have all contributed to a backlash against globalization. These problems arise for a multiplicity of reasons, but differing cultures, value systems, forms of government, socioeconomic systems, and underhanded and ill-motivated business exploits have all been contributing factors.

The balancing of home and host country standards, global codes of conduct, the integration of ethical considerations into corporate strategy, the option of suspending activities, the use of ethical impact statements, and the adherence to international rights and moral guidelines offer some hope that global business can be better managed. Despite any resistance, current trends point to a growth in business activity in the transnational economy, and consequently these issues will become more rather than less important in the future. Indeed, it could easily be argued that business's greatest ethical challenges in the future will be at the global level.

KEY TERMS

bribes (page 110)

cultural relativism (page 112)

ethical impact statements (page 113)

globalization, globalism (page 102)

global codes of conduct (page 113)

grease payments (page 111)

infant formula controversy (page 106)

internationalization (page 104)

Maquila Solidarity Network (MSN) (page 109)

multinational corporations (MNCs) (page 104)

sweatshops (page 108)

DISCUSSION QUESTIONS

1. Do you think globalization will offer more "good" or more "harm" to all those affected by this phenomenon?

2. As an MNC seeks to balance and honour the ethical standards of both the home and host countries, conflicts inevitably will arise. What criteria do you think managers should consider as they try to decide whether to use home or host country ethical standards?

3. Differentiate between a bribe and a grease payment. Give an example of each.

4. What kind of ethical guidelines should be applied to judge the ethics of MNC's? Whose ethics matter most – the MNC's home country or the host country?

5. Drawing on the notions of moral, amoral, and immoral management (discussed in Chapter 10), categorize your impressions of Nestlé, in the infant formula controversy.

ENDNOTES

1. Paul Beamish, Allen Morrison, Philip Rosenzweig, and Andrew Inkpen, *International Management: Text and Cases* (Boston: Irwin McGraw Hill, 2000), 3.

2. Herman E. Daly, "Globalization and Its Discontents," *Philosophy & Public Policy Quarterly* (Vol. 21, No. 2/3, Spring/Summer 2001), 17.

3. *Ibid.*, 17.

4. "Backlash Behind the Anxiety over Globalization," *Business Week* (April 24, 2000), 38.

5. Ernesto Zedillo, "Globaphobia," *Forbes* (March 19, 2001), 49.

6. *Ibid.*; "The Meaning of Seattle" (1999), 5.

7. Robert Batterson and Murray Weidenbaum, *The Pros and Cons of Globalization* (St. Louis: Center for the Study of American Business, January 2001), i.

8. Nicholas Stern, "Businesses Are Helping to Overcome Global Poverty," *Ivey Business Journal* (Vol. 66, No. 1, September/October 2001), 9–13.

9. John Garland and Richard N. Farmer, *International Dimensions of Business Policy and Strategy* (Boston: Kent Publishing Company, 1986), 166–173.

10. *Ibid.*, 167–168.

11. *Ibid.*, 169.

12. *Ibid.*, 170–171.

13. *Ibid.*, 172.

14. *Ibid.*

15. "Ethical Dilemmas of the Multinational Enterprise," *Business Ethics Report*, Highlights of Bentley College's Sixth National Conference of Business Ethics (Waltham, MA: The Center for Business Ethics at Bentley College, October 10 and 11, 1985), 3. See also Richard T. DeGeorge, *Competing with Integrity in International Business* (New York: Oxford University Press, 1993).

16. James E. Post, "Assessing the Nestlé Boycott: Corporate Accountability and Human Rights," *California Management Review* (Winter 1985), 115–116.

17. *Ibid.*, 116–117.

18. Rogene A. Buchholz, William D. Evans, and Robert Q. Wagley, *Management Response to Public Issues* (Englewood Cliffs, NJ: Prentice Hall, 1985), 80.

19. *Ibid.*, 81–82.

20. Oliver Williams, "Who Cast the First Stone?" *Harvard Business Review* (September–October, 1984), 155.

21. "Nestlé's Costly Accord," *Newsweek* (February 6, 1984), 52.

22. Alix M. Freedman, "Nestlé to Restrict Low-Cost Supplies of Baby Food to Developing Nations" and "American Home Infant-Formula Giveaway to End," *The Wall Street Journal* (February 4, 1991), B1.

23. For further discussion, see S. Prakash Sethi, *Multinational Corporations and the Impact of Public Advocacy on Corporate Strategy: Nestlé and the Infant Formula Case* (Boston: Kluwer Academic, 1994).

24. Mark Clifford, Michael Shari, and Linda Himelstein, "Pangs of Conscience: Sweatshops Haunt U.S. Consumers," *Business Week* (July 29, 1996), 46–47. See also Keith B. Richburg and Anne Swardson "Sweatshops or Economic Development?" The *Washington Post National Weekly Edition* (August 5–11, 1996), 19; *Unite Magazine* (Summer 1999), http://www.uniteunion.org/magazine/sum99/canada.html .

25. "Stamping Out Sweatshops," *The Economist* (April 19, 1997), 28–29.

26. Clifford, Shari, and Himelstein, 46.

27. Andrew Young, "A Debate over Child Labor: The World's Next Moral Crusade," *The Atlanta Journal* (March 9, 1997), R2.

28. *Ibid.*

29. *Ibid.*

30. Maquila Solidarity Network, http://www.web.net/~msn/3codehistory.htm; Murray MacAdam, *The CCPA Monitor* (March 2003); Canadian Centre for Policy Alternatives, http://www.policyalternatives.ca.

31. UNITE Canada, http://www.unite-svti.org/En/en.html.

32. Maquila Solidarity Network, http://www.maquilasolidarity.org/.

33. "Clothing label Info May Not Help Battle Sweatshops: Conference Board," *CBC Online* (June 3, 2003), http://www.cbc.ca/.

34. Maquila Solidarity Network, http://www.maquilasolidarity.org/.

35. Dwight R. Ladd, "The Bribery Business," in Tom L. Beauchamp (ed.), *Case Studies in Business, Society and Ethics* (Englewood Cliffs, NJ: Prentice Hall, 1983), 251.

36. Richard T. DeGeorge, *Business Ethics* (New York: Macmillan, 1982), 53.

37. Neil Ford, "Turning Water into Money," *African Business* (Issue 291, October 2003), 48.

38. Bruce Lloyd, "Bribery, Corruption and Accountability," *Insights on Global Ethics* (Vol. 4, No. 8, September 1994), 5.

39. Ian I. Mitroff and Ralph H. Kilmann, "Teaching Managers to Do Policy Analysis: The Case of Corporate Bribery," *California Management Review* (Fall 1977), 50–52.

40. "The Destructive Costs of Greasing Palms," *Business Week* (December 6, 1993), 133–138; See also Henry W. Lane and Donald G. Simpson, "Bribery in International Business: Whose Problem Is It?" (Reading 12) in H. W. Lane, J. J. DiStefano, and M. L. Maznevski (eds.), *International Management Behavior*, 4th ed., (Oxford: Blackwell Publishers, 2000), 469–487.

41. G. Pascal Zachary, "Levi Tries to Make Sure Contract Plants in Asia Treat People Well," *The Wall Street Journal* (July 28, 1994), A1.

42. Gene R. Laczniak and Jacob Naor, "Global Ethics: Wrestling with the Corporate Conscience," *Business* (July–September 1985),

43. "A Code of Worldwide Business Conduct," in Frederick D. Sturdivant (ed.), *The Corporate Social Challenge: Cases and Commentaries* (Homewood, IL: Richard D. Irwin, 1985), 159–169.

44. "General Dynamics Standards of Business Ethics and Conduct" (August 1985), 17.

45. "Mattel, Inc. Launches Global Code of Conduct," unpublished press release, November 20, 1997; See also "Global Manufacturing Principles" (1997), 1–11.

46. Robert D. Haas, "Ethics in the Trenches," *Across the Board* (May 1994), 12–13.

47. "Starbucks Pays Premium Price to Benefit Workers," *Business Ethics* (March/April 1998), 9.

48. Laczniak and Naor, 7–8.

49. Archie B. Carroll, Frank Hoy, and John Hall, "The Integration of Corporate Social Policy into Strategic Management," in S. Prakash Sethi and Cecilia M. Falbe (eds.), *Business and Society: Dimensions of Conflict and Cooperation* (Lexington, MA: Lexington Books, 1987), 449–470.

50. Laczniak and Naor, 8.

51. Haas, 12.

52. Toby Heaps, "After Talisman's Exit from Sudan, Other Canadian Resource Companies in Focus," *Corporate Knights*, http://www.corporateknights.ca/index.asp.

53. David H. Blake, William C. Frederick, and Mildred S. Myers, *Social Auditing: Evaluating the Impact of Corporate Programs* (New York: Praeger, 1976), 3.

54. Mattel press release, November 20, 1997.

7

GOVERNMENT AS A STAKEHOLDER IN BUSINESS

CHAPTER OBJECTIVES

After studying this chapter, you should be able to:

1   Appreciate the complex interactions among business, government, and the public.

2   Identify and describe government's nonregulatory influences, especially the concepts of industrial policy and privatization.

3   Explain government regulation and identify the major reasons for regulation, the types of regulation, and issues arising out of regulation.

4   Discuss the issues surrounding regulation versus deregulation.

Over the past 40 years, the depth, scope, and direction of government's involvement in business has made the business/government relationship one of the most hotly debated issues of modern times. Government's role, particularly in the regulation of business, has ensured its place among the major stakeholders with which business must establish an effective working relationship if it is to survive and prosper.

Business has never been fond of government's having an activist role in establishing the ground rules under which it operates. In contrast, public interest has been cyclical, going through periods when it has thought that the federal government had too much power and other periods when it has thought that government should be more activist.

The traditional relationship between government and business is clearly undergoing change across the world. Canada like many other countries has experienced a marked shift toward reduced government involvement in the business sector, reflected in such trends as deregulation and privatization. It has been suggested that what we are witnessing is a significant decrease in government involvement as public preferences shift toward a more purely private market system. It seems that many observers view the decrease in the level of government influence in business as a positive change. However, some believe that there is good reason for advocating a continued—and, perhaps, increased—role for government in business. What kind of role should government play in the business sector?

In this chapter, we will examine the relationship between business and government, although the general public will assume an important role in the discussion as well. A central concern in this chapter is the government's role in influencing business. Exploring this relationship carefully will provide an appreciation of the complexity of the issues surrounding business/government interactions.

THE ROLES OF GOVERNMENT AND BUSINESS

We do not intend to philosophize in this chapter on the ideal role of government in relation to business, because this is outside our stakeholder frame of reference. However, we will strive for an understanding of current major issues as they pertain to this vital relationship. For effective management, government, as a stakeholder, must be understood.

The fundamental question underlying our entire discussion of business/government relationships is, "What should be the respective roles of business and government in our socioeconomic system?" This question is far easier to ask than to answer, but as we explore it, some important basic understandings begin to emerge.

The issue could be stated in a different fashion: Given all the tasks that must be accomplished to make our society work, which of these tasks should be handled by government and which should be handled by business? This poses the issue clearly, but there are other questions that remain to be answered. If we decide, for example, that it is best to let business handle the production and distribution roles in our society, the next question becomes "How much autonomy are we willing to allow business?" If our goals were simply the production and distribution of goods and services, we would not have to constrain business severely. In modern times, however, other goals have been added to the production and distribution functions: for example, a safe working environment for those engaging in production, equal employment opportunities, fair pay, clean air, safe products, employee rights, and so on. When these goals are superimposed on the basic economic goals, the task of business becomes much more complex and challenging.

Because these latter, more socially oriented goals are not automatically factored into business decision making and processes, it often falls on government to ensure that those goals that reflect concerns of the public interest be achieved. Thus, whereas the marketplace dictates economic production decisions, government becomes one of the citizenry's designated representatives charged with articulating and protecting the public interest.

A CLASH OF ETHICAL BELIEF SYSTEMS

A clash of emphases partially forms the crux of the antagonistic relationship that has evolved between business and government over the years. This problem has been termed "a clash of ethical systems." The two ethical systems (systems of belief) are the **individualistic ethic of business** and the **collectivistic ethic of government**. Figure 7–1 summarizes the characteristics of these two philosophies.[1]

Figure 7-1

The Clash of Ethical Systems Between Business and Government

Business Beliefs	Government Beliefs
• Individualistic ethic	• Collectivistic ethic
• Maximum concession to self-interest	• Subordination of individual goals and self-interest to group goals and group interests
• Minimizing the load of obligations society imposes on the individual (personal freedom)	• Maximizing the obligations assumed by the individual and discouraging self-interest
• Emphasizes inequalities of individuals	• Emphasizes equality of individuals

The clash of these two ethical systems partially explains why the current business/government relationship is adversarial in nature. In elaborating on the adversarial nature of the business/government relationship, Jacoby offered the following comments:

> Officials of government characteristically look upon themselves as probers, inspectors, taxers, regulators, and punishers of business transgressions. Businesspeople typically view government agencies as obstacles, constraints, delayers, and impediments to economic progress, having much power to stop and little to start.[2]

The business/government relationship not only has become adversarial but also has been deteriorating. The goals and values of our pluralistic society have become more complex, more numerous, more interrelated, and, consequently, more difficult to reconcile. The result has been increasing conflicts among diverse interest groups, with trade-off decisions becoming harder to make. In this process, it has become more difficult to establish social priorities, and consensus has in many cases become impossible to achieve.[3]

SOCIAL, TECHNOLOGICAL, AND VALUE CHANGES

As we attempt to understand why all this has happened, it is only natural to look to changes in the social and technological environments for some explanations. According to Daniel Bell, since World War II four major changes have had profound impacts on North American society in general and on the business/government relationship in particular. **First**, out of local and regional societies a truly national one has arisen.[4] **Second**, we have seen a "communal society" arise, characterized by a great emphasis on public goods. **Third**, the revolution of rising expectations has brought with it the demand for "entitlements"—good jobs, excellent housing, and other amenities. **Fourth**, a rising concern has emerged for an improved "quality of life."[5]

The value changes that have taken place "have multiplied the number of political decisions that have to be made relative to the number of decisions made in markets."[6] To the extent that these political decisions affect business—and they do to a great extent—we can understand the basic conflict arising once again in a clash between individualist and collectivist belief systems. Government's responses to changes taking place in society have put it in direct opposition to business in terms of both philosophy and mode of operation. Although one might argue that this clash of belief systems is not as severe today as it once was, the basic differences still serve to frame the positions of the two groups.

INTERACTION OF BUSINESS, GOVERNMENT, AND THE PUBLIC

This section offers a brief overview of the influence relationships among business, government, and the public. This should be helpful in understanding both the nature of the process by which public policy decisions are made and the current problems that characterize the business/government relationship. Figure 7–2 illustrates the pattern of these influence relationships.

Figure 7-2

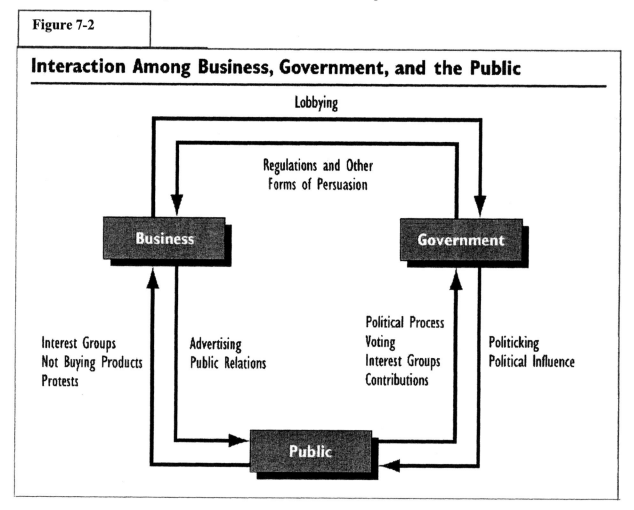

Interaction Among Business, Government, and the Public

One might rightly ask at this point, "Why include the public? Isn't the public represented by government?" In an ideal world, perhaps this would be true. To help us appreciate that government functions somewhat apart from the public, it has been depicted separately in the diagram. In addition, the public has its methods of influence that need to be singled out.

The public uses the political processes of voting and electing officials (or removing them from office) to influence government. It also exerts its influence by forming special-interest groups (farmers, small business owners, educators, senior citizens, truckers, manufacturers, etc.) to wield more targeted influence. Government, in turn, uses politicking, public policy formation, and other political influences to have an impact on the public.

BUSINESS/PUBLIC RELATIONSHIP

Business influences the public through advertising, public relations, and other forms of communication. The public influences business through the marketplace or by forming special-interest or advocacy groups (e.g., Greenpeace, Aboriginal Rights Coalition, Canadian Federation of Humane Societies).

Earlier we raised the question of whether government really represents the public. This question may be stated another way: "Who determines what is in the public interest?" In our society, determining the public interest is not a simple matter. Whereas government may be the official representative of the public, we should not assume that representation occurs in a straightforward fashion. As we saw in Figure 7–2, the public takes its own initiatives both with business and with government. The three major groups, therefore, are involved in a dynamic interplay of influence processes that determine what is currently considered to be in the public interest.

Our central concern in this chapter is with government's role in influencing business, and we now turn our attention to that topic. Here we will begin to see more clearly how government is a major stakeholder of business. Government's official priority is in representing the public interest as it sees and interprets the public's wishes. But, like all large bureaucratic organizations, government also takes on a life of its own with its own goals and agenda.

GOVERNMENT'S NONREGULATORY INFLUENCE ON BUSINESS

Given its magnitude, it is not difficult to appreciate the significant effect government actions have on all institutions in society. We will limit our treatment to the federal government's influence on business, but we must remain mindful of the presence and influence of provincial and local governments as well.

Broadly speaking, we may categorize the kinds of influence government has on business as *nonregulatory* and *regulatory*. In the next major section, we will focus on government regulation, but in this section let us consider the wide range of nonregulatory influences that government has on business.

Two major issues merit consideration before we examine some of the specific policy tools or mechanisms government uses to influence business. These two major issues are (1) industrial policy and (2) privatization. Industrial policy is concerned with the role that our government plays in the world of international trade, and privatization zeroes in on the question of whether current public functions (e.g., public education, public transit, health care, social security, fire service) should be turned over to the private (business) sector. Both of these issues have important implications for the business/government relationship. They are both important, because they seem to come into and out of popularity on a fairly regular basis.

INDUSTRIAL POLICY

Important initial questions include: "What does industrial policy mean, and why has it become such a hotly debated issue?" An **industrial policy** may be defined as follows: "Any selective government measure that prevents or promotes changes in the structure of an economy."[7]

This very broad definition by itself does not give us enough focus to understand the concept. Let us elaborate. One school of thought thinks of industrial policy as some variation of the British model, wherein government provides help for older, declining industries. Therefore, when steel company executives in Canada argue for tax breaks and tariffs that would enable them to survive and compete with foreign competition, they are asking for an industrial policy.[8]

Another school of thought is exemplified by Robert Reich in his book *The Next American Frontier*, wherein he argues for a national industrial policy that attempts to identify winning (or sunrise) industries and foster their growth. As for losing (or sunset) industries, industrial policy would have as its goal redirecting resources into growth fields.[9]

ARGUMENTS FOR INDUSTRIAL POLICY

Proponents of an industrial policy (more active role of government in the business sector) cite a variety of reasons for supporting it. **First**, of course, is the threatened competitiveness of Canada in world markets. A **second** argument is the use of industrial policy by other world governments, including Germany, Britain, France, and Italy. A **third** major argument is that Canada does not have a comprehensive industrial policy, but rather operates based on the haphazard results of unplanned taxes, tariffs, regulatory policies, and research and development policies. Our current system has been called an ad hoc industrial policy because the government has, in fact, intervened in many specific industries as emergencies have arisen.

In Canada, though the relationship has not been shaped by a clear industrial policy, we have a long history of government involvement in business in the sense of promoting and protecting our industries. For example, tariff and nontariff barriers on imported goods were designed to protect our domestic business by making foreign goods more expensive relative to Canadian goods. In fact, it can be argued that a large portion of Canada's industrial development is due to protectionism through tariffs first imposed in 1879 by Sir John A. Macdonald's National Policy. Eventually, the government also offered direct incentives for industrial and resource development.

The pervasiveness of globalization has demanded that governments reconsider the extent to which they feel obligated to maintain a relationship with the private business sector. Thomas Friedman, in his book *The Lexus and the Olive Tree*, asserts that globalization is, in fact, increasing the importance of government while changing the roles that it plays:

> The ability of an economy to withstand the inevitable ups and downs depends in large part on the quality of its legal system, financial system and economic management—all matters still under the control of governments and bureaucrats. Chile, Taiwan, Hong Kong, and Singapore all survived the economic crises of the 1990s so much better than their neighbours because they had better-quality states running better-quality software and operating systems.

Among the important roles governments can play in the global business scene are:

Nurturing Young Industries.
The infant-industry argument asserts that the government should help a young domestic industry to grow and develop by ensuring that the industry maintains a dominant share of the domestic market until it is mature enough to compete against foreign competition. Consequently, this philosophy is still applied, particularly, among developing countries. The rationale is that the infant industry may be less competitive, particularly because of initially high output costs; however, with maturity, the production will become more efficient, and protection will no longer be necessary.

Protecting Domestic Business from Unfair Competition
There is a concern among some businesses that foreign competitors will offer their products at extremely low prices as a means of monopolizing their share of the target country's market. The ultimate consequence would be that domestic producers could potentially be driven out of business and replaced

by the foreign imports. A foreign competitor who manages to export the products at such low prices may be accused of dumping—which is pricing the product below cost or below the cost in the target country. In other words, a foreign supplier who sells a product at a loss or for less than the price of the seller's domestic market would be considered guilty of dumping.

Steel companies have been among the most avid users of anti-dumping legislation in Canada and the United States. Hamilton-based Dofasco Inc. lodged a dumping complaint against steel mills in Asia and South America. The aim was to seek government assistance, which in this case resulted in a decision by the Canadian government to place antidumping tariffs on low-cost imported steel from these foreign suppliers. In total, these antidumping tariffs were aimed at blocking the dumping of steel shipments from nine countries. This echoes similar action taken in the United States. Steel producers in both the United States and Canada have blamed increasing foreign imports of steel for reducing demand for their product domestically and, consequently, reducing product prices and revenue.

Maintaining Adequate Levels of Domestic Employment
A government knows that society holds it responsible for ensuring the unemployment rates are not high. Imports that come to dominate an industry bring the threat of causing domestic industries to go bankrupt. Consequently, where businesses claim they are under threat of bankruptcy due to foreign competition, the government is forced to consider what action it can take to combat this threat. In the past, the government protected Canadian business and employment from the risk of foreign competition via the implementation of tariffs. Clearly, such an option is complicated by the fact that reducing imports is not necessarily feasible under trade agreements. Protectionist policies are not compatible with the sentiments of free trade, and thus governments are sometimes placed in the unenviable position of balancing the needs of the domestic economy with the need to honour the rules governing global business. A case in point is the issue of government subsidies.

Offering Subsidies to Compete Globally
Whether it is for the purpose of maintaining employment levels or of assisting businesses in the global marketplace, the issue of government subsidies to business has become much more controversial in the context of globalization. Whether it is cash payments, low-interest loans, or tax breaks, such financial assistance is referred to as a subsidy. And in the case of the global context, such subsidies are intended to help domestic industry deal with global competition.

ARGUMENTS AGAINST INDUSTRIAL POLICY

Critics of industrial policy argue that government interference reduces the market's efficiency. How do you keep politics out of what ought to be economic decisions? Some politicians, as well as experts, think Canada should focus on rescuing flagging or "sunset" industries. Others argue we ought to promote emerging "sunrise" industries, such as breakthrough products in high technology.

Those who oppose industrial policy say that foreign success with it has been highly variable. Japan, for example, has had as many failures as successes with its government's development agency, Ministry of International Trade and Industry (MITI). MITI was generally credited with helping to build Japan's computer, semiconductor, and steel industries, but efforts to promote the aluminum-refining, petrochemical, shipping, and commercial aircraft industries were viewed as failures.[10] One economist, Gary Saxonhouse, reports that Japanese support for research and development is less than that in North America. He says that less than 2 percent of nondefence business research and development is financed by government in Japan, compared with 22 percent in the United States.[11] Further, Japan's favourable industrial policies (keiretsu), combined with lifetime employment, are ill suited to surviving economic recessions: The Japanese business system has produced too few entrepreneurial risk-takers.[12]

Finally, attempts at forming an industrial policy have been criticized as being irrational and uncoordinated and composed largely of "voluntary" restrictions on imports, occasional bailouts for near-bankruptcy companies, and a wide array of subsidies, loan guarantees, and special tax benefits for particular firms and industries. Thus, such efforts have constituted an industrial policy by default.[13] One could argue that Canada is incapable of developing a successful and planned industrial policy, given its experience and the composition of the public policy process that has characterized past decision making. Moreover, many critics would suggest that business must learn to survive on its own without looking to government involvement whenever it is in need. Based on that sentiment, any kind of industrial policy that requires government to come to the aid of business in order to help it compete internationally is problematic.

Government interventions in the international context may be viewed as another form of undesirable protectionism. For example, while Canadian steel producers welcomed government intervention to restrict access to cheaper foreign competitors' imports, other domestic players were not happy with the implementation of antidumping tariffs. These tariffs effectively raised the price of the foreign-produced goods. Many Canadian steel businesses argued that they would lose access to cheaper foreign sources and be forced to rely on costlier steel sources in Ontario. The argument of these businesses is that they feel that they should have access to the lowest-cost sources of steel, whether these sources are from Canada or from foreign producers. In this regard, they are opposed to the government's protectionist policy of imposing antidumping tariffs.

Government assistance to business in the form of subsidies has significant implications in the global business context. Subsidies have been identified as either cash payments, low-interest loans, or potentially reduced taxes. Specifically, subsidies in the global context are intended to assist domestic industry to compete against foreign businesses, whether in the home country or through exports. One central argument against subsidies, whether in the domestic or global context, is that businesses should be required to manage their costs without external help, or "hand-outs," from the government. This is part of the requirement of fair competition, according to the critics. In addition, it is argued that consumers essentially pay for these subsidies. The government collects revenues through income and sales taxes, and it is these funds, collected from the general public, that are used to help some businesses. The question is: Are subsidies to business an unfair drain on public funds? There is no clear resolution to this ongoing debate.

From the global perspective, there is a second central criticism aimed at companies that receive subsidies from their local government. The criticism asserts that subsidies are not merely harmless forms of assistance to businesses; rather, they constitute a form of trade barrier, just like tariffs, and they create unfair competition. According to some critics, the recent Canada–U.S. softwood lumber dispute was an example of the difficulty in establishing the degree to which government should aid business in the global context. The U.S lumber industry accused the Canadian government of unfairly subsidizing the Canadian softwood lumber industry.

PRIVATIZATION

Privatization, generally speaking, refers to the process of "turning over to" the private sector (business) some function or service that was previously handled by some government body.[14] More than $700 billion in assets have been privatized worldwide, with emerging economies accounting for almost 40 percent of that.[15] Privatization is an integral part of the twenty-first century strategies of both developed and developing countries, with the intent being to capture both the discipline of the free market and a spirit of entrepreneurial risk-taking.[16]

To understand privatization, we need to differentiate two functions government might perform: (1) producing a service and (2) providing a service.[17] A city government would be *providing a service* if it employed a private security firm to work at the coliseum during the local basketball playoffs. This same city government would be *producing a service* if its own police force provided security at the same basketball tournament. The terminology can be confusing, but the distinction must be made, because sometimes government provides a service (has a program for and actually pays for a service) and at other times it also produces a service (has its own employees who do it).[18]

WHY SHOULD GOVERNMENT PRODUCE OR PROVIDE SERVICES? Traditionally, Canada embraced the need for Crown corporations. Such public enterprises are organizations accountable, through a minister, to Parliament for its operations. Crown corporations may be federal (e.g., Canada Post, the Canadian Broadcasting Corporation, the Canadian Wheat Board) or provincial (e.g., the Liquor Control Board of Ontario). Governments establish Crown corporations for a number of possible reasons:

- *To implement public policy that includes protecting or safeguarding national interests.* For example, federal Crown corporations, such as Air Canada and Petro-Canada, helped facilitate government policy in the area of cross-Canada transportation and Canadian ownership in the domestic oil industry.
- *To protect industries deemed to be vital to the economy.* The reason for taking control of the Canadian National Railways (CNR) in 1919 was in order to safeguard the government's large investment in the railways and to protect Canada's image in foreign capital markets. While few municipal governments have traditionally held significant corporate holdings, they have been owners of public transit systems, recreational centres, and other facilities that are intended to enhance the quality of life in society.
- *To provide special services that could not otherwise be made available by private business.* For example, Trans Canada Airlines (Air Canada) was established in the 1930s, after it was observed that no private business was willing or able to provide domestic air services. Consider also the Bank of Canada. The Bank of Canada, created in 1935, was established to serve first as a control agent for the chartered banks—for example, requiring the banks to report regularly on their operations and to hold deposit reserves with the Bank of Canada. Second, the Bank of Canada is responsible for developing monetary policy and regulating monetary operations in Canada.
- *To nationalize or federalize industries considered to be "natural monopolies," including the generation and distribution of electricity.* It is not hard to imagine that in the early days of Canadian society the private sector was too small to undertake the creation of a national electricity supply grid. On the other hand, government was capable of raising the necessary capital and, consequently, it took on the establishment of public utilities, including things like water supply, sewage treatment plants, and electricity generating plants, in addition to road construction and the like.

THE PRIVATIZATION DEBATE

Proponents of privatization suggest that the functions of entire bureaucracies need to be contracted out to the private sector. They maintain that government at all levels is involved in thousands of businesses in which it has no real comparative advantage and no basic reason for being involved. They also argue that publicly owned enterprises are less efficient and less flexible than competitive private firms.[18] Opponents of privatization contend that there are certain activities that cannot be safely or effectively handled by the private sector. For example, in the U.S., following the September 11 terrorist attacks, there were many calls for **federalization** of airport security (the return of airport security to the government sector).

Privatization efforts are always undertaken with the hope that they will lead to improvements in efficiency and overall performance. In some cases, these hopes are realized but in many they are not. On average, a privatized firm's performance improves, but there is considerable variance in post-privatization performance among individual firms.[19] This variance is likely to be caused by differences in the ways that firms implement privatization programs. The nature of top management, the functioning of the board, and the strategic actions the firms undertake will all contribute to the likelihood of a privatization strategy's success.[19]

These two issues—industrial policy and privatization—are largely unresolved. As a result, they continue to be discussed and debated. As we have seen, the success of these efforts is largely dependent on their context—both the environments in which they are adopted and the ways in which they are implemented. It is clear that both industrial policy and privatization will have significant implications for the business/government relationship for years to come.

GOVERNMENT'S REGULATORY INFLUENCES ON BUSINESS

For more than two decades, government regulation has been the most controversial issue in the business/government relationship. Government regulation has affected virtually every aspect of how business functions. It has affected the terms and conditions under which firms have competed in their respective industries. It has touched almost every business decision ranging from the production of goods and services to packaging, distribution, marketing, and service. Most people agree that some degree of regulation has been necessary to ensure that consumers and employees are treated fairly and are not exposed to unreasonable hazards and that the environment is protected. However, they also think that government regulation has often been too extensive in scope, too costly, and inevitably burdensome in terms of paperwork requirements and red tape.

REGULATION: WHAT DOES IT MEAN?

Generally, **regulation** refers to the act of governing, directing according to rule, or bringing under the control of law or constituted authority. Although there is no universally agreed-upon definition of federal regulation, we can look to the definition provided by the Economic Council of Canada as "the imposition of constraints, backed by the authority of a government, that are intended to modify economic behaviour in the private sector significantly."

There has been a relatively wide scope for government regulation in business activity: for example, regulation focused on consumer protection, regulation aimed at environmental protection, and regulation regarding the nature of competition. One obvious set of regulations exists fundamentally to protect the consumer, and the Canadian government has initiated a number of programs designed for consumer protection, many of which are administered by Health Canada. Among the numerous regulations, there is the Food and Drug Act, which was designed to protect the public from potential risks to health as well as from fraud or deception as it relates to food, drugs, cosmetics, and the like. Similarly, the Hazardous Products Act serves to protect public safety by either banning products because they are deemed dangerous or requiring warning labels on products that might be considered hazardous. Ecological regulations are designed to protect the environment, and include legislation such as the Environmental Contaminants Act, which creates regulations to limit any dangerous byproducts of industrial production that could be harmful to people's health.

REASONS FOR REGULATION

Why does the government need to intervene in the functioning of the business enterprise system? Regulations have come about over the years for a variety of reasons. There are several legitimate reasons why government regulation has evolved, although many businesspeople may not entirely agree with them. For the most part, however, government regulation has arisen because some kind of **market failure** (failure of the free-enterprise system) has occurred and government, intending to represent the public interest, has chosen to take corrective action. In addition, regulations can be encouraged through the efforts of special-interest groups that have lobbied successfully for them.

Major reasons or justifications for regulation include (1) controlling natural monopolies, (2) controlling negative externalities, (3) achieving social goals.

CONTROLLING NATURAL MONOPOLIES

One of the earliest circumstances in which government felt a need to regulate occurred when a natural monopoly existed. A **natural monopoly** exists in a market where the economics of scale are so great that the largest firm has the lowest costs and thus is able to drive out its competitors. Such a firm can supply the entire market more efficiently and cheaply than several smaller firms. Local telephone service is a good example, because parallel sets of telephone wires would involve waste and duplication that would be much more costly.

Monopolies such as this may seem "natural," but when left to their own devices could restrict output and raise prices. This potential abuse justifies the regulation of monopolies. As a consequence, we have seen telephone service providers (e.g., Bell Canada) subject to government regulators like the Canadian Radio-television and Telecommunications Commission (CRTC). Among other issues, such government regulators would determine the rates that the company may charge its customers.[20]

Related to the control of natural monopolies is the government's desire to intervene when it thinks companies have engaged in anticompetitive practices. A famous, recent example of this was the U.S. Justice Department's investigation of the Microsoft Corporation case in which the company was accused of anticompetitive trade practices. The U.S. Court of Appeals in a mixed ruling overturned an initial court ruling, recommending that Microsoft be split in two. The appeals court reprimanded the judge for publicly criticizing Microsoft but upheld the finding of fact that the Windows operating system constitutes a monopoly in the PC market and that Microsoft violated the Sherman Antitrust Act with its marketing tactics. Microsoft would bundle new features into their Windows operating system as a way of breaking into new markets. They then designed their operating system so that it worked more smoothly with Microsoft products than with others—giving it a clear and, according to the courts, unfair marketing advantage.[21] A *Business Week* editorial opined, "The courts should insist that Windows is a common carrier that must be open to all competitors, much like phone lines and cable . . . Microsoft must accept the legal finding that it is a monopoly. As such, it has an obligation to open its operating system to competitors. If it does, it should be able to do the very thing it says is essential to its future—bundle new features into Windows that consumers want."[22]

CONTROLLING NEGATIVE EXTERNALITIES

Another important rationale for government regulation is that of controlling the **negative externalities** (or spillover effects) that result when the manufacture or use of a product gives rise to unplanned or unintended side effects on others (other than the producer or the consumer). Examples of these negative externalities are air pollution, water pollution, and improper disposal of toxic wastes. The consequence of such negative externalities is that neither the producer nor the consumer of the product directly "pays" for all the "costs" that are created by the manufacture of the product. The "costs" that must be borne by the public include an unpleasant or a foul atmosphere, illness, and the resulting health-care costs. Some have called these **social costs**, because they are absorbed by society rather than incorporated into the cost of making the product.

Preventing negative externalities is enormously expensive, and few firms are willing to pay for these added costs voluntarily. This is especially true in an industry that produces an essentially undifferentiated product, such as steel, where the millions of dollars needed to protect the environment would only add to the cost of the product and provide no benefit to the purchaser. In such situations, therefore, government regulation is seen as reasonable, and even welcomed, because it requires all firms competing in a given industry to operate according to the same rules. By forcing all firms to incur the costs, regulations level the competitive playing field.

Just as companies do not voluntarily take on huge expenditures for environmental protection, individuals often behave in the same fashion. For example, automobile emissions are one of the principal forms of air pollution. But how many private individuals would voluntarily request an emissions control system if it were offered as optional equipment? In situations such as this, a government standard that requires everyone to adhere to the regulation is much more likely to address the public's concern for air pollution.[23]

ACHIEVING SOCIAL GOALS

Government not only employs regulations to address market failures and negative externalities but also seeks to use regulations to help achieve certain **social goals** it deems to be in the public interest. Some of these social goals are related to negative externalities in the sense that government is attempting to correct problems that might also be viewed as negative externalities by particular groups. An example of this might be the harmful effects of a dangerous product or the unfair treatment of minorities resulting from employment discrimination. These externalities are not as obvious as air pollution, but they are just as real.

Another important social goal of government is to keep people informed. One could argue that inadequate information is a serious problem and that government should use its regulatory powers to require firms to reveal certain kinds of information to consumers. Thus, Health Canada's Product Safety Programme requires firms to warn consumers of potential product hazards through labelling requirements. Other regulatory mandates that address the issue of inadequate information include grading standards, weight and size information, truth-in-advertising requirements, product safety standards, and so on. A prime example of recent labelling requirements can be seen on canned goods and other products at the grocery store. Most canned goods now carry a "Nutrition Facts" label that provides consumer information on calories, fat content, and quantities of sodium, cholesterol, carbohydrates, proteins, and vitamins.

Other important social goals that have been addressed include preservation of national security (deregulation of oil prices to lessen dependence on imports), considerations of fairness or equity (employment discrimination laws), protection of those who provide essential services (farmers), allocation of scarce resources (gasoline rationing), and protection of consumers from excessively high price increases (natural gas regulation).[24]

Finally, the issue of protecting or preserving Canadian culture has been an issue of concern to the government and one that has been reflected in the rationale for some types of government regulation. For example, the media has often been viewed as an instrument to promote Canadian culture and consequently the government has at times been called upon to consider whether any regulations would help or harm the media's impact on Canadian culture. The notion of preserving national identity or culture has been an argument for regulating the extent of foreign ownership in Canadian businesses involved in cultural activities, such as television and publishing.

TYPES OF REGULATION

Broadly speaking, government regulations have been used for two central purposes: achieving certain economic goals and achieving certain social goals. Therefore, it has become customary to identify two different types of regulation: economic regulation and social regulation.

ECONOMIC REGULATION. Economic regulation is best exemplified by such regulatory bodies as the Transport Canada or the CRTC. These regulatory bodies typically operate along industry lines and were created for the purpose of regulating business behaviour through the control of or influence over economic or market variables such as prices (maximum and minimum), entry to and exit from markets, and types of services that can be offered.

The government has also established a competition policy to control the nature of competition in the business sector. The competition policy, set out in the Competition Act, is intended to stimulate open competition and eliminate any restrictive business practices with the aim of encouraging maximum production, distribution, and employment opportunities. While it is not specific to any one industry, the Competition Bureau's aim is in many ways reflective of the notion of economic regulation.

Competition policy is aimed at creating equity in the marketplace among all the different and potentially competing interests, including consumers and producers; wholesalers and retailers; dominant players and minor players; and the public interest and the private interest. The Competition Bureau (under the auspices of Industry Canada) is responsible for enforcing and administering the Competition Act, and it has four main functions:

1. The Bureau informs companies of what they can and cannot do under competition law. It also informs consumers with regard to their rights.

2. It takes on an advocacy role in promoting greater competition in the business sector. For example, the Bureau has been actively involved in the deregulation process of the telecommunications sector, including its numerous appearances before the CRTC to urge regulators to take the least restrictive action possible so as to minimize the level of regulation, and therefore maximize potential competition.

3. The Bureau closely reviews mergers prior to their occurrence in order to ensure that they do not lead to undue concentration that would limit competition.

4. It seeks to rectify anticompetitive activities, including the use of suasion (warning letters, visits, interviews, etc.); enforcing compliance by obtaining injunctions, consent orders, adoption of voluntary codes; or prosecuting for violations of the Competition Act.[25]

SOCIAL REGULATION. The 1960s ushered in a new form of regulation that for all practical purposes has become what regulation means to modern-day business managers. This new form of regulation has come to be known as social regulation, because it has had as its major thrust the furtherance of societal objectives quite different from the earlier focus on markets and economic variables. Whereas the older form of economic regulation focused on markets, the new social regulation focuses on business's impacts on people. The emphasis on people essentially addresses the needs of people in their roles as employees, consumers, and citizens.

Two major examples of social regulations having specific impacts on people as employees were Employment Equity regulations and Occupational Safety and Health regulations. In 1986 the Employment Equity Act was passed with its purpose to "achieve equality in the workplace so that no person shall be denied employment opportunities or benefits for reasons unrelated to ability and, in the fulfillment of the goals, to correct the conditions of disadvantage in employment experienced by women, Aboriginal peoples, persons with disabilities, and visible minority people..."

The goal of occupational health and safety regulation is to ensure that the nation's workplaces are safe and healthful. Health and safety legislation regulates the standards of workplace safety with the objective of preventing workplace accidents and injury. Regulations cover a variety of issues, including the bases for refusal to work (because of unsafe conditions), workers' compensation, substance abuse in the workplace, violence in the workplace, and employees working alone. Often Workers Compensation Boards act as insurance boards responsible for compensating workers for costs and lost income relating to workplace injury or illness.

A key body governing regulation in both the areas of occupational health and safety and employment equity is the Ministry of Labour. It was created in 1919 to develop and enforce labour legislation, and advance safe, fair, and harmonious workplace practices that are essential to the social and economic well-being of the Canadian citizens.[26] While the Ministry is responsible for establishing, communicating, and enforcing workplace standards, there are a host of commissions and agencies that assist the Ministry of Labour with this mandate. The Canadian Human Rights Commission, for example, is one instrument for helping to reduce barriers to equality in employment and access to services. Figure 7-3 summarizes the nature of economic versus social regulations along with pertinent examples.

Figure 7-3		
Comparison of Economic and Social Regulations		
	Economic Regulations	Social Regulations
Focus	Market conditions, economic variables (entry, exit, prices, services)	People in their roles as employees, consumers, and citizens
Industries Affected	Often industry specific (e.g., breweries, transportation, telecommunications)	Virtually all industries
Examples	Transport Canada	Human Rights Commission

DEREGULATION

Quite frequently, trends and countertrends overlap with one another. Such is the case with regulation and its counterpart, **deregulation**. There are many reasons for this overlapping, but typically they include both the economic and the political. From an economic perspective, there is a continual striving for the balance of freedom and control for business that will be best for society. From a political perspective, there is an ongoing interplay of different societal goals and means for achieving those goals. The outcome is a mix of economic and political decisions that seem to be in a constant state of flux. Thus, in the economy at any point in time, trends that appear counter to one another can coexist simultaneously. These trends are the natural result of competing forces seeking some sort of balance or equilibrium.

This is how we can explain the trend toward deregulation that evolved in a highly regulated environment. Deregulation represents a counterforce aimed at keeping the economy in balance. It also represents a political philosophy that was prevailing during the period of its origin and growth.

Deregulation may be thought of as one kind of regulatory reform. But, because it is unique and quite unlike the regulatory reform measures discussed earlier, we will treat it separately. Deregulation has taken place primarily with respect to economic regulations, and this, too, helps to explain its separate treatment.

PURPOSE OF DEREGULATION

The basic idea behind deregulation has been to remove certain industries from the old-line economic regulations of the past. The purpose of this deregulation, or at least a reduced level of regulation, has been to increase competition with the expected benefits of greater efficiency, lower prices, and enhanced innovation. These goals have not been uniformly received, and it is still undecided whether deregulation works as a method of maximizing society's best interests.

TREND TOWARD DEREGULATION

When the trend toward deregulation began in the 1980s, most notably exemplified in the financial industry, the telecommunications industry, and the transportation (trucking, airline, railroad) industry, it represented business's first major redirection in 50 years.[27] The result seemed to be a mixed bag of benefits and problems. On the benefits side, prices fell in many industries, and better service appeared in some industries along with increased numbers of competitors and innovative products and services.

Several problems arose also. Although prices fell and many competitors entered some of those industries, more and more of those competitors were unable to compete with the dominant firms. They were failing, going bankrupt, or being absorbed by the larger firms. Entry barriers into some industries were enormous and had been greatly underestimated. This has been shown to be the case in airline, trucking, railroad, and long-distance telephone service.[28]

DILEMMA WITH DEREGULATION

The intent of deregulation was to deregulate the industries, thus allowing for freer competition. The intent was not to deregulate health and safety requirements. The dilemma with deregulation is how to enhance the competitive nature of the affected industries without sacrificing the applicable social regulations. This is the second major problem with deregulation that needs to be discussed. Unfortunately, the potential competition unleashed by economic deregulation can force many companies to cut corners in ways that endanger the health and/or safety of their customers. This pattern, which seems to occur in any deregulated industry, was apparent in the trucking and airline industries.[29]

In addition, critics of deregulation point out that in many cases, the deregulation did not achieve the goal of increased competition and consequently may fail to benefit the consumer. While advocates of deregulation feel that the benefits of increased competition will ultimately prevail, opponents believe that public ownership should continue to exist for essential services in order to ensure that all members of society will be guaranteed access to the same service at a reasonable price.

SUMMARY

Business cannot be discussed without considering the paramount role played by government. Although the two institutions have opposing systems of belief, they are intertwined in terms of their functioning in our socioeconomic system. In addition, the public assumes a major role in a complex pattern of interactions among business, government, and the public. Government exerts a host of nonregulatory influences on business. Two influences with a macro orientation include industrial policy and privatization.

One of government's most controversial interventions in business is direct regulation. Government regulates business for several legitimate reasons, and in the past two decades social regulation has been more dominant than economic regulation. While numerous industries have undergone deregulation, bad experiences in key industries have caused many to wonder whether the government has gone too far in that direction.

KEY TERMS

collectivistic ethic of government (page 121)

deregulation (page 134)

economic regulation (page 132)

federalization (page 129)

individualistic ethic of business (page 121)

DISCUSSION QUESTIONS

1. Briefly explain how business and government represent a clash of ethical systems (belief systems). With which do you find yourself identifying most? Explain. With which would most business students identify? Explain.

2. Explain why the public is treated as a separate group in the interactions among business, government, and the public. Doesn't government represent the public's interests? How should the public's interests be manifested?

3. What is regulation? Why does government see a need to regulate? Differentiate between economic and social regulation. What social regulations do you think are most important, and why? What social regulations ought to be eliminated? Explain.

4. What is the current mood of Canada regarding deregulation? What evidence can you present to substantiate your opinion?

ENDNOTES

1. L. Earle Birdsell, "Business and Government: The Walls Between," in Neil H. Jacoby (ed.), *The Business–Government Relationship: A Reassessment* (Santa Monica, CA: Goodyear, 1975), 32–34.

2. Jacoby, 167.

3. *Ibid.*, 168.

4. For a view somewhat counter to this, see Kevin Phillips, "The Balkanization of America," *Harper's* (May 1978), 37–47.

5. Daniel Bell, "Too Much, Too Late: Reactions to Changing Social Values," in Jacoby, 17–19.

6. Jacoby, 168.

7. Arthur T. Denzau, "Will an 'Industrial Policy' Work for the United States?" (St. Louis: Center for the Study of American Business, Washington University, September 1983), 1.

8. *Ibid.*, 2.

9. Robert B. Reich, *The Next American Frontier* (New York: Penguin Books, 1983).

10. Monroe W. Karmin, "Industrial Policy: What Is It? Do We Need One?" *U.S. News & World Report* (October 3, 1983), 47.

11. Robert J. Samuelson, "The New (Old) Industrial Policy," *Newsweek* (May 23, 1994), 53.

12. Hiroyuki Tezuka, "Success as the Source of Failure? Competition and Cooperation in the Japanese Economy," *Sloan Management Review* (Vol. 38, No. 2, March 1997), 83–93.

13. Ira C. Magaziner and Robert B. Reich, *Minding America's Business: The Decline and Rise of the American Economy* (New York: Vintage Books, 1983), 255.

14. Steve Coll, "Retooling Europe," *The Washington Post National Weekly Edition* (August 22–28, 1994), 6–7.

15. Alvaro Cuervo and Bélen Villalonga, "Explaining the Variance in the Performance Effects of Privatization," *Academy of Management Review* (July 2000), 581–590.

16. Shaker A. Zahra, R. Duane Ireland, Isabel Gutierrez, and Michael A. Hitt, "Privatization and Entrepreneurial Transformation: Emerging Issues and a Future Research Agenda," *Academy of Management Review* (July 2000), 509–524.

17. Ted Kolderie, "What Do We Mean by Privatization?" (St. Louis: Center for the Study of American Business, Washington University, May 1986), 2–5.

18. *Ibid.*, 3–5.

19. *Ibid.*, 581–590.

20. *Congressional Quarterly's Federal Regulatory Directory*, 5th ed. (1985–1986), 9.

21. "Microsoft: Time to Change," *Business Week* (July 16, 2001), 100.

22. *Ibid.*, 100.

23. *Congressional Quarterly's Federal Regulatory Directory*, 5th ed. (1985–1986), 10–11.

24. *Ibid.*, 12.

25. Based on statement by Konrad von Finckenstein, Q. C. Commissioner of Competition Bureau to the "Meet the Competition Bureau," Forum Insight Conference, Toronto, May 3, 1999.

26. http://www.gov.on.ca/LAB/english/about.

27. "Deregulating America," *Business Week* (November 28, 1983), 80–89.

28. "Is Deregulation Working?" *Business Week* (December 22, 1986), 50–55.

29. Frederick C. Thayer, "The Emerging Dangers of Deregulation," *The New York Times* (February 23 1986), 3.

8

CONSUMER STAKEHOLDERS

CHAPTER OBJECTIVES

After studying this chapter, you should be able to:

1   Discuss the fundamental expectations of consumers.

2   Identify concerns with regard to product information practices, including advertising.

3   Describe the major issues surrounding product quality and safety and the notion of product liability.

4   Consider the variety of consumer regulations that exist and their nature.

5   Explain some of the types of business responses aimed at better addressing consumer interests.

How important are consumers as stakeholders? According to management expert Peter Drucker, there is only one valid definition of business purpose: to create a customer.[1] Of course, retaining that customer is essential, too. In *The Loyalty Effect*, Frederick Reichheld showed that small increases in customer retention rates can lead to dramatic increases in profits.[2] Clearly, businesses must create and retain customers if they are to succeed in today's competitive marketplace. It is not surprising, therefore, that customer relationship management (CRM) has become the mantra of marketing.[3] Customer relationship management is "the ability of an organization to effectively identify, acquire, foster, and retain loyal profitable customers."[4] With CRM guiding businesses in their customer relations, one would expect consumers to be pleased, or at least satisfied, with the way they have been treated. Unfortunately, that hasn't been the case. The consumer is still "often ignored"[5] and, in practice, CRM has been said to be "an awful lot of bland talk and not a lot of action."[6]

The issue of business and the consumer stakeholder is at the forefront of discussions about business and its relationships with and responsibility to the society in which it exists. Products and services are the most visible manifestations of business in society. For this reason, the whole issue of business and its consumer stakeholders deserves a careful examination.

Product information issues compose a major area in the business/consumer stakeholder relationship. Foremost among these is advertising, an issue we address in this chapter. Attention is also given to the concern by consumer stakeholders over product quality and safety. In connection with safety, we consider the product liability issue and we identify the role that regulation plays in protecting the consumer. Finally, we will discuss business's response to consumer stakeholder concerns, include an examination of quality improvement initiatives like TQM and Six Sigma.

CONSUMERISM IN TWENTY-FIRST CENTURY

Many groups make up the loose confederation known as the consumer movement. For example, the Consumers Council of Canada is an independent, not-for-profit organization designed to provide a voice for consumer concerns. Its members work with the federal and provincial governments, industry, and consumers in order to help manage current consumer issues. The Consumers' Association of Canada (CAC), established in 1947, is similarly aimed at ensuring that consumers have a role in government and industry decisions that substantially affect the public. This organization also offers information and advice to consumers on marketplace rights and responsibilities. The CAC has successfully represented consumers in government decisions resulting in mandatory seat belts, safety standards for children's car seats, a voluntary code for advertising directed at children, a hazardous products symbol program, and a ban on DDT and other hazardous pesticides.

Although organized groups are not being recognized as effective lobbyists, the grassroots activism of consumers has never been stronger. In England, a relatively small group of disgruntled consumers brought the country to a halt by protesting the price of gas. They set up blockades that emptied roads, closed schools, and caused panic buying in supermarkets. The Internet has made it easier for consumer groups to respond to issues more quickly and more forcefully. It makes it possible to not only inform consumers of concerns that have arisen but also to rally the troops to take action. This is of special concern for global companies whose interests are far-flung. According to Cordelia Brabbs of *Marketing* magazine, "Global companies find themselves under the watchful eye of their customers. If they fail to behave impeccably at all times, they risk finding their misdemeanors broadcast on a high-speed information network."[7]

It is fruitful to look in more detail at some of the issues that have become prominent in the business/consumer relationship. It is impossible to list them all, but Figure 8-1 lists examples of major problems that consumers worry about in terms of business' products and services.

Figure 8-1

Examples of Consumer Problems with Business

- The high prices of many products
- The poor quality of many products
- The failure of many companies to live up to claims made in their advertising
- The poor quality of after-sales service
- Too many products breaking or going wrong after you bring them home
- Misleading packaging or labelling
- The feeling that it is a waste of time to complain about consumer problems because nothing substantial will be achieved
- Inadequate guarantees and warranties
- Failure of companies to handle complaints properly
- Too many products that are dangerous
- The absence of reliable information about various products and services
- Not knowing what to do if something is wrong with a product you have bought

Broadly, we may classify the major kinds of issues into two groups: product information and the product itself.

PRODUCT INFORMATION ISSUES: ADVERTISING

Why have questions been raised about business's social and ethical responsibilities in the area of product information? Most consumers know the answer. Companies understandably want to portray their products in the most flattering light. However, efforts to paint a positive portrait of a product can easily cross the line into misinformation regarding the product's attributes. Hence, the ethics of advertising continue to merit attention in any discussion that focuses on responsibilities to consumer stakeholders.

The debate over the role of advertising in society has been going on for decades. Most observers have concentrated on the economic function of advertising in our market system, but opinions are diverse as to whether advertising is beneficial or detrimental as a business function. Critics charge that it is a wasteful and **inefficient tool of business** and that our current standard of living would be even higher if we could be freed from the negative influence of advertising. These critics argue that advertising raises the prices of products and services because it is an unnecessary business cost whose main effect is to circulate superfluous information that could better and more cheaply be provided on product information labels or by salespeople in stores. The result is that significant amounts of money are spent that produce no net consumer benefit.[8]

In response, others have claimed that advertising is a **beneficial component of the market system** and that the increases in the standard of living and consumer satisfaction may be attributed to it. They argue that, in general, advertising is an efficient means of distributing information because there is such an enormous and ever-changing array of products about which consumers need to know. Advertising is an effective and relatively inexpensive way to inform consumers of new and improved products.[9]

It has been argued that even uninformative advertising still tells consumers a lot. Advertising heavily, even if vaguely, helps attract shoppers to retail stores through a kind of they-must-be-doing-something-right logic. The increased traffic then enables the retailer to offer a wider selection of goods, raising the incentive to invest in cost-reduction technologies such as computerized inventory, modern warehouses, and quantity discounts, thus further lowering marginal costs. The advertising can promote efficiency, even if it provides no hard information, by **signalling to consumers** where the big-company, low-price, high-variety stores are. Economists have argued that retail juggernauts such as Wal-Mart and Home Depot have taken advantage of this phenomenon. Viewed in this way, advertising is seen as a net plus for society because it tends to lower prices and increase variety.[10]

The debate over whether advertising is a productive or wasteful business practice will undoubtedly continue. As a practical matter, however, advertising has become the lifeblood of the free-enterprise system. It **stimulates competition** and makes available information that consumers can use in comparison buying. It also provides competitors with information with which to respond in a competitive way and contains a mechanism for immediate feedback in the form of sales response. So, despite its criticisms, advertising does provide social and economic benefits to consumers.

With the thousands of products and their increasing complexity, the consumer today has a real **need for information** that is clear, accurate, and adequate. Clear information is that which is direct and straightforward and on which neither deception nor manipulation relies. Accurate information communicates truths, not half-truths. It avoids gross exaggeration and innuendo. Adequate information provides potential purchasers with enough information to make the best choice among the options available.[11]

Whereas providing information is one legitimate purpose of advertising in our society, another legitimate purpose is **persuasion**. Most consumers today expect that business advertises for the purpose of persuading them to buy their products or services, and they accept this as a part of the commercial system.

Ethical issues in advertising usually arise as companies attempt to inform and persuade consumer stakeholders. The frequently heard phrase "the seamy side of advertising" alludes to the economic and social costs that derive from advertising abuses.

In Canada, the Competition Act, enforced by the Competition Bureau, is intended to prohibit false or misleading advertising. Any company that employs false or misleading advertising can face fines or be punished under the act. Of course, what constitutes misleading advertising is not always easily identifiable, and consumers consequently need to remain vigilant in their attention to product or service promotions.

In 2003, the Competition Bureau ruled that Sears Canada practised "deceptive marketing" in 1999 by advertising false sale prices on five lines of automobile tires. The bureau's commissioner said Sears intentionally deceived consumers by pretending to offer them special prices on major lines of all-season tires, while having little intention of selling substantial quantities of the tires at the regular prices.[12]

REGULATION OF MARKETING PRACTICES

Both the federal and provincial governments have responsibilities in dealing with marketplace issues. The federal government oversees national marketplace standards in an effort to ensure a fair, efficient, and competitive marketplace for producers, traders, and consumers. Current federal consumer statutes govern issues of product safety (except electrical equipment), competition, labelling, and weights and measures. On the other hand, the provincial government enforces provincial statutes over such issues as the conditions of sale, guarantees, and licensing. Typically, services are regulated by the provinces or, in some cases, by municipalities. Most provinces have a statute to regulate unfair business practices. Though provincial acts can vary from province to province, the nature of consumer protection is similar across the country.[13] The Competition Bureau along with other government bodies such as Health Canada and Environment Canada are actively involved in these issues.

Cases of deceptive or unfair advertising are handled through such government regulatory bodies as the Competition Bureau. In addition to this regulatory approach, however, self-regulation of advertising has become an important business response, primarily in the past two decades. Under the regulatory approach, advertising behaviour is controlled through various governmental rules that are backed by the use of penalties. **Self-regulation**, on the other hand, refers to the control of business conduct and performance by business itself rather than by government or by market forces.[14]

TYPES OF SELF-REGULATION. Business self-regulation of advertising may take on various forms. One is self-discipline, where the firm itself controls its own advertising. Another is pure self-regulation, where the industry (one's peers) controls advertising. A third type is co-opted self-regulation, where the industry, of its own volition, involves nonindustry people (e.g., consumer or public representatives) in the development, application, and enforcement of norms. A fourth type is negotiated self-regulation, where the industry voluntarily negotiates the development, use, and enforcement of norms with some outside body (e.g., a government department or a consumer association). Finally, a fifth type is mandated self-regulation (which may sound like a contradiction of terms), where the industry is ordered or designated by the government to develop, use, and enforce norms, whether alone or in concert with other bodies.[15]

The most prominent instance of self-regulation in the advertising industry is the program sponsored by Advertising Standards Canada (ASC). ASC (formerly the Canadian Advertising Foundation) is an industry body committed to establishing and maintaining community confidence in advertising. ASC administers the Canadian Code of Advertising Standards, the main instrument of advertising self-regulation.

The Canadian Code of Advertising Standards, designed in 1963 and continually revised, was developed to promote the professional practice of advertising. It provides criteria for acceptable advertising and establishes the basis upon which advertising is assessed in response to consumer, trade, or special interest group complaints. The code's provisions deal with a variety of issues related to responsible advertising practices, including:

- accuracy and clarity

- disguised advertising techniques

- price claims

- advertising aimed at children and minors (see Figure 8-2)

- unacceptable depictions and portrayals.

The code has been widely endorsed by advertisers, advertising agencies, media that exhibit advertising, and suppliers to the advertising process. Consumer complaints to Advertising Standards Canada about alleged violations of advertising standards are reviewed and adjudicated by the English national and regional Consumer Response Councils. These autonomous bodies are composed of senior industry and public representatives and are independent from ASC.

Figure 8-2

Principles of Advertising to Children

A number of basic principles underlie the Broadcast Code for Advertising to Children, as presented by Advertising Standards Canada and the Canadian Association of Broadcasters:

1. Advertisers need to consider and abide by requirements regarding the avoidance of sex-role stereotyping and violence consistent with the principles of industry broadcast self-regulatory codes such as those endorsed by the Canadian Association of Broadcasters (CAB), Advertising Standards Canada (ASC), and the Canadian Broadcasting Corporation (CBC).

2. Children, especially the very young, live in a world that is part imaginary, part real, and sometimes do not distinguish clearly between the two. Children's advertising should respect and not abuse the power of the child's imagination.

3. Products and content which are inappropriate for use by children should not be advertised or promoted directly to children.

4. Advertisers should communicate information in a truthful and accurate manner and in language understandable to young children.

5. Children's advertising must not encourage or portray a range of values that are inconsistent with the moral, ethical, or legal standards of contemporary Canadian society.

6. It is recognized, of course, that it remains the primary responsibility of parents "to instruct a child in the way that he/she should go." The code and the guidelines that are issued from time to time are designed to help advertisers avoid making that task more difficult.

Source: Advertising Standards Canada, http://www.adstandards.com/en/Clearance/childrencode.asp2003.

PRODUCT QUALITY AND PRODUCT SAFETY

Although product information is a pivotal issue between business and consumer stakeholders, product and service issues such as quality and safety occupy centre stage. The quest to improve product and service quality has been driven by the demands of a competitive marketplace and an increasingly sophisticated consumer base. With **product safety**, an additional driving force has been the threat of product liability lawsuits and the damage they can wreak to both the balance sheet and the reputation.

The Ford Motor Company provides a notable example of the havoc that can result from product quality and safety problems. On October 30, 2001, Ford CEO Jacques Nasser departed the post after two years in the position. His tenure had been tumultuous. Product quality problems had plagued the launches of new products, even before the problems with Firestone-brand tires hit the news in August 2000. The tire problems were eventually traced to production problems at a Bridgestone/Firestone plant, but the tire maker's accusations against Ford, coupled with the high number of Ford recalls on other vehicles, made the Ford image easier to tarnish.[16] According to J.D. Power and Associates, the company went from the best in car quality, among Detroit automakers, to the worst in just three years. Ford's profits plunged 11 percent, double the decline of the other U.S. automakers.[17] Of course, the decline was not only due to product quality and safety: Unsuccessful diversification attempts were a factor as well. However, for a company that once boasted "Quality Is Job One," the decline in the J.D. Power ranking must have been a bitter pill to swallow. The fall of 2001 was a difficult time for all car companies, but the host of problems

Ford faced, beyond the falling economy, made it even more difficult for them to weather the storm. As *Newsweek* commented, "This hasn't been easy for Ford, which just 2 years ago was revered as America's best automaker."[18]

With respect to **product quality**, it is not clear whether North American business has fully appreciated the spectrum of meanings that quality takes on for the consumer stakeholder. As David Garvin has expressed, there are at least eight critical dimensions of product or service quality that must be understood if business is to respond strategically to this factor.[19] These eight dimensions include (1) performance, (2) features, (3) reliability, (4) conformance, (5) durability, (6) serviceability, (7) aesthetics, and (8) perceived quality.

Performance refers to a product's primary operating characteristics. For an automobile, this would include such factors as handling, steering, and comfort. *Features* are the "bells and whistles" of products that supplement their basic functioning. *Reliability* reflects the probability of a product malfunctioning or failing. *Conformance* is the extent to which the product or service meets established standards. *Durability* is a measure of product life. *Serviceability* refers to the speed, courtesy, competence, and ease of repair. *Aesthetics* is a subjective factor that refers to how the product looks, feels, tastes, and so on. Finally, *perceived quality* is a subjective inference that the consumer makes on the basis of a variety of tangible and intangible product characteristics.

RESPONSIBILITIES TO CONSUMER STAKEHOLDERS

What responsibilities does business have toward its consumers? To what lengths should business go in order to ensure they do not violate the trust of consumer stakeholders? Consumer trust and business integrity are sometimes shaken with periodic media reports of business neglect for consumer health and safety. For example, in 2003, the Canadian Food Inspection Agency launched an investigation into nutritional supplements such as power drinks, energy bars, and weight-loss preparations. A report by federal inspectors questioned the safety of energy bars and power drinks, saying they contain ingredients not stated on the label and consequently those products could jeopardize the health of people who are allergic to certain ingredients. The report also asserts that those products make health and performance claims that can't be substantiated.[20]

Business clearly has a duty to consumer stakeholders to sell them safe products and services. The concept of safety, in a definitional sense, means "free from harm or risk" or "secure from threat of danger, harm, or loss." In reality, however, the use of virtually any consumer product or service entails some degree of risk or some chance that the consumer may be harmed by the product or service.

In the 1800s, the legal view that prevailed was *caveat emptor* ("let the buyer beware"). The basic idea behind this concept was that the buyer had as much knowledge of what she or he wanted as the seller and, in any event, the marketplace would punish any violators. In the 1900s, *caveat emptor* gradually lost its favour and rationale, because it was frequently impossible for the consumer to have complete knowledge about manufactured goods.[21] Today, manufacturers are held responsible for all products placed on the market. We have a weak version of *caveat vendor*—"let the seller take care."[22]

Through a series of legal developments as well as changing societal values, business has become significantly responsible for product safety. Court cases and legal doctrine now hold companies financially liable for harm to consumers. Yet this still does not answer the difficult question, "How safe are manufacturers obligated to make products?" It is not possible to make products totally "risk free"; experience has shown that consumers seem to have an uncanny ability to injure themselves in novel and creative ways, many of which cannot be anticipated. The challenge to management, therefore, is to make products as safe as possible while at the same time making them affordable and useful to consumers.

Successfully meeting such a challenge is critical to establishing and maintaining consumer confidence and trust in business. The importance of building consumer trust is highlighted in Industry Canada's discussion of "the Consumer Connection":

> Consumer confidence and participation are critical to the performance of the national economy, to the efficient functioning of Canadian markets, and to our ability to compete in other countries' markets. Consumer expenditures contribute about 60% to Canada's gross national product, and traditionally have been the leading force in "kick-starting" the economy out of a recession.... Because of the consumer's importance to the Canadian economy, relatively small improvements to the consumer framework could provide important dividends to our overall economic well-being.[23]

Today the public is concerned about a variety of hazards (see Figure 8–3 for an example). Food scares, both real and imagined, have occupied much of the public's attention. Although they occur everywhere, consumers in the European Union have been especially hard hit. The discovery of cancer-causing dioxin in Belgian food products caused many countries to temporarily halt imports from Belgium. Then, Coca-Cola recalled 2.5 million bottles of soft drinks that originated in two Belgian factories after children who drank it complained of stomach-aches, nausea, and headaches.

Figure 8-3

Questioning the Safety of Our Food

Greenpeace Canada ran the following recent campaign to protest the trend toward genetically modified food:

Our Wheat Is in Danger

Monsanto is trying to introduce genetically engineered wheat in Canada.

Monsanto and other big biotech companies are tinkering with a mainstay of Canadian farming and a staple food for many people around the world—wheat. Monsanto, in collaboration with the government of Canada, is developing genetically engineered (GE) wheat that is designed to resist its "Roundup Ready" herbicide when applied to a farmer's field to kill weeds. The company plans to bring it to market by 2005 or so.

Take Action

Help Greenpeace stop the introduction of GE wheat in Canada: Send a free fax to your Member of Parliament, sign our petition against GE wheat and let people know that GE wheat is a risk to Canadians.

Why Is GE Wheat Risky?

Greenpeace is opposed to the environmental release of genetically engineered organisms due to the harm, possibly irreversible, they may cause to the environment.

What Can the Food Industry Do?

Health and scientific authorities have identified possible health risks associated with GE food. These possible health risks might be exacerbated with the introduction of GE wheat into the food supply, since wheat is so widely consumed globally, often in a minimally processed form. So we think the food industry has a special responsibility to protect consumers and the environment from the introduction of GE wheat.

We are asking companies such as Loblaws to use their influence in Ottawa to oppose the introduction of GE wheat, and to stop using other GE ingredients in their products. In the interim, all GE food should be labelled so that consumers concerned about impacts to human and environmental health can choose to avoid food produced with GE ingredients. But the food companies need to hear this from you, the consumer. Please let your grocery store and favourite food manufacturers know that you do not want them to use GE ingredients. Ask them to publicly state their opposition to GE wheat and to use their influence in Ottawa to stop its introduction.

Source: Greenpeace Canada, http://www.greenpeace.ca/e/campaign/gmo/depth/wheat/index.php. Reprinted by permission.

In recent years, a variety of health threats connected with food products have shaken consumer confidence in a number of industries. Bovine spongiform ecephalopathy (BSE), or "mad cow" disease, precipitated a crisis for beef farmers throughout Europe. Beef consumption dropped by 27 percent in the 15 member states of the European Union, with Greece reporting a 50 percent drop.[24] In Canada, the beef industry was shaken in the summer of 2003 when it was announced that a single breeder cow in northern Alberta tested positive for mad cow disease. Following the discovery, prices collapsed, costing 90 000 producers across the country more than $11 million a day.[25] Because of reduced consumption, including a U.S. ban on Canadian beef imports, production was reduced, with consequent job losses and damages to many businesses in Alberta and Saskatchewan and other related Canadian businesses.[26]

Manufactured products create hazards not only because of unsafe product design but also as a result of consumers being given inadequate information regarding the hazards associated with using the products. Consequently, it is not surprising in product liability claims to find that the charges are based on one or more of several allegations. *First*, it may be charged that the product was improperly manufactured. Here the producer failed to exercise due care in the product's production, and this failure contributed directly to the accident or injury. *Second,* if the product was manufactured properly, its design could have been defective in that alternative designs or devices, if used at the time of manufacture, may have prevented the accident. *Third*, it may be charged that the producer failed to provide satisfactory instructions and/or warnings and that the accident or injury could have been prevented if such information had been provided. *Fourth*, it may be charged that the producer failed to foresee a reasonable and anticipated misuse of the product and warn against such misuse.[27]

PRODUCT LIABILITY

Product liability has become a monumental consumer issue, particularly due to the sheer number of cases where products have resulted in illness, harm, or death. In addition, more and more consumers are resorting to legal action against the alleged offender when faced with situations about which they are unhappy. While the U.S. has traditionally been among the most litigious societies, Canada has also experienced a growing trend in litigation.

In 2002, an individual from British Columbia filed a class action lawsuit against Shell Canada. The suit alleged that Shell didn't do enough to notify consumers about a problem with its gasoline. Shell subsequently admitted that an additive in its gas was responsible for causing damage to fuel gauges or pumps in certain cars. The lawsuit also claimed that Shell continued to sell the product even though it was aware of problem. A Shell representative issued a news release that offered a "sincere apology for any inconvenience this problem may have caused." Shell also had discretely compensated consumers for months by offering Air Miles or free gas. In response to Shell's behaviour, a representative of the Automobile Protection Association, a consumer advocacy group, commented that "It's a longstanding principle that when you put out something that's defective, you put the word out. It would appear the company sort of ducked when they had a decision to make."[28]

Closely paralleling the rise in the number of lawsuits in North America has been the growing size of the financial awards given by the courts. A path-breaking award in the product liability category was obtained in the United States in 1978. The US$128.5 million award was granted in the case of a 19-year-old who at age 13 was severely injured. He was riding with a friend in a Ford Pinto that was struck from behind. The Pinto's gas tank ruptured, and the passenger compartment was filled with flames that killed his friend and severely burned him over 90 percent of his body. The badly scarred teenager underwent more than 50 operations. Ford was required by the jury to pay US$666 280 to the dead driver's family and to pay the survivor US$2.8 million in compensatory damages and US$125 million in punitive damages.[29] The Pinto case was the beginning, but the awards have grown since then. The largest judgment in a personal injury case since then was the US$4.9 billion a jury awarded to six people in

1999. Six years earlier they had been seriously burned in a collision that allegedly caused the gas tank in their 1970 Malibu to explode. The average jury award went from US$520 000 in 1993 to US$1 million in 1999, an increase of 93 percent. Also from 1993 to 1999, jury awards rose 79 percent for medical malpractice cases, 128 percent in business negligence cases, and 410 percent in cases involving product liability.[30]

Since the Pinto case, multimillion-dollar lawsuits have become commonplace in North America, particularly in the U.S. Some major North American companies have been hit so hard by lawsuits that they have filed for bankruptcy protection. One famous example of this is the Johns Manville Corporation, which faced an avalanche of asbestos-related lawsuits that totalled 16 500 suits demanding over US$12 billion.[31] In April 2001, W. R. Grace & Co. filed for bankruptcy protection to shield it from asbestos-related claims.[32] Other companies encountering large lawsuits have included Union Carbide, with its poison gas explosion in Bhopal, India; Dow Chemical, with its Agent Orange defoliant; and Bridgestone/Firestone, with its defective tires.

It is useful to point out that, according to some critics, one major source of the relatively greater presence of consumer-related lawsuits in the U.S. compared to Canada may be partly a result of legal differences in the conceptions of product liability. In the U.S., product liability has been reinforced by the doctrine of **strict liability** and the expansion of this concept in the courts. In its most general form, the doctrine of strict liability holds that anyone in the value chain of a product is liable for harm caused to the user if the product as sold was unreasonably dangerous because of its defective condition. This applies to anyone involved in the design, manufacture, or sale of a defective product. Beyond manufacturing, courts have ruled against plaintiffs from a broad array of functions, such as selling, advertising, promotion, and distribution.[33] For example, the U.S. Department of Transportation holds warehouses liable for violations of hazardous materials regulations even when the warehouse relied on information provided by the customer (the depositor) when documenting the shipment.[34] In other words, there is no legal defence for placing on the market a product that is dangerous to a consumer because of a known or knowable defect.

Canada's legal view of product liability differs somewhat from the U.S. notion of strict liability. Canada did not adopt the doctrine of strict liability for defective products. Instead, product liability in Canada is governed by contract law and basic negligence law. That means that in addition to proving what the doctrine of strict liability requires, the plaintiff must also prove that the product's defect arose due to the defendant's negligence. In this sense, Canadian law is "fault-based," whereas U.S. law holds companies accountable for preventing defects, not simply for taking all reasonable steps to prevent them (hence, the notion of strict liability).

Which system is better for the consumer? While some critics view the U.S. system as more protective of the consumer, others see the systems as essentially producing similar results. As Bruce Feldthusen points out, "In negligence, we employ a doctrine in Canadian law called *res ipsa loquitur* (the thing speaks for itself) that permits the jury to infer negligence from the accident itself, which in practice brings us close to strict liability. There are few cases in Canadian law reports where the plaintiff has succeeded on all the elements of the action including proof of defect, but lost on the issue of negligence."[35] In practice then, the Canadian context may in fact be enforcing the spirit of the strict liability doctrine. Given the importance of this concept to both the U.S. and Canada, it is useful to consider that the law in both countries may eventually lead to even higher corporate standards of diligence toward consumer safety concerns.

TOWARD ABSOLUTE LIABILITY

Certain countries and parts of the U.S. have established a standard that is much more demanding than even the standard U.S. concept of strict liability. This concept is called **absolute liability**. The ruling that established this new concept was handed down by the New Jersey Supreme Court in *Beshada v. Johns Manville Corporation* (1982). The plaintiffs in the Beshada case were employees of Johns Manville and other companies who had developed asbestos-related diseases as a result of exposure in the workplace.[36] The court ruled in this case that a manufacturer could be held strictly liable for failure to warn of a product hazard, even if the hazard was scientifically unknowable at the time of manufacture and sale. Therefore, a company cannot use as its defence the assurance that it did its best according to the state of the art in the industry at that time. Under this ruling, the manufacturer is liable for damages even if it had no way of knowing that the product might cause a problem later. Similarly in 2000, the Supreme Court of India upheld the absolute liability of a common carrier, in this case Patel Roadways Ltd., for goods destroyed by fire. The court ruled that, in the case of damage or loss, it is not necessary for the plaintiff to establish negligence.[37]

The absolute-liability rule frequently involves cases involving chemicals or drugs. For example, a drug producer might put a drug on the market (with government approval) thinking that it is safe based on current knowledge. Under the doctrine of absolute liability, the firm could be held liable for side effects or health problems that develop years, or even decades, later. The result is that a large amount of uncertainty is injected into the production process.[38]

CONSUMER NEEDS AND CONSUMER PROTECTION

The system of consumer law and policy in Canada has been viewed as a "patchwork" rather than a framework for governing business activity. The system evolved incrementally within the social, economic, and political systems present in Canada about 30 years ago. Responsibilities for consumer law are shared between the federal and provincial governments. This shared responsibility distinguishes the consumer system from most of the other marketplace laws within Industry Canada (competition law, insolvency law, intellectual property statutes), which are largely within the federal domain. In addition, with the government reorganization of 1993, federal responsibilities for implementing federal consumer laws were transferred to different federal agencies, including Industry Canada, Health Canada, Agriculture and Agrifood, Natural Resources, and Fisheries and Oceans. Prior to 1993, the Department of Consumer and Corporate Affairs had central responsibility for most federal consumer statutes and took a leadership role in establishing consumer policy within the government of Canada.[39]

HEALTH CANADA

Health Canada is a federal government department that acts in cooperation with provincial bodies to protect the health of Canadians. Figure 8–4 offers an organizational chart of the branches of Health Canada. As you can see, Health Canada is the umbrella department for a wide-ranging body of government responsibilities.

Figure 8-4

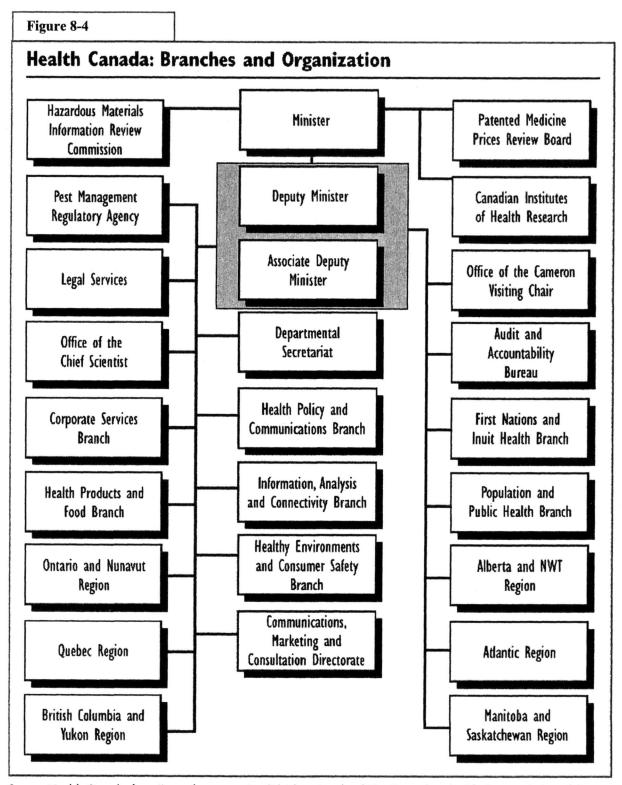

Health Canada: Branches and Organization

Source: Health Canada, http://www.hc-sc.gc.ca/english/about/org.html#9a. Reproduced with the permission of the Minister of Public Works and Government Services Canada, 2004.

Among its numerous responsibilities, Health Canada administers the Food and Drugs Act and releases advisories and warnings on foods, drugs, medical devices, natural health products, and consumer products. More recent responsibilities have come to include providing information and policies on genetically modified foods, nutrition labelling, and biotechnology products such as blood, tissues, and reproductive technologies in the Canadian marketplace and health system. Health Canada also monitors health and safety risks related to the sale and use of drug products, natural health products, medical devices, pesticides, radiation-emitting devices, and certain other consumer products.[40]

Through its Healthy Environments and Consumer Safety Branch (HECS), Health Canada also administers the Product Safety Programme (PSP). This program is aimed at protecting the health of Canadians by researching, assessing, and collaborating in the management of the health risks and safety hazards associated with consumer products, cosmetics, new chemical substances, products of biotechnology, workplace chemicals, radiation-emitting devices, environmental noise, solar UV radiation. The PSP mandate is governed by a variety of legislation, including the Hazardous Products Act, Radiation Emitting Devices Act, Canadian Environmental Protection Act, New Substances Notification Regulations, Canada Labour Code, Treasury Board Regulations (Health and Safety), and Food and Drugs Act (including the Cosmetics Regulations).[41]

The consumer products portion of the PSP, referred to as Consumer Product Safety (CPS), is aimed at protecting consumers from product-related hazards and promoting the safe use of products through raising consumer awareness. CPS also encourages the design of safer products for the Canadian market by providing importers and manufacturers with hazard and product technical information, including the following:

- *Chemical hazards.* Consumer chemical products such as detergents, paints, solvents, and glues are assessed for potential hazards or harm from their use.

- *Flammability hazards.* Textile products including children's sleepwear, clothing, tents, bedding, and mattresses are assessed.

- *Mechanical hazards.* Possible hazards such as strangulation are assessed in children's products including toys, cribs, and bunk beds, and in products intended for household or recreational use.[45]

FOOD AND DRUG SAFETY ADMINISTRATION IN CANADA

The Minister of Health is responsible for a number of activities related to consumer safety, including establishing policies and safety standards for food sold in Canada; administering those provisions of the Food and Drugs Act that relate to public health, safety, and nutrition; and assessing the effectiveness of various government agencies in regard to food safety.

Branches of Health Canada which are particularly pertinent to food and drug safety administration include: the Healthy Environments and Consumer Safety Branch (HECS) and the Health Products and Food Branch (HPFB). In addition, the Canadian Food Inspection Agency (CFIA) plays an important role in product safety.

THE HEALTHY ENVIRONMENTS AND CONSUMER SAFETY BRANCH (HECS). The objectives of the HECS are broader than simply product safety concerns. This branch of Health Canada aims to do the following: Promote safe living, working, and recreational environments, with a special emphasis on health in the work environment and delivering occupational health and safety services; Assess and reduce health risks posed by environmental factors; Promote initiatives to reduce and prevent the harm caused by tobacco and the abuse of alcohol and other controlled substances; Regulate tobacco and controlled substances, and provide drug analytical services; Regulate the safety of industrial and consumer products in the Canadian marketplace, and promote their safe use.[42] HECS's principal programs include the following: Drug Strategy and Controlled Substances; Product Safety; Safe Environments; Sustainable Development; Tobacco Control; Workplace Health and Public Safety.

HEALTH PRODUCTS AND FOOD BRANCH (HPFB). Another branch of Health Canada with responsibilities for consumer health and safety is the HPFB. Its main objectives include:Minimizing health risk factors to Canadians while maximizing the safety provided by the regulatory system for health products and food; Promoting conditions that enable Canadians to make healthy choices and providing information so that they can make informed decisions about their health.[43] The major programs operated through HFPB are focused on the following areas:Therapeutic products (medical devices and drugs); Food, including all Health Canada nutrition activities;Natural health products; Biologics and genetics (e.g., blood and blood products, viral and bacterial vaccines, genetic therapies and diagnostics, tissues, organs, and reproductive technologies).

CANADIAN FOOD INSPECTION AGENCY (CFIA). The CFIA (established in 1997) is another instrument through which the Canadian government can maintain product safety. This body consolidated the delivery of all federal food, animal, and plant health inspection programs previously provided through the activities of four federal government departments (Agriculture and Agri-Food Canada, Fisheries and Oceans Canada, Health Canada, and Industry Canada).

The CFIA aims to protect consumers by contributing to food safety, the protection of plants, and the health of animals in Canada. Among the central responsibilities of the CFIA is the enforcement of food safety and nutritional quality standards established by Health Canada. Specific activities include inspecting federally registered meat-processing facilities, inspecting borders for foreign pests and diseases, enforcing practices related to fraudulent labelling, conducting food investigations and recalls, and performing laboratory testing and environmental assessments of seeds, plants, feeds, and fertilizers.[44] Figure 8–5 outlines the responsibilities of the CFIA.

Figure 8-5

The Work of the Canadian Food Inspection Agency (CFIA)

- CFIA veterinarians and inspectors conduct rigorous inspections in some 1800 meat- and fish-processing establishments across Canada.
- CFIA inspectors check shipments from abroad—examining plants, animals, foods, and even packaging materials that can harbour diseases and pests, such as beetles or moths.
- CFIA agricultural officers inspect potato fields and greenhouses, hatcheries, feed mills, and live-stock premises.
- CFIA laboratory scientists analyze food samples for impurities, drug residues, or disease-causing agents.
- CFIA regulators evaluate the safety of the newest kinds of seeds, feeds, fertilizers, and animal health products, such as vaccines, for use in Canada.
- CFIA officers review food labels for honesty and accuracy, investigate complaints, and prosecute offenders.

Source: Canadian Food Inspection Agency, http://www.inspection.gc.ca/english/toce.shtml.

THE U.S. FOOD AND DRUG ADMINISTRATION (FDA)

Given the increasing integration of activities between Canadian and U.S. business and consumers, Health Canada and its branches often work together with the U.S. Food and Drug Administration (FDA). In 2003, Health Canada and the FDA signed a Memorandum of Understanding (MOU) that "builds on existing collaborative efforts between Health Canada and the U.S. FDA. In general, it will better enable the two regulatory authorities to share information on the post-market safety of therapeutic products, information related to the review and evaluation of new product submissions and information on product investigations and enforcement activities."[45]

The FDA's goals are largely the same as Health Canada, and as it describes on its Web site, its mission includes the following:[46]

1. To promote the public health by promptly and efficiently reviewing clinical research and taking appropriate action on the marketing of regulated products in a timely manner.

2. With respect to such products, protect the public health by ensuring that foods are safe, wholesome, sanitary, and properly labelled; human and veterinary drugs are safe and effective; there is reasonable assurance of the safety and effectiveness of devices intended for human use; cosmetics are safe and properly labelled; public health and safety are protected from electronic product radiation.

3. Participate through appropriate processes with representatives of other countries to reduce the burden of regulation, harmonize regulatory requirements, and achieve appropriate reciprocal arrangements.

4. As determined to be appropriate by the Secretary, carry out paragraphs (1) through (3) in consultation with experts in science, medicine, and public health, and in cooperation with consumers, users, manufacturers, importers, packers, distributors and retailers of regulated products.

BUSINESS RESPONSE TO CONSUMER STAKEHOLDERS

Business's response to consumerism and consumer stakeholders has varied over the years. The history of business's response to consumers parallels its perceptions of the seriousness, pervasiveness, effectiveness, and longevity of the consumer movement. When the consumer movement first began, business's response was casual, perhaps symbolic, and hardly effective. Today, the consumer movement has matured, and formal interactions with consumer stakeholders have become more and more institutionalized. Business has realized that consumers today are more persistent than in the past, more assertive, and more likely to use or exhaust all appeal channels before being satisfied. Armed with considerable power, consumer activists have been a major stimulus to more sincere responses on behalf of business. These responses have included the creation of toll-free hotlines, user-friendly Web sites, consumer service representatives, the designation of specific consumer affairs officers, and the creation of specific company departments to handle consumer affairs.

Early attempts to be responsive to consumer stakeholders involved the creation of organizational units such as consumer affairs offices. Today, these kinds of responses have become an institutionalized part of business's response to consumers. Programs like Six Sigma and total quality management have become part of the strategic responses. These responses merit brief consideration.

CONSUMER AFFAIRS OFFICES

There are various ways of organizing the corporate response to consumers. A company might appoint a consumer affairs officer or create a consumer affairs task force or committee, but a more sophisticated way is to establish a consumer affairs office or department. To be sure, the establishment of such a formalized unit is not a substitute for a consumer-stakeholder focus on the part of all members of the organization. But it does provide a hub around which a dedicated consumer-stakeholder thrust might be built.

BASIC MISSION. The basic mission of a consumer affairs office is to heighten management responsiveness to consumer stakeholders. In accomplishing this mission, consumer affairs professionals have to execute two key roles: One is the role of consumer advocate in the company, and the other is the role of consumer specialist making managerial recommendations about corporate practices that mesh well with the needs of both consumers and the company. Some companies take one or the other of these two postures, whereas other companies use both approaches and/or additional approaches. There are potential conflicts between the two roles, but they need not create conflicts if consumer affairs professionals and management have a sympathetic understanding of each other's goals.[47]

ESSENTIAL FUNCTIONS. Consumer affairs practitioners have suggested that there are at least four essential functions of an effective consumer affairs office:

- *Establish a comprehensive, complete, and accurate database* that assesses the levels of consumer satisfaction and dissatisfaction with the company's products and services in all important areas involving consumers, such as billing and collection practices, repair services, guarantee policy and practice, handling of complaints, quality of products and services, and pricing.

- *Audit the company's programs* to determine how adequate they are in responding to consumer complaints and interests. Use company records, special task forces, outside consultants, and consumer groups.

- *Recommend specific consumer programs, policies, and practices* in all areas where needed.

- *Establish programs to ensure effective communication* between the company and consumers to build public confidence and understanding of company policy and practice.[48]

In general, the appropriate response of a company to consumer stakeholders is to ensure an understanding of the consumer movement throughout the organization, especially at top management levels, where it is easy for executives to get isolated from company activities.

TOTAL QUALITY MANAGEMENT PROGRAMS

Total quality management (TQM). TQM has many different characteristics, but it essentially means that all of the functions of the business are blended into a holistic, integrated philosophy built around the concepts of quality, teamwork, productivity, and customer understanding and satisfaction.[49] Figure 8–6 depicts one useful view of the principles, practices, and techniques of TQM. It should be noted that the customer, or consumer stakeholder, is the focus of the process.

A vital assumption and premise of TQM is that the customer is the final judge of quality. Therefore, the first part of the TQM process is to define quality in terms of customer expectations and requirements.

Figure 8-6

Principles, Practices, and Techniques of Total Quality Management

	Customer Focus	Continuous Improvement	Teamwork
Principles	• Paramount importance of customers • Providing products and services that fulfill customer needs; requires organization-wide focus on customers	• Consistent customer satisfaction can be attained only through relentless improvement of processes that create products and services	• Customer focus and continuous improvement are best achieved by collaboration throughout an organization as well as with customers and suppliers
Practices	• Direct customer contact • Collecting information about customer needs • Using information to design and deliver products and services	• Process analysis • Re-engineering • Problem solving • Play/do/check/act	• Search for arrangements that benefit all units involved in a process • Formation of various types of teams • Group skills training
Techniques	• Customer surveys and focus groups • Quality function deployment (translates customer information into product specifications)	• Flowcharts • Pareto analysis • Statistical process control • Fishbone diagrams	• Organizational development methods, such as the nominal group technique • Team-building methods (e.g., role clarification and group feedback)

Source: James W. Dean, Jr., and David E. Bowen, "Management Theory and Total Quality: Improving Research and Practice Through Theory Development," *Academy of Management Review* (Vol. 19, No. 3, July 1994), 395.

Customer expectations and requirements are then converted to standards and specifications. Finally, the entire organization is realigned to ensure that both conformance quality (adherence to standards and specifications) and perceived quality (meeting or exceeding customer expectations) are achieved.[50] It is clear in TQM that "delighted customers" is the overarching goal of management's efforts.[51]

Opportunities for recognition have helped to propel quality efforts. In North America and the rest of the industrialized world, the Malcolm Baldrige Award, ISO 9000, and the Deming Quality Award have enhanced the reputations of firms that undertake quality initiatives and complete them successfully. However, TQM became the buzzword of the 1980s, and many of its slogans, such as "Getting it right the first time" became viewed as clichés. It is against that backdrop that other tools developed, such as just in time (JIT) and business process re-engineering (BPR).

Six Sigma. Critics of TQM argued that "TQM never did anything to define quality, which is conformance to standards."[52] Consequently, the need for a more rigorous definition of quality was part of the appeal of Six Sigma, another quality-based management approach to product and service generation. Six Sigma is a development in total quality management under which are grouped a body of methodologies and techniques directed at improving quality and reducing costs.[53] Dow, DuPont, Sony, Honeywell, Nokia, GlaxoSmithKline, and Raytheon that have relied on the Six Sigma methodology. According to Jack Welch, former CEO of GE, "[Six Sigma—the Breakthrough Strategy] is the most important initiative GE has ever taken ... it is part of the genetic code of our future leadership."[54]

Although some deride Six Sigma as "TQM on steroids," it has brought new commitment and energy to the quest for quality in the new millennium. It is even said to have brought "more prominence to the quality world than it has enjoyed since the glory days of the mid-1980s."[55]

Motorola first developed Six Sigma, and Allied Signal later experimented with it, but most observers believe that GE perfected it. *Sigma* is a statistical measure of variation from the mean; higher values of sigma mean fewer defects. The six sigma level of operation is 3.4 defects per million. Most companies operate around the four sigma level (i.e., 6000 defects per million). Corporations adopting the program must develop "black belts"—people specifically trained to fill sponsorship roles, provide assistance, and see the program through. They must also find "champions" at senior levels of management who are committed to shepherding the program when needed.[56]

One of Six Sigma's strengths has been the clarity of the process and the steps companies must take to adopt it. However, Six Sigma is more than a toolbox with clear instructions. The program also represents a philosophy that stresses the importance of customers as well as careful measurement. Six Sigma practitioners look for facts rather than opinions, and they believe in fixing the process rather than the product.[57] Of course, these underlying principles are the foundation of TQM and most other quality efforts. The basis for all of these is the satisfaction of the consumer. Figure 8–7 outlines a consumer-stakeholder satisfaction model.

Figure 8-7

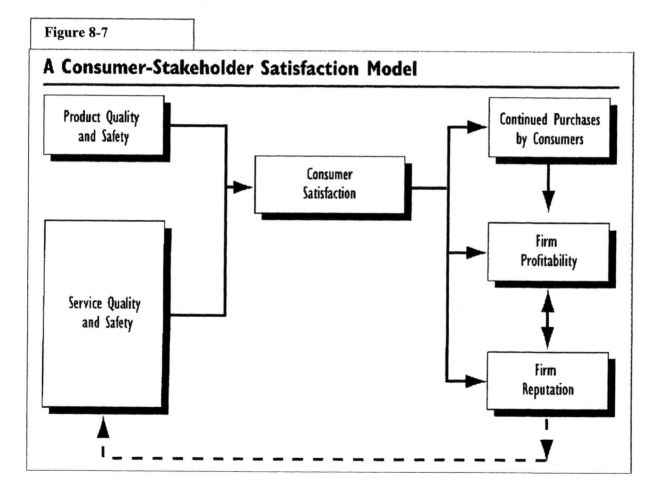

A Consumer-Stakeholder Satisfaction Model

Summary

In a consumption-driven society, business must be especially attentive to the issues that arise in its relationships with consumer stakeholders. Product information issues compose a major area in the business/consumer stakeholder relationship. Foremost among these is advertising. In addition, consumer stakeholders have become concerned with product quality and safety, largely because businesses have failed to meet their needs reliably on these two fronts. One major challenge has been to identify and understand all the different dimensions of the quality issue. An extremely important and related issue has been product safety, which has become one of the most crucial consumer issues for firms. Health and safety issues related to foods, drugs, and medical devices have propelled the various branches in Health Canada and the Canadian Food Inspection Agency into prominent roles.

With regard to corporate responses to these challenges, quality improvement initiatives like TQM and Six Sigma, have the potential for addressing the problems in a significant way if they are properly formulated and implemented. In addition to these specific responses, a consumer focus and orientation needs to permeate management decision making if the concerns of consumers are to be handled effectively. In today's business environment, consumers have many choices. Consequently, companies have no alternative but to internalize the consumer focus if they are to succeed.

Key Terms

absolute liability (page 149)

Canadian Food Inspection Agency (page 152)

Health Canada (page 149)

perceived quality (page 145)

persuasion (page 142)

product quality (page 145)

product safety (page 144)

reliability (page 145)

self-regulation (page 143)

signalling to customer (page 142)

Six Sigma (page 155)

strict liability (page 148)

Total Quality Management (TQM) (page 154)

DISCUSSION QUESTIONS

1. What expectations do you think consumer stakeholders should have of business beyond basic product information and safety issues?

2   Give an example of a major abuse of advertising from your own observations and experiences. How do you feel about this as a consumer?

3   Identify the dimensions of quality. Give an example of a product or service in which each of these characteristics is important.

4. Given the current business and consumer climate, do you anticipate business becoming more responsive to consumer expectations? What role does politics play in your answer?

ENDNOTES

1. Peter F. Drucker, *Management: Tasks, Responsibilities, Practices* (New York: Harper & Row, 1973), 61.

2. Frederick F. Reichheld, *The Loyalty Effect* (Cambridge, MA: Harvard Business School Press, 1996).

3. Russell S. Winer, "A Framework for Customer Relationship Management," *California Management Review* (Summer 2001), 89–105.

4. "The Customer Is Often Ignored," *Marketing Week* (September 27, 2001), 3.

5. Camilla Ballesteros, "Don't Talk About CRM; Do It," *Marketing Week* (September 27, 2001) 49.

6. *Ibid.*

7. Cordelia Brabbs, "Web Fuels Consumer Activism," *Marketing* (September 21, 2000), 23.

8. William Leiss, Stephen Kline, and Sut Jhally, *Social Communication in Advertising* (Toronto: Methuen, 1986), 13.

9. *Ibid.*

10. Rob Norton, "How Uninformative Advertising Tells Consumers Quite a Bit," *Fortune* (December 26, 1994), 37.

11. William Shaw and Vincent Barry, *Moral Issues in Business*, 4th ed. (Belmont, CA: Wadsworth, 1989), 389–414.

12. Simon Tuck, "Tribunal Hears First Allegations of 'Deceptive Marketing' by Sears," *Globe and Mail* (October 28, 2003), http://www.globeandmail.com.

13. http://strategis.ic.gc.ca/epic/internet/inoca-bc.nsf/vwGeneratedInterE/ca00179e.html.

14. J. F. Pickering and D. C. Cousins, *The Economic Implications of Codes of Practice* (Manchester, England: University of Manchester Institute of Science and Technology, Department of Management Sciences, 1980), 17. Also see J. J. Boddewyn, "Advertising Self-Regulation: Private Government and Agent of Public Policy," *Journal of Public Policy and Marketing* (1985), 129.

15. *Ibid.*, 135.

16. Terril Yue Jones, "Ford Board Deposes CEO Nasser," *Los Angeles Times* (October 30, 2001), part 3, page 1.

17. Keith Naughton, "Ford's Perfect Storm," *Newsweek* (September 17, 2001), 48.

18. *Ibid.*

19. David A. Garvin, "Competing on the Eight Dimensions of Quality," *Harvard Business Review* (November–December 1987), 101–109.

20. Francine Schwadel, "Robins and Plaintiffs Face Uncertain Future," *The Wall Street Journal* (August 23, 1985), 4.

21. Yair Aharoni, *The No Risk Society* (Chatham, NJ: Chatham House Publishers, 1981), 62–63.

22. Velasquez, 348.

23. Industry Canada, http://strategis.ic.gc.ca/epic/internet/inoca-bc.nsf/vwGeneratedInterE/ca00321e.html.

24. Douglas Herbert, "Food Frights Mount in Europe," *CNN.com* (March 13, 2001).

25. CNEWS, http://cnews.canoe.ca/CNEWS/Canada/Canadiana/2003/06/26/120540-cp.html.

26. *The National Post*, http://www.nationalpost.com/home/index.html

27. E. Patrick McGuire, "Product Liability: Evolution and Reform" (New York: The Conference Board, 1989), 6.

28. Terry Morehead Dworkin and Mary Jane Sheffet, "Product Liability in the 1980s," *Journal of Public Policy and Marketing* (1985), 69.

29. "Ford's $128.5 Million Headache," *Time* (February 10, 1978), 65.

30. Robert P. Hartwig, "Whatever Happened to Tort Reform?" *National Underwriter* (November 20, 2000), 31–33.

31. Andrew Hacker, "The Asbestos Nightmare," *Fortune* (January 20, 1986), 121.

32. Kristine Henry, "Chapter 11 Fails to Hurt Grace Much," *The Sun* (July 26, 2001), 2C.

33. Fred W. Morgan and Karl A. Boedecker, "A Historical View of Strict Liability for Product-Related Injuries," *Journal of Macromarketing* (Spring 1996), 103–117.

34. Ann Christopher, "Avoiding a Hazardous Violation," *Warehousing Management* (August, 2001), 20.

35. Bruce Feldthusen, "Civil Liability in Canada: No Tip, No Iceberg," http://oldfraser.lexi.net/publications/books/laws_markets/civil_liability_in_canada_no_tip.html.

36. Dworkin and Sheffet, 69.

37. "Business Line: India Supreme Court Ruling on Damage Liability of Common Carrier," *Businessline* (June 30, 2000), 1.

38. Roger Leroy Miller, "Drawing Limits on Liability," *The Wall Street Journal* (April 4, 1984), 28.

39. Industry Canada, http://strategis.ic.gc.ca/epic/internet/inoca-bc.nsf/vwGeneratedInterE/ca00321e.html.

40. Health Canada, http://www.hc-sc.gc.ca/english/protection/index.html.

41. Health Canada, http://www.hc-sc.gc.ca/hecs-sesc/psp/index.htm.

42. Health Canada, http://www.hc-sc.gc.ca/english/about/org.html#13.

43. Health Canada, http://www.hc-sc.gc.ca/hpfb-dgpsa/index_e.html.

44. Canadian Food Inspection Agency, http://www.inspection.gc.ca/english/corpaffr/publications/prog/agence.shtml

45. Health Canada, http://www.hc-sc.gc.ca/english/media/index.html.

46. Food and Drug Administration, http://www.fda.gov.

47. Mary Gardner Jones, "The Consumer Affairs Office: Essential Element in Corporate Policy and Planning," *California Management Review* (Summer 1978), 63.

48. *Ibid.*, 64–69.

49. *Ibid.*, 70–72.

50. Lawrence A. Crosby, "Measuring Customer Satisfaction," in E. E. Scheuing and W. F. Christopher (eds.), *The Service Quality Handbook* (New York, AMACOM, 1993), 392.

51. A. Blanton Godfrey and E. G. Kammerer, "Service Quality vs. Manufacturing Quality: Five Myths Exploded," *The Service Quality Handbook*, 5.

52. Ron Basu, "Six Sigma to Fit Sigma," *IIE Solutions* (July 2001), 28–33.

53. Michael Hammer and Jeff Godling, "Putting Six Sigma in Perspective," *Quality* (October 2001), 58–62.

54. The Six Sigma Academy Website (http://www.6-sigma.com).

55. Hammer and Godling, 58.

56. Basu, 28–33.

57. *Ibid.*

9

COMMUNITY
STAKEHOLDERS

CHAPTER OBJECTIVES

After studying this chapter, you should be able to:

1   Discuss reasons for community involvement and various types of community involvement.

2   Explain the pros and cons of corporate philanthropy and explain why and to whom companies give.

3. Examine the nature of public purpose partnerships, strategic philanthropy and global philanthropy.

4   Identify reasons for business and plant closings.

5   Consider how business might address concerns of community stakeholders in the context of a plant closing.

When we speak of a community, we usually mean the immediate locale—the town, city, or province—in which a business resides. In our modern age of global business, instantaneous communication, and speedy travel, however, the region, the nation, or even the world can become the relevant community. Businesses are affected by events throughout the world. Traditional geographic boundaries have been eclipsed by communications technology and high-speed travel. The business community now encompasses the entire world.

When we think of business and its community stakeholders, two major kinds of relationships come to mind. One is the positive contribution business can make to the community. Examples of these positive contributions include volunteerism, company contributions, and support of programs in education, culture, urban development, the arts, civic activities, and other health and welfare endeavours. On the other hand, business can also cause harm to community stakeholders. It can pollute the environment, put people out of work by closing a plant, abuse its power, and exploit consumers and employees.

In this chapter, we will concentrate on community involvement and corporate philanthropy as community stakeholder issues. In addition, we will discuss the topic of business or plant closings as community stakeholder concerns. This discussion should provide us with an opportunity to explore both the positive and the detrimental effects that characterize business/community relationships. We will begin with the positive.

In addition to being profitable, obeying the law, and being ethical, a company may create a positive impact in the community by giving in basically two ways: (1) donating the time and talents of its managers and employees and (2) making financial contributions. The first category manifests itself in a wide array of voluntary activities in the community. The second category involves corporate philanthropy or business giving. We should note that there is significant overlap between these two categories, because companies quite frequently donate their time and talents and give financial aid to the same general projects. First, we will discuss community involvement and the various ways in which companies enhance the quality of life in their communities. Second, we will identify the ways that business can contribute to community stakeholders through philanthropy. In addition to the potential beneficial effects on community stakeholders, we will also consider the detrimental effects as well by examining the specific issue of business or plant closings. What responsibilities does business have toward community stakeholders in deciding to close a facility? This chapter will address that question.

COMMUNITY INVOLVEMENT

There are a variety of Canadian-based organizations that encourage corporations to increase their commitment to their communities. For example, the Canadian Centre for Philanthropy focuses on increasing corporate funding of Canadian charities. In 1988, it launched the Imagine campaign, whose goals include encouraging companies to increase their charitable donations and to increase their support for employee volunteering.

Deloitte & Touche is a professional services firm that employs more than 6600 people in 46 locations across Canada. The Canadian Centre for Philanthropy's Imagine program recently lauded Deloitte & Touche for their strong community involvement.[1] Perhaps one of the most compelling arguments for increased **community involvement** was offered by the chairman and chief executive officer of Deloitte & Touche:

> We have an absolutely enormous stake in the communities where our people live and work. If we have good educational systems, good safety, and good activity programs for young people, we're going to be much more effective in attracting and retaining quality people.[2]

Therefore, business must—not only for a healthier society, but also for its own well-being—be willing to give the same serious consideration to human needs that it gives to its own needs for production and profits. Robert Cushman, former president of the Norton Company, enumerates six reasons for business involvement in the community:[3]

1. Businesspeople are efficient problem solvers.

2. Employees gain satisfaction and improved morale from involvement in community programs.

3. A positive image in the community facilitates hiring.

4. Often a company gains prestige and greater acceptance in a community when it gets actively involved.

5. Social responsibility in business is the alternative to government regulation.

6. Business helps itself by supporting those institutions that are essential to the continuation of business.

Business involvement in the community can be enlightened self-interest. Businesses are in a position to help themselves in the process of helping others. This dual objective of business clearly illustrates that making profits and addressing social concerns are not mutually exclusive endeavours. Other rationales for business involvement in community affairs provide moral justification, beyond that of enlightened self-interest. For example, utilitarianism has been used to support corporate giving, with arguments that improvement of the social fabric creates the greatest good for the greatest number. This need not contradict the mandates of self-interest, because the corporation is a community member that will benefit.[4] Although justifications for corporate involvement in the community can be made from various perspectives, one thing is clear: Business has a public responsibility to build a relationship with the community and to be sensitive to its impacts on the world around it.

This point is driven home in Petro-Canada's *2003 Community Report*:

> Petro-Canada's success as an energy company depends on the support of Canadians, so we work hard to invest and participate in the communities where we work and live across the country.[5] ... Petro-Canada has played an active role in Canadian communities for 27 years. We know that we must continually earn Canadians' support, so we work hard to invest and participate in the communities where we work and live across the country.[6]

VOLUNTEER PROGRAMS

One of the most pervasive examples of business involvement in communities is a **volunteer program**. Corporate volunteer programs reflect the resourcefulness and responsiveness of business to communities in need of increasing services. Canadian businesses are increasingly giving attention to volunteerism. From the period 1997 to 2000, the number of employed volunteers who reported receiving approval from their employer to modify their work hours in order to volunteer increased from 22 percent to 27 percent. In addition, more employed volunteers indicated that they received recognition from their employer for their volunteer work (from 14 percent in 1997 to 22 percent in 2000).[7]

The activities used by companies to encourage employee volunteerism include:

- Recognition through articles, awards, and commendations

- Publicity about community volunteer opportunities

- Board membership (encouraging executives to serve on boards)

- Company-sponsored projects involving multiple volunteers

- Ongoing endorsement of programs by CEOs

There are numerous examples of corporations making a difference in communities through volunteer activities. CIBC, Canadian National, Hewlett-Packard (Canada) Ltd., Suncor Energy Inc., and TransCanada PipeLines Ltd. joined together in 2002 to establish a project called "Taking Pulse." This private-sector effort is aimed at increasing the participation of Aboriginal people in the Canadian work force. In the words of Rick George, the president of Suncor Energy Inc., "This is an excellent opportunity for involvement in creating a long-term strategy that will benefit Aboriginal people and indeed the great economy.... We are committed to corporate social responsibility and strongly believe our workforce should be reflective of the communities in which we work." [8] Microsoft Canada engaged in a partnership with the nonprofit organization Boys and Girls Club of Canada to increase computer accessibility for children who lacked the opportunity. Microsoft Canada received high accolades for its contributions to the community, including its financial donations in the millions of dollars, software, resources, online support, and training by employee volunteers.[9]

Communities obviously benefit from such volunteer programs, but how do companies benefit from employee volunteerism? Among the variety of benefits that company executives have indicated are as follows:[10]

- *Indirect community benefits*
  Creation of "healthier" communities
  Improved corporate public image
  Enhanced impact of monetary contributions

- *Employee benefits*
  Building of teamwork skills
  Improved morale
  Attraction of better employees

- *Bottom-line benefits*
  Facilitation of attainment of strategic corporate goals
  Increased employee productivity
  Positive impacts on company productivity

How might involvement in volunteer activities make employees more productive? Kristin Smith, the director of corporate relations for Volunteer Canada, has offered insights into the potential value of employer-supported volunteer initiatives. Smith has observed that volunteerism can enhance interpersonal skills, improve communication abilities, strengthen organizational and management/leadership capacities, and offer new skills that directly apply to the employee's paid job. In addition, such involvement can improve morale by making employees feel good about working for an association that supports them in their interests.[11]

Figure 9–1 presents a sample of corporate community contributions and illustrates the range of activities in which companies can and have become involved.

Figure 9-1

Examples of Corporate Commitments to Communities

Company	Community Service Commitment
CN	Established the CN Safe Community Fund which offers an annual $25 000 incentive award to encourage communities across the country to incorporate rail safety initiatives and campaigns with local school participation.
Sears	Sears works together with the Boys and Girls Clubs of Canada to offer support and funding for youth-focused programs such as *I Can Swim* and the *Sears Ontario Drama Festival*. *Sears Young Futures* initiative has contributed over $3 million to youth groups across Canada
TELUS	Working in cooperation with the Alberta School Boards, TELUS provides a portion of the funding, office space, and the technology to help teachers and educators develop the necessary skills to effectively use the Internet as a teaching tool and to develop online educational materials.
Petro-Canada	Provides financial support, and assists the Canadian Association of Food Banks with business planning and marketing communications directed at providing food to those in need and raising public awareness about hunger in Canada.
Home Depot Canada	Provides funding and materials to community-based organizations for the development and building of safe community playgrounds across Canada (in 2002 provided $1 million for this cause).

RESOURCE-BASED GIVING

The increasingly competitive global environment has heightened pressure for efficiency in all areas, including community service. A key goal of corporate community service is to get the most good possible from each dollar spent on giving. Companies often find that they can achieve the greatest good by providing services that fit their resources and competencies. For example, LensCrafters can provide vision care more efficiently and effectively than can a business that does not specialize in eye care. TELUS uses its high-tech expertise to help educators exploit the benefits of computer and Internet-based education. CN is obviously an expert for the promotion of rail safety.

Resource-based giving involves assessing a firm's resources and competencies and determining where sharing those resources and competencies would accomplish the most good. In the aftermath of the attack on New York's World Trade Center, rescue workers were using cell phones around the clock in a situation where they couldn't afford to have a dead battery but didn't have the time or electricity to recharge phones. Electric Fuel Corporation donated 500 Instant Power cell phone chargers and batteries to keep the phones working. With their head office located in lower Manhattan, only a 10-minute walk from the scene of the tragedy, they were able to hand over their entire inventory to the rescue effort.[12] Information technology (IT) firms have found their capabilities to be in great demand. Because many nonprofits are technologically behind, the skills and resources of technology-based firms can make significant differences in nonprofit operations. For example, Hewlett-Packard (Canada) Co. has supported the nonprofit group Computers for Schools since 1996 with donations of used PCs and equipment.

Drug companies have also found they can accomplish more by drawing on their specific resources. In conjunction with the World Health Organization (WHO), SmithKline Beecham recently launched a 20-year, US$1.7 billion program to eradicate elephantiasis, a disease that affects about 120 million people in Asia, South America, and Africa. The plan is to give annual doses of albendazole to the 1.1 billion people worldwide who are at risk of infection by the disease. To accomplish its goal, SmithKline will donate several billion doses of the drug, as well as technical assistance and health-education support. Similarly, Merck has worked with WHO to provide free ivermectin to treat patients with river blindness in Africa, and it will help support the elephantiasis project by donating ivermectin for clinical trials to determine the drug's ability to treat elephantiasis when used jointly with albendazole.[13]

CORPORATE PHILANTHROPY OR BUSINESS GIVING

The dictionary defines **philanthropy** as "a desire to help mankind as indicated by acts of charity; love of mankind."[14] Robert Payton, an expert on philanthropy, argues that philanthropy is defined as three related activities: voluntary service, voluntary association, and voluntary giving for public purposes.[15] He goes on to state that it includes "acts of community to enhance the quality of life and to ensure a better future."[16] These definitions of philanthropy suggest a broad range of activities.

One more restricted contemporary usage of the word "philanthropy" is "business giving." In this section, we will concentrate on the voluntary giving of financial resources by business. One problem with the dictionary definition is that the motive for the giving is characterized as charitable, benevolent, or generous. In actual practice, it is difficult to assess the true motives behind businesses'—or anyone's—giving of themselves or their financial resources.

In 2003, *Business Week* featured its first ranking of corporate philanthropists. General Mills figured prominently in this ranking because of its tradition of corporate generosity that dates back to the late 1800s, and which includes its effort to reduce crime in U.S. communities, its support of food backs, and its generous donation of US$65 million to a variety of charitable causes in 2002. In addition, *Business Week's* poll of companies in the Standard & Poor's 500-stock index revealed that only four out of 218 respondents agreed with the notion that the sole responsibility of business is to make profits. That is, corporations appear to see increasing value in philanthropy. Among the highest ranked corporate donors in 2002 were Wal-Mart Stores Inc. (US$156 million), Ford Motor (US$131 million), Altria Group (US$113.4 million), SBC Communications (US$100 million), Exxon Mobil (US$97.2 million) and General Mills (US$65 million).[17]

Although Canada's charitable sector receives financial support from business, it is a relatively small portion of the total funding currently received. Individual donations make up a larger source of revenue for the nonprofit and voluntary sector than corporate donations. With recent estimates indicating that corporate donors account for only 1 percent of total sector revenues, it is fair to say that, traditionally, the corporate sector in Canada has not been a generous donor to charitable causes.[18]

During the course of any budget year, companies receive numerous requests for contributions from a wide variety of applicants. Companies must then weigh both quantitative and qualitative factors to arrive at decisions regarding the recipients of their gifts. Data on corporate contributions show that business giving is distributed among five major categories of recipients in the following order of emphasis: (1) education, (2) health and human services, (3) community activities, (4) culture and the arts, and (5) other or unspecified.

WHY DO COMPANIES GIVE?

Perhaps it would be more worthwhile to know why companies give to charitable causes rather than to know how much they give. There are several ways to approach this question. We get initial insights when we consider five categories of corporate contributions programs as shown in Figure 9–2.[19] The motivations that are reflected in these categories range from pure self-interest to a desire to practise good corporate citizenship by supporting both traditional and innovative programs in the community.

Figure 9-2

Categories of Corporate Contributions Programs

1. *The Nondonor*—This is a firm for which no evidence of charitable giving was found.

2. *The "What's in It for Us" Donor*—With this firm, most contributions relate to the company's direct interest or to the welfare of its employees.

3. *The "Company President Believes in Art Support" Donor*—With this firm, most contributions relate to the company's direct interest, employees' welfare, or management's interest.

4. *The "We Are a Good Citizen" Donor*—Here a substantial portion of the company's giving provides support for traditional nonprofit institutions.

5. *The "We Care" Donor*—Here some funds go to newer organizations and established organizations that deal with nontraditional issues.

Saiia, Carroll, and Buchholtz found that corporate giving managers believe their firms are becoming more strategic in their giving and that top managers are requiring greater strategic accountability in their corporate giving programs. They also found that firms that are more "exposed" to the environment (i.e., more open and vulnerable to the environment) are more likely to engage in strategic philanthropy.[20] In another study, Fry, Keim, and Meiners found that corporate contributions are motivated by profit considerations that influence both advertising expenditures and corporate giving. They concluded that corporate giving is a complement to advertising and is, therefore, a profit-motivated expense.[21]

As economic pressures and increased international competitiveness force companies to be more careful with their earnings, we should not be surprised to see the profit motive co-existing with loftier goals in corporate contributions programs. Indeed, in a subsequent section of this chapter, we show that philanthropy can be "strategic," which means that corporate giving can be aligned with the firm's economic or profitability objectives.

The authors of *Business Week*'s 2003 special report on corporate philanthropy made the following observations:

> Many big companies are upfront about their desire to use philanthropy to polish their image. In an age of social activism and instant communication, when a Web log can energize a mass boycott overnight, some say it's essential to build a public narrative about your company as a good global citizen. Thus, we found pharmaceutical companies Merck and Pfizer working to stem the spread of infectious diseases; network-equipment maker Cisco providing voice mail to the homeless; and bank Washington Mutual building affordable housing near its branches.... Of course, just because a company gives lots of its shareholders' money away doesn't mean that it has a heart of gold. Enron Corp. donated heavily to board member John Mendelson's cancer research center. And L. Dennis Kozlowski, the former CEO of Tyco International Ltd. who is now in court fighting charges that he looted the company, allegedly used more than [US]$40 million of Tyco funds to make charitable contributions that either benefited him or that he represented as his personal donations.[22]

PUBLIC PURPOSE PARTNERSHIPS

A report by the Voluntary Sector Initiative (VSI) indicated that there has been a significant shift in the nature of corporate giving to the nonprofit sector:

> The larger trend ... has been the pervasive shift away from corporate donations to corporate sponsorships. Marketing departments are now in control of "philanthropic" budgets. Corporations very carefully seek out potential nonprofit and voluntary sector partners to form strategic relationships that will deliver defined benefits, value and return for their investments in the form of heightened community profile and increased customer loyalty. There are fewer and fewer sources of unrestricted donations or funds. Rather, decisions are taken to maximize positive corporate exposure.[23]

As a broad response to this growing need to reconcile financial and social goals, both of which were deemed by business to be desirable and necessary, the concept of public purpose partnerships evolved.[24] A **public purpose partnership** occurs when a for-profit business enters into a cooperative arrangement with a nonprofit organization for their mutual advantage. Businesses see in public purpose partnerships the opportunity for simultaneous achievement of economic and philanthropic objectives. An example of a public purpose partnership is the one between 3M Company and the University of Minnesota. The 3M Company gave US$1 million to the MBA program at Minnesota. Rather than just give the money and run, 3M officials formed a committee with university officials to discuss how the two organizations could work together. This was seen as a smart move on 3M's part, because about 15 percent of its employees are alumni of the university.[25]

Nortel Networks has developed collaborative relationships with a number of universities across Canada, including the University of Toronto, Carleton University, and the University of Calgary. Nortel provides funding for university chairs, new faculty positions, and cooperative education programs across Canada. This obviously helps universities in attract high-calibre faculty and enhance curricula. For example, with Nortel's support, the University of Toronto established a new Master's of Engineering Degree in Telecommunications (MET) and created a comprehensive summer school program focused on advanced telecommunications topics. Nortel's collaborative efforts will also benefit the company itself. Nortel's involvement generates a closer network of highly qualified recruits that may look first to Nortel when they are considering the job market.[26]

Public purpose sponsorship, particularly in the university setting, has attracted both controversy and criticism. One common question raised is: Does private sector funding of university programs and research generate any constraints or threats to academic freedom and integrity? A commentary in the Canadian Association of University Teachers (CAUT) bulletin entitled "Canada's Universities Mean Business" referred to this criticism of public purpose sponsorship in an academic setting:

> Increased corporate funding poses serious threats to the quality and integrity of the university. Nowhere has this been more apparent than in research. There are a growing number of examples of corporate interests infringing on research practices and ethics. University of Toronto clinician, Dr. Nancy Olivieri, received widespread attention recently when her research at the Hospital for Sick Children led her to believe that a new drug treatment posed serious dangers to some patients. The corporate co-sponsor of the research objected to her findings, threatened legal action should she publish her results, and had her removed as the study's principal investigator. Dr. Olivieri was only reinstated after the intervention of the Canadian Association of University Teachers and the University of Toronto Faculty Association.[27]

This sentiment was shared in a recent report on public-private partnerships (PPPs) in universities in Ontario conducted by the Canadian Centre for Policy Alternatives.[28] The report suggests that public purpose partnerships between the universities and the private sector are adversely affecting the quality of education and appropriate research practices. The report alleges that academic programs favoured by Canadian industry will prosper, while those not considered valuable will be ignored and suffer from underfunding. Specifically, according to this report, this form of university funding (facilitated by both the private sector as well as such government initiatives as SuperBuild and the Ontario Challenge Research and Development Fund) tends to overemphasize support for science and technology disciplines and underemphasize support for the liberal arts programs. These concerns led one of the authors of this report to argue that "these vehicles of PPPs have begun to transform public-serving universities into contracted-out centres for private-sector R & D initiatives, particularly as the public funding for research is often tied to securing private funding."[29]

Public purpose partnerships can take on many different forms. Two of the most important are strategic philanthropy and cause-related marketing. Other partnership options include sponsorships, vendor relationships, licensing agreements, and in-kind donations.[30]

STRATEGIC PHILANTHROPY

Strategic philanthropy is an approach by which corporate giving and other philanthropic endeavours of a firm are designed in a way that best fits with the firm's overall mission, goals, or objectives. This implies that the firm has some idea of what its overall strategy is and that it is able to articulate its missions, goals, or objectives. One goal of all firms is profitability. Therefore, one requirement of strategic philanthropy is to **make as direct a contribution as possible to the financial goals of the firm**. Philanthropy has long been thought to be in the long-range economic interest of the firm. Strategic philanthropy simply presses for a more direct or immediate contribution of philanthropy to the firm's economic success.

An important way in which philanthropy can be made strategic is to **bring contribution programs into sharper alignment with business endeavours**. This means that each firm should pursue those social programs that have a direct rather than an indirect bearing on its success. Thus, a local bank should logically pursue people-oriented projects in the community in which it resides; a manufacturer might pursue programs having to do with environmental protection or technological advancement.

A third way to make philanthropy strategic is to **ensure that it is well planned and managed** rather than handled haphazardly and without direction. When a program is planned, this implies that it has clearly delineated goals, is properly organized and staffed, and is administered in accordance with certain established policies. Figure 9–3 presents one company's views on what constitutes an effective strategic corporate contributions program.

Figure 9-3

Characteristics of an Effective Strategic Corporate Contributions Program

An effective strategic corporate contributions program will have most of the following characteristics:

1. It will be based on the longer-term, strategic self-interest of the company.
2. It will have a clearly stated strategy, agreed to by top management.
3. It will have clear, well-defined guidelines.
4. By definition, it will be planned. (But not all planned giving programs are necessarily strategic.)
5. It will be based on objective criteria understood by all concerned.
6. It will be actively managed and evaluated for results.
7. It will focus on programs, not on capital or endowments. (Strategies change.)
8. It will be recognized as another function or tool in the entire public affairs process—not simply as a measure of corporate conscience.

Sources: Gerald S. Gendell, Manager, Public Affairs Division, Procter & Gamble. Excerpted from his talk at the Public Affairs Council's conference on strategic uses of philanthropy in public affairs. Diane R. Shayon, "Strategic Philanthropy Beginning to Take Hold," *Impact* (October 1984), 2. Reprinted with permission.

Timothy Mescon and Donn Tilson elaborate on the need for managing the philanthropic function:

> A professionally run contributions program requires a set of strategic plans, goals, and objectives which are reviewed regularly; a set of guidelines for determining how much money will be allocated to it; criteria for making and evaluating grants; and either an in-house staff or access to competent consultants.[67]

An example of a firm that turned its philanthropic program around by making it more strategic is Burger King. For years, Burger King was an average corporate good citizen, quietly dribbling out US$200 000 to the United Way along with small contributions to arts organizations and a scattering of other causes. At the same time, McDonald's, its major competitor, was gaining a reputation for strong social programs through its strategically focused Ronald McDonald Houses for children with terminal cancer. Then, suddenly, Burger King woke up and turned its corporate image around with a contributions strategy that sought to make a social statement. This Pillsbury subsidiary began pumping US$4 million a year into highly focused programs to help students, teachers, and schools. Much of Burger King's philanthropy began to consist of scholarships to its own teen work force, designed to reduce the high turnover rate among those workers. As one direct result of the firm's education focus, its turnover rate dropped by more than half during the first six months of its national effort.[68]

Another example of strategic philanthropy was the decision of *People* magazine to promote charities that have particular significance to its readers. Thus, in one year, the magazine planned to give up more than US$3 million worth of advertising space to charities that represent such causes as women with ovarian cancer, children with AIDS, and homeless children. The magazine planned to go even further. It decided to experiment with a program whereby it would eliminate many of the usual "perks" offered to its best advertisers—golf outings, expensive dinners, Broadway theatre tickets—and, instead, invite these companies' executives to engage in charitable activities themselves.[69]

In recent years, popular social causes adopted by corporations have included hunger, community and economic development, literacy, school reform, and environmentalism.[31] In his book titled *Corporate Social Investing*, Curt Weeden details the importance of selecting the right corporate giving manager to oversee philanthropic activities. First, the giving manager should be no more than one executive away from the CEO or chief operating officer (COO), with both a title and a level of compensation that reflect her or his position in the hierarchy. That person should have basic business skills as well as a solid knowledge of the profit-and-loss activities of the company. In addition, the giving manager should be aware of and interested in the nonprofit sector. Last, the giving manager must have the respect of fellow executives and the ability to be an effective company representative.[32]

GLOBAL PHILANTHROPY

Formal international philanthropy efforts are now part of global business strategies. Companies among the top ten global contributors state that their contributions go where they have operations as well as a strong presence. In general, giving programs tend to focus on infrastructure needs, education, the environment, and health care. Some companies, such as IBM and Merck & Co., donate large quantities of product, especially to undeveloped countries.[33]

One recent example of global philanthropy involves firms that do business in sub-Saharan Africa, a region where AIDS has killed 17 million people and infected 25 million more. These companies have seen the disease take a devastating toll on their employees. They often must train two people for the same job so that they will be prepared if the employee or a family member becomes ill. Frequent absences, caused by the disease, are the norm. In response, companies such as Chevron, Coca-Cola, and the Ford Motor Company have undertaken sweeping initiatives to address the problem.[34]

Chevron provides AIDS education, psychological counselling, and free medical facilities for its employees. Although employees do not have access to retroviral treatments, they have had success using available antibiotics to treat the opportunistic infections so common with AIDS. Coca-Cola also sponsors two-day AIDS seminars, provides condoms in all restrooms, and makes health coverage available for all employees. It provides AIDS benefits based on reasonable and customary allowances. The Ford Motor Company also promotes education and prevention while providing health coverage. It takes a three-pronged approach that includes programs for the employees, joint efforts with other employers, and a community outreach program.[35]

Executives claim several advantages of global contributions programs,[36] including:

- An improved corporate image

- A boost in market penetration

- Improved personal relations

- Improved government relations

Executives also note, however, that it can be difficult to administer programs in some cultures that do not place a high priority on voluntary activity. In addition, getting information about the impacts of their programs is difficult.

It is expected that global philanthropy will continue to be an integral and growing part of corporate contributions programs. As long as companies continue to generate revenues and profits abroad, involvement in these countries and their communities will continue.[37]

BUSINESS AND PLANT CLOSINGS

We now shift our focus to business and plant closings. In the preceding sections, we considered the ways in which business firms might have positive, constructive, and creative impacts on community stakeholders. Firms can also have detrimental impacts on communities. We see a most pervasive example of such negative effects when a business or plant closes and its management does not carefully consider the community stakeholders affected.

In the remainder of this chapter, we will examine the nature of the business or plant closing problem, identify some reasons for these occurrences, and consider some actions and strategies that businesses might employ to minimize their negative impacts on community stakeholders.

REASONS FOR CLOSINGS

There is no single reason why so many businesses and plants close. The recession in the 1980s provided a major catalyst for these shutdowns. Some of the affected companies were in declining industries; some had outdated facilities or technology; some moved to less unionized areas; some sought access to new markets; some were victims of the merger/acquisition frenzy; and many were victims of global competition. Plant closings continued in the 1990s. As we entered the new millennium, the sharp decline in the technology sector resulted in the sudden closing of dot-coms and other technology-based firms. It is clear that closings will continue to occur and to profoundly impact employees and the community. Therefore, it is important to understand why they happen.

In the mid-1980s, when plant closings became rampant in North America, a major survey was conducted among public affairs executives to ascertain why they thought business closings were occurring. Figure 9–4 summarizes the reasons that were cited. The major reasons included economic recession, consolidation of company operations, outmoded technology/facilities, changes in corporate strategy, and unmet corporate objectives.[38] In later years, foreign competition became a vital factor. It is clear from these findings and other studies that the primary reasons for companies deciding to close down plants have been related to economics.[39]

[CATCH Figure 14–6; see US 465]

Figure 9–4 Reasons Cited for Business/Plant Closings

WHAT SHOULD BUSINESS DO?

Although the right to close a business or plant has long been regarded as a management prerogative, the business shutdowns of the past two decades—especially their dramatic effects—have called attention to the question of what place rights and responsibilities business has in relation to employee and community stakeholders. The literature of business social responsibility and policy has documented corporate concern with the detrimental impact of its actions. Indeed, business's social response patterns over the past 20 years have borne this out. Management expert Peter Drucker has suggested the following business position regarding social impacts of management decisions:

> Because one is responsible for one's impacts, one minimizes them. The fewer impacts an institution has outside of its own specific purpose and mission, the better does it conduct itself, the more responsibly does it act, and the more acceptable a citizen, neighbor, and contributor it is.[40]

The question is raised, therefore, whether business's responsibilities in the realm of plant closings and their impacts on employees and communities are any different from the host of responsibilities that have already been assumed in areas such as employment discrimination, employee privacy and safety, honesty in advertising, product safety, and concern for the environment. From the perspective of the employees affected, their role in plant and business closings might be considered an extension of the numerous employee rights issues.

Of the executives who have spoken out on this issue, several have indicated that there is an obligation to employees and to the community when a business opens or decides to close. As one observer noted:

> A corporation has a responsibility not only to its employees but to the community involved. It's a simple question of corporate citizenship. Just as an individual must conduct himself [or herself] in a way relating to the community, so must a corporation. As a matter of fact, a corporation has an even larger responsibility since it has been afforded even greater advantages than the individual. Just as a golfer must replace divots, a corporation must be prepared at all times to deal with hardships it may create when it moves or closes down.[41]

Others have also argued that there is a moral obligation at stake in the business-closing issue. In an extensive consideration of plant closings, philosopher John Kavanagh has asserted that companies are not morally free to ignore the impact of a closing on employees and the community. His argument is similar to those that have been given on many other social issues—namely, that business should minimize the negative externalities (unintended side effects) of its actions.[42]

Business has an opportunity to be responsive to employee and community stakeholders in shutdown situations by taking certain actions before the decision to close is made.

BEFORE THE DECISION TO CLOSE IS MADE

Before a company makes a decision to close down, it has a responsibility to itself, its employees, and its community to thoroughly and diligently study whether the closing is the only option available. A decision to leave should be preceded by critical and realistic investigations of economic alternatives.

After a careful study has been made, it may be concluded that finding new ownership for the plant or business is the only feasible alternative. Two basic options exist at this point: (1) find a new owner or (2) explore the possibility of employee ownership.[43]

New Ownership.
Malcolm Baldrige argued that the first obligation a company has to its employees and the community is to try to sell the business as a going unit instead of shutting down. This is often not possible, but it is an avenue that should be explored.[44] Quite often, the most promising new buyers of a firm are residents of the region who have a long-term stake in the community and are willing to make a strong commitment.

For example, when Viner Brothers, an American shoe manufacturer filed for bankruptcy, its three plants presented an attractive investment opportunity for area shoe companies. Within several weeks, Wolverine, the maker of Hush Puppies, was the new owner. Part of the multimillion-dollar sale agreement was that Wolverine hire at least 60 percent of the laid-off workers. About 90 percent of the 900 workers who were laid off were eventually rehired.[45]

Employee Ownership.
The idea of a company selling a plant to the employees as a way of avoiding a closedown is appealing at first glance. Hundreds of North American companies with at least ten workers are **employee owned**. Most of these arrangements are the results of last-ditch efforts to stay in business. Such firms as General Motors, Algoma Steel, Spruce Falls Power and Paper Co. Ltd, Spruce Falls/Tembec, Great Western

Brewery, Creo, and Pacific Regeneration Technologies have sold plants to employees—typically plants that otherwise would have been closed.

Algoma Steel in Sault St. Marie, Ontario, remains one of the most prominent examples of an employee buyout in Canada. Confronted by huge losses due to poor economic conditions, outdated production processes, and low productivity, the steel maker in Canada was taken over by Dofasco Steel in 1989. Because the losses continued, Dofasco decided that, in the absence of prospective purchasers, it would shut down the business. Faced with pending job losses, the United Steel Workers union, with support from the Ontario government, facilitated an employees buyout of the company in 1992, acquiring 60 percent of the voting shares. In addition, procedures for employee involvement in decision-making were established, including employee representation on the board of directors. Following the buyout, the company also gained in strength due to a renewed demand for the company's product, along with productivity improvements.[46]

According to researchers such as Dr. Carol Beatty, director of the School of Industrial Relations at Queen's University, there is a great strength in employee ownership evidenced by some Canadian success stories. With reference to several such stories, Dr. Beatty made the following comments:

> One of the stories I really love is Pacific Regeneration Technologies. Here was a bunch of civil servants—who everybody looks down upon because "they are not living in the real world"—who bought the company and made it into a hugely successful corporation. Now they are taking over other operations all across Canada and they are going to go into the States.... I also really love the Spruce Falls/Tembec story because here is a turn-around of an old economy company that was really sinking. It is a Canadian story too because the American owners wanted to get rid of their Canadian assets and here you had the whole town of Kapuskasing completely dependent on this mill. Employee ownership saved the mill, they got their investment back in spades and they continued to have their jobs. It is a real happy ending.[47]

Of course not all employee buyouts result in happy endings. While the buyout of Algoma Steel and other such companies in distress saved jobs, the longer-term experiences of many of these firms have not been extremely favourable.[48] In numerous cases, employees have been forced to take significant wage and benefit reductions to make the business profitable. In other cases, morale and working conditions have not been satisfactory under the new method of ownership and management.

One such case in point is the U.S.-based Weirton Steel. Negotiators worked out an agreement whereby the employees of the National Steel's Weirton, West Virginia, mill would purchase the mill. The new company, Weirton Steel, became what was then the U.S.'s largest employee-owned enterprise, as well as its eighth-largest producer of steel. Experts gave the mill a surprisingly good chance of succeeding, although Weirton's workers had to take a pay cut of about 32 percent. The mill's union president argued, "32 percent less of $25 an hour is a whole lot better than 100 percent of nothing."[49] In 1990, however, as demand sank for the steel sheet it produced, Weirton Steel found itself in the unenviable position of actually having to lay off some of its employee-owners. By 1991, Weirton had eliminated 1000 of its 8200 jobs, had furloughed another 200 workers, and had plans to cut 700 more jobs. After a decade as owners of the company, Weirton employees became extremely frustrated and angry that employee ownership did not guarantee them that they would not lose their jobs. One employee posed the question many were asking: "How can we be laid off if we own the company?" The reality of the situation, however, is that even an employee-owned company must take whatever actions are necessary if it is to remain solvent and profitable. One of the major pitfalls of worker ownership is that it does not rewrite the laws of capitalism—the bottom line is still the bottom line.[50]

SUMMARY

Because business has a vital stake in the community, it engages in a variety of community projects. Business also contributes to community stakeholders through philanthropy. Companies give for a variety of reasons—some altruistic, some self-interested. Major recipients of business giving include education, health and welfare, community activities, and culture and the arts.

Just as firms have beneficial effects on community stakeholders, they can have detrimental effects as well. Business or plant closings are a prime example of these detrimental effects. Plant closings have a pervasive influence in the sense that a multitude of community stakeholders—employees, local government, other businesses, and the general citizenry—are affected. There is no single reason why these closings have occurred, but among the major reasons are economic conditions, consolidation of company operations, outmoded technology or facilities, changes in corporate strategy, and international competition. Before management makes the decision to close a facility, it has a responsibility to itself, its employees, and the community to study thoroughly whether closing is the only or the best option. Finding a new owner for the business and pursuing the possibility of employee ownership are reasonable and desirable alternatives.

KEY TERMS

community involvement (page 164)

employee owned (page 175)

global philanthropy (page 173)

philanthropy (page 168)

public purpose partnerships (page 170)

resource-based giving (page 167)

strategic philanthropy (page 171)

volunteer program (page 165)

DISCUSSION QUESTIONS

1. Explain the pros and cons of community involvement and corporate philanthropy, and explain why and to whom companies give.

2. Differentiate among public purpose partnerships and strategic philanthropy. Provide an example of each that is not discussed in the text.

3. In your opinion, why does a business have a responsibility to community stakeholders in a business-closing decision? Enumerate what you think are the major reasons.

4. Identify and discuss briefly what you think are the major trade-offs that firms face as they think about possible plant closings or substantial layoffs and their responsibility to their employees and their communities.

ENDNOTES

1. Imagine, http://www.imagine.ca/.

2. Carole Schweitzer, "Corporate Assets," *Association Management* (January 1998), 30–37.

3. *Community Action Manual* (Worcester, MA: Norton Company, April 1978), 1–2.

4. Bill Shaw and Frederick Post, "A Moral Basis for Corporate Philanthropy," *Journal of Business Ethics* (October 1993), 745–751.

5. Petro-Canada, http://www.petro-canada.ca/eng/about/environment/7087.htm.

6. Petro-Canada, http://www.petro-canada.ca/eng/about/environment/7088.htm.

7. National Survey of Giving Volunteering and Participating, http://www.nsgvp.org/.

8. National Aboriginal Achievement Foundation, http://www.naaf.ca/news_releases/Release17.html.

9. Imagine, http://www.imagine.ca/content/awards&recognition/partnership_awards_2003_Microsoft.asp?section=awards.

10. Cathleen Wild, *Corporate Volunteer Programs: Benefits to Business* (New York: The Conference Board, 1993), 37.

11. *Association Magazine*, http://www.associationmagazine.com/client/csae/AM.nsf/0/C119FFA8A7F3264D85256B5F007895FF?OpenDocument.

12. "Electric Fuel Donates 500 Instant Power™ Chargers & Batteries to Keep New York Rescue Workers' Cellphones Working," *PR Newswire* (September 17, 2001).

13. Clive Cookson, "Drug Group in Bid to Wipe Out Elephantiasis," *Financial Times* (January 27,

14. *Webster's New World Dictionary* (Cleveland: World Publishing Company, 1964), 1098.

15. Robert L. Payton, *Philanthropy: Voluntary Action for the Public Good* (New York: Macmillan, 1988), 32.

16. Robert L. Payton, "Philanthropy in Action," in Robert L. Payton, Michael Novak, Brian O'Connell, and Peter Dobkin Hall, *Philanthropy: Four Views* (New Brunswick: Transaction Books, Inc.), 1.

17. Michelle Conlin and Jessi Hempel, Joshua Tanzer and David Polek, "The Corporate Donors," *BusinessWeek* (December 1, 2003), http://www.businessweek.com/magazine/content/03_48/b3860616.htm.

18. Voluntary Sector Initiative, http://www.vsi-isbc.ca/eng/funding/fundingmatters/02.cfm.

19. Sam Sternberg, *National Directory of Corporate Charity* (San Francisco: Regional Young Adult Project, 1984), 14.

20. David Saiia, Archie Carroll, and Ann Buchholtz, "Does Philanthropy Begin at Home? The Strategic Motivation Underlying Corporate Giving Programs," Presented at the 2001 Academy of Management Conference, Washington, D.C.

21. Louis W. Fry, Gerald D. Keim, and Roger E. Meiners, "Corporate Contributions: Altruistic or For-Profit?" *Academy of Management Journal* (March 1982), 94–106.

22. Conlin, et al., "The Corporate Donors."

23. "Funding Matters: The Impact of Canada's New Funding Regime on Nonprofit and Voluntary Organizations" (2003), http://www.vsi-isbc.ca/eng/funding/fundingmatters/02.cfm.

24. Public purpose partnerships are discussed in Richard Steckel and Robin Simons, *Doing Best by Doing Good* (New York: Dutton Publishers, 1992).

25. Andrew E. Serwer, "Company Givers Get Smart," *Fortune* (August 22, 1994), 16.

26. NSERC, http://www.nserc.ca/synergy/articles/98nortel_e.htm.

27. "Canada's Universities Mean Business," CAUT Commentary (Vol. 1, No. 1, May–June 1999), http://www.caut.ca/english/publications/commentary/199905_business.asp.

28. "For Cash and Future Considerations: Ontario Universities and Public-Private Partnerships" (2003), http://www.policyalternatives.ca/.

29. *Ibid.*

30. Steckel and Simons.

31. Craig Smith, "The New Corporate Philanthropy," *Harvard Business Review* (May–June 1994), 106; *Business Week* (December 1, 2003), http://www.businessweek.com/magazine/toc/03_48/B38600348giving.htm.

32. Weeden (1998), 202–205.

33. Anne Klepper, *Global Contributions of U.S. Corporations* (New York: The Conference Board, 1993), 6–7.

34. Judy Greenwald, "Employers Confront AIDS in Africa," *Business Insurance*, (July 23, 2001) 15–22.

35. *Ibid.*

36. Klepper (1993), 6–7.

37. *Ibid.*

38. Archie B. Carroll, Elizabeth J. Gatewood, and James J. Chrisman, "Plant Closings: PAOs Respond to a Survey on an Increasingly Troublesome Issue," *Public Affairs Review* (1984), 64.

39. Cooper and Lybrand, *Closing Plants: Planning and Implementing Strategies* (Morristown, NJ: Financial Executives Research Foundation, 1986), 2.

40. Peter F. Drucker, *Management: Tasks, Responsibilities, Practices* (New York: Harper & Row, 1974) 327–328.

41. Quoted in "A Firm's Obligations: To Employees, Community," *The Atlanta Journal* (September 19, 1977), 4–C.

42. John P. Kavanagh, "Ethical Issues in Plant Relocation," *Business and Professional Ethics Journal* (Winter 1982), 21–33.

43. Archie B. Carroll, "When Business Closes Down: Social Responsibilities and Management Actions,' *California Management Review* (Winter 1984), 131.

44. Quoted in *The Atlanta Journal* (September 19, 1977), 4–C.

45. Jeff Strout, "Viner Shoe Expected to Be in Full Swing Soon," *Bangor News* (January 21, 1981), 9.

46. Richard Long, "Employee Buyouts: The Canadian Experience," *Canadian Business Economics* (1995), http://www.cabe.ca/cbe/vol3_4/34-long.pdf.

47. David Creelman, Interview with Dr. Carol Beatty on Employee Ownership, for *HR.com* http://startribune.hr.com/HRcom/index.cfm/WeeklyMag/825C5B69-090D-4CF7-B48F9E902E3D59EF?ost=wmFeature.

48. Terri Minsky, "Gripes of Rath: Workers Who Bought Iowa Slaughterhouse Regret That They Did," *The Wall Street Journal* (December 2, 1981), 1.

48. "A Steel Town's Fight for Life," *Newsweek* (March 28, 1983), 49.

50. Maria Mallary, "How Can We Be Laid Off If We Own the Company?" *Business Week* (September 9, 1991), 66.

10

BUSINESS RESPONSIBILITIES AND BUSINESS ETHICS

CHAPTER OBJECTIVES

After studying this chapter, you should be able to:

1 Define business ethics and appreciate the complexities of making ethical judgments.

2 Identify and explain three approaches to understanding business ethics.

3 Discuss the factors affecting an organization's moral climate and provide examples of these factors at work.

4 Describe and explain actions or strategies that management may take to improve an organization's ethical climate.

As we have indicated earlier, corruption and scandal have rocked countless corporate boardrooms in these early years of the 21st century. Among those companies devastated by scandal was telecom giant WorldCom Inc. with a US$11 billion fraud, one of the biggest in corporate history. As of October 2003, 11 former Enron executives were facing criminal charges. In addition, several of North America's most important financial institutions, including Merrill Lynch and J. P. Morgan, admitted to helping enable the Enron fraud. Three Merrill Lynch bankers were indicted, and Citi as well as J. P. Morgan settled their cases with the U.S. government, along with an agreement to change the way they do business.[1] Leading drug maker Pfizer Inc. was forced to pay US$49 million to settle charges of overcharging the U.S. government health insurance program for its cholesterol drug Lipitor. Arthur Anderson, Global Crossings, Tyco, Xerox and HealthSouth Corp were also among the companies tainted by scandal in recent years.

Corruption and scandal have not been the sole domain of big business. Toronto native Daniel Duic, agreed to pay back $1.9 million in ill-gotten gains for his role in a large insider trading scandal stemming from his involvement with a friend and former RBC Dominion Securities executive, Andrew Rankin. New York Times newspaper reporter, Jayson Blair, was guilty of journalistic fraud by fabricating parts of his reports and plagiarizing material for many of his stories. Years earlier, the tragedy at Walkerton, Ontario, involving the deaths of seven people and thousands of illnesses, was ultimately connected to simple acts of fraudulent behavior. Individuals responsible for managing the Walkerton Public Utilities failed to maintain the water system in a satisfactory manner and consistently reported false chlorination levels, leading to widespread water contamination. One of Canada's most prestigious law schools was shaken with the revelation that about 30 law students had lied to prospective employers about the academic grades achieved in their first year of law school in order to help secure jobs at prestigious firms. An inquiry launched by the Dean of the University of Toronto's Law School indicated that approximately 30 of the 170 students were guilty of this offence

All these organizations and individuals share at least one common characteristic – at some point they ignored the responsibilities that go along with their profession/business/career. As we have emphasized in this book, business responsibilities are responsibilities to stakeholders. Who are the stakeholders of your business? Who has a stake in your decision or actions? Whose stakes are accommodated or violated by your behavior? These questions are too important for any individual to ignore – regardless of whether the individual is the CEO of a corporation, a journalist for a newspaper or a student in a university program. And, like it or not, these questions are fundamentally questions of ethics.

The growing list of scandals and corrupt behaviour draws clear attention to the urgency of understanding the role of ethics in business management. Mark Pastin, a respected writer on business ethics, once observed that managers don't simply manage people or assets, above all, managers manage interests. In fact, the workplace can be viewed, in Pastin's terms, as a "tangled web of conflicting interests vying for scarce resources."[2] A manager is required to balance the interests of many different parties: shareholders, employees, customers, creditors, etc. Clearly, the existence of different stakeholders, with often differing interests, requires a thoughtful approach to the task of managing organizations. An organization that is managed without a consideration of stakeholder interests is destined to fail – an organization that ignores its responsibilities cannot function effectively in the long-run.

The challenge of stakeholder management and responsibilities to stakeholders has a clear ethical dimension. This begs for a greater understanding of the ethical nature and challenges of business activity. This is the topic is explored in this chapter. Specifically, we will examine the notion of business ethics and identify three major approaches to thinking about business ethics: conventional approach, principles approach and ethical tests approach. We will also examine how organizations can influence and manage their ethical climates.

BUSINESS ETHICS: WHAT DOES IT REALLY MEAN?

All business professionals would readily agree that business must respect and follow the law – no one would condone criminal activity. However, much less talked about is the moral activity of business – business ethics. Consider the following example of an organization that allegedly respected the law yet ignored the ethical implications of their behaviour.

According to evidence documented in the book *IBM and the Holocaust*, IBM played an important role in some of the most horrific events of the 1930s and 1940s in Europe. Specifically, IBM's production of hundreds of Hollerith machines, the precursor to the computer, played a central role in the first racial censuses conducted by the Nazis. Beginning in 1933, the Hollerith machine was used by the German government to identify its intended targets. As Black comments in his book:

> Nearly every Nazi concentration camp operated a Hollerith Department ... in some camps ... as many as two dozen IBM sorters, tabulators and printers were installed ... [I]t did not matter whether IBM did or did not know exactly which machine was used at which death camp. All that mattered was that the money would be waiting—once the smoke cleared.

The book's author, Edwin Black, suggests that IBM's involvement with Nazi Germany helps explain one mystery of the Holocaust—how so many people were killed in so little time. With the knowledge of top IBM management in the United States, IBM's European subsidiaries actually perfected the means for the Nazis to quickly collect census data for its murderous plans. Hitler awarded IBM chairman Thomas Watson a medal for his company's work.[3]

The above is a striking example of the need to consider what, if any, ethical guidelines or frameworks might be employed to judge the ethics of business decision making and practices. Consequently, we need to explore the notion of business ethics and identify the approaches that have been commonly applied to make sense if this topic.

Ethics is the discipline that deals with what is good and bad and with moral duty and obligation. Ethics can also be regarded as a set of moral principles or values. Morality is a doctrine or system of moral conduct. Moral conduct refers to that which relates to principles of right and wrong in behaviour. For the most part, then, we can think of ethics and morality as being so similar to one another that we may use the terms interchangeably to refer to the study of fairness, justice, and right and wrong behaviour in business.

Business ethics, therefore, is concerned with good and bad or right and wrong behaviour and practices that take place within a business context. Concepts of right and wrong are increasingly being interpreted today to include the more difficult and subtle questions of fairness, justice, and equity.

To gain an appreciation of the kinds of issues that are important under the rubric of business ethics, Figure 10–1 presents an inventory of business ethics issues. Here we see business ethics issues categorized on the basis of stakeholder relationships.

Figure 10-1

Inventory of Ethical Issues in Business

This checklist is designed to stimulate thought and discussion on important ethical concerns in your company and the larger business community.

For each of the following issues indicate whether ethical problems are:
5 = Very serious; 4 = Serious; 3 = Not very serious; 2 = Not a problem; 1 = No opinion.

Column I = In the business world in general   Column II = In your company

Employee—Employer Relations

_____ _____ 1. Work ethic—giving a full day's work for a full day's pay
_____ _____ 2. Petty theft (i.e., supplies, telephone, photocopying, etc.)
_____ _____ 3. Cheating on expense accounts
_____ _____ 4. Employee acceptance of gifts or favours from vendors
_____ _____ 5. Distortion or falsification of internal reports
_____ _____ 6 Cheating or overreaching on benefits (sick days, insurance, etc.)

Employer—Employee Relations

_____ _____ 7. Sexual or racial discrimination in hiring, promotion, or pay
_____ _____ 8. Sexual harassment
_____ _____ 9. Invasions of employee privacy
_____ _____ 10. Unsafe or unhealthy working conditions
_____ _____ 11. Discouragement of internal criticism re: unfair, illegal, or improper activities
_____ _____ 12. Unfair or insensitive handling of assignment changes or major reorganizations
_____ _____ 13. Improper dealing with persons with disabilities
_____ _____ 14. Failure to give honest, fair, and timely work appraisals
_____ _____ 15. Recruiting for employee's replacement without telling employee being replaced
_____ _____ 16. Using strategies or technical justifications to deny employees earned benefits
_____ _____ 17. Dealing peremptorily or unfairly with employee complaints
_____ _____ 18. Misleading employees about the likelihood of layoffs, terminations, or job changes
_____ _____ 19. Inadequate training or supervision to ensure employee's success
_____ _____ 20. Inadequate participation by qualified staff in major policy decisions
_____ _____ 21. Unfair demands on or expectations of paid staff
_____ _____ 22. Inadequate compensation
_____ _____ 23. Inadequate recognition, appreciation, or other psychic rewards to staff
_____ _____ 24. Inappropriate blame-shifting or credit-taking to protect or advance personal careers
_____ _____ 25. Unhealthy competition among employees about "turf," assignments, budget, etc.
_____ _____ 26. Inadequate communication among departments and divisions for the wrong reasons
_____ _____ 27. Inadequate mutual support and teamwork; individuals focus primarily on their own narrow jobs

Company—Customer Relations

_____ _____ 28. Unfair product pricing
_____ _____ 29. Deceptive marketing/advertising
_____ _____ 30. Unsafe or unhealthy products
_____ _____ 31. Unfair and/or legalistic handling of customer complaints
_____ _____ 32. Discourtesy or arrogance toward customers

THE CONVENTIONAL APPROACH TO BUSINESS ETHICS

The **conventional approach to business ethics** is essentially an approach whereby we compare a decision or practice with prevailing norms of acceptability. We call it the conventional approach because it is believed that this is the way that conventional or general society thinks. The major challenge of this approach is answering the questions "Whose norms do we use?" in making the judgment, and "What norms are prevailing?" This approach may be depicted by highlighting the major variables to be compared with one another:

Decision or Practice ⟷ Prevailing Norms of Acceptability

There is considerable room for variability on both of these issues. With respect to whose norms are used as the basis for ethical judgments, the conventional approach would consider as legitimate those norms emanating from family, friends, religious beliefs, the local community, one's employer, law, the profession, and so on. In addition, one's conscience, or the individual, would be seen by many as a legitimate source of ethical norms.

In many circumstances, the conventional approach to ethics may be useful and applicable. What does a person do, however, if norms from one source conflict with norms from another source? Also, how can we be sure that societal norms are really appropriate or defensible? Our society's culture sends us many and often conflicting messages about what is appropriate behaviour. We get these messages from television, movies, music, and other sources in the culture. There is little doubt that media representations of what is acceptable behaviour have changed dramatically over the last two decades.

Another example of the conflicting messages people get today from society occurs in the realm of sexual harassment in the workplace. On the one hand, today's television, movies, advertisements, and music are replete with sexual innuendo and the treatment of women and men as sex objects. This would suggest that such behaviour is normal, acceptable, even desired. On the other hand, the law and the courts are stringently prohibiting sexual gestures or innuendo in the workplace. In this example, we see a norm arising from culture and society clashing with a norm evolving from employment law and business ethics.

MAKING ETHICAL JUDGMENTS

When a decision is made about what is ethical (right, just, fair) using the conventional approach, there is room for variability on several counts (see Figure 10–2). Three key elements compose such a decision. First, we observe the *decision, action,* or *practice* that has been committed. Second, we *compare the practice with prevailing norms of acceptability*—that is, society's or some other standard of what is acceptable or unacceptable. Third, *we must recognize that value judgments are being made* by someone as to what really occurred (the actual behaviour) and what the prevailing norms of acceptability really are. This means that two different people could look at the same behaviour, compare it with their concepts of what the prevailing norms are, and reach different conclusions as to whether the behaviour was ethical or not. This becomes quite complex as perceptions of what is ethical inevitably lead to the difficult task of ranking different values against one another.

Figure 10-2

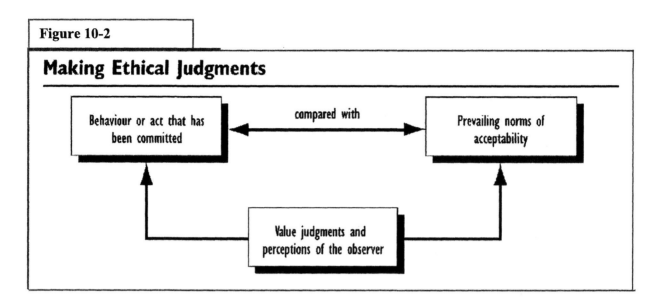

Making Ethical Judgments

If we can put aside for a moment the fact that perceptual differences about an incident do exist, and the fact that we differ among ourselves because of our personal values and philosophies of right and wrong, we are still left with the problematic task of determining society's prevailing norms of acceptability of business behaviour. As a whole, members of society generally agree at a very high level of abstraction that certain behaviours are wrong. However, the consensus tends to disintegrate as we move from the general to specific situations.

The conventional approach to business ethics can be valuable, because we all need to be aware of and sensitive to the total environment in which we exist. We need to be aware of how society regards ethical issues. It has limitations, however, and we need to be cognizant of these as well. The most serious danger is that of falling into an **ethical relativism** where we pick and choose which source of norms we wish to use based on what will justify our current actions or maximize our freedom. We will argue that a principles approach, described below, is needed to augment the conventional approach. The principles approach looks at general guides to ethical decision making that come from moral philosophy.

THE PRINCIPLES APPROACH TO BUSINESS ETHICS

The principles approach to ethics or ethical decision making is based on the idea that managers may desire to anchor their decisions on a more solid foundation than the conventional approach to ethics. Several principles of ethics have evolved over the centuries as moral philosophers and ethicists have attempted to organize and codify their thinking. This raises the question of what constitutes a principle of business ethics and how it might be applied. A principle of business ethics is a concept, guideline, or rule that, if applied when you are faced with an ethical dilemma, will assist you in making an ethical decision.[4]

There are many different principles of ethics, but we must limit our discussion to a number of those that have been deemed most useful in business settings. Therefore, we will concentrate on three major principles: utilitarianism, rights, and justice.

PRINCIPLE OF UTILITARIANISM

Many have held that the rightness or fairness of an action can be determined by looking at its results or consequences. If the consequences are good, the action or decision is considered good. If the consequences are bad, the action or decision is considered wrong. The **principle of utilitarianism** is, therefore, a *consequential* principle. In its simplest form, **utilitarianism** asserts that "we should always act so as to produce the greatest ratio of good to evil for everyone."[5] Another way of stating utilitarianism is to say that one should take that course of action that represents the "greatest good for the greatest number." Two of the most influential philosophers who advocated this consequential view were Jeremy Bentham (1748–1832) and John Stuart Mill (1806–1873).

The attractiveness of utilitarianism is that it forces us to think about the general welfare. It proposes a standard outside of self-interest by which to judge the value of a course of action. It also forces us to think in stakeholder terms: What would produce the greatest good in our decision, considering stakeholders such as owners, employees, customers, and others, as well as ourselves? Finally, it provides for latitude in decision making in that it does not recognize specific actions as inherently good or bad but rather allows us to fit our personal decisions to the complexities of the situation.

A weakness of utilitarianism is that it ignores actions that may be inherently wrong. By focusing on the ends (consequences) of a decision or an action, the means (the decision or action itself) may be ignored. Thus, we have the problematic situation where one may argue that the end justifies the means, using utilitarian reasoning. Therefore, the action or decision is considered objectionable only if it leads to a lesser ratio of good to evil. Another problem with the principle of utilitarianism is that it may come into conflict with the idea of justice. Critics of utilitarianism say that the mere increase in total good is not good in and of itself because it ignores the distribution of good, which is also an important issue. Another stated weakness is that, when using this principle, it is very difficult to formulate satisfactory rules for decision making. Therefore, utilitarianism, like most ethical principles, has its advantages and disadvantages.[6]

PRINCIPLE OF RIGHTS

One major problem with utilitarianism is that it does not handle the issue of **rights** very well. That is, utilitarianism implies that certain actions are morally right (i.e., they represent the greatest good for the greatest number) when in fact they may violate another person's rights.[7] **Moral rights** are important, justifiable claims or entitlements. The right to life or the right not to be killed by others is a justifiable claim in our society. The Declaration of Independence referred to the rights to life, liberty, and the pursuit of happiness. We also speak of human rights. Some of these are **legal rights** and some are moral rights.

The basic idea undergirding the **principle of rights** is that rights cannot simply be overridden by utility. A right can be overridden only by another, more basic or important right. Let us consider the problem if we apply the utilitarian principle. For example, if we accept the basic right to human life, we are precluded from considering whether killing someone might produce the greatest good for the greatest number. To use a business example, if a person has a right to equal treatment (not to be discriminated against), we could not argue for discriminating against that person so as to produce more good for others.[8] However, some people would say that this is precisely what we do when we advocate affirmative action.

The rights principle expresses morality from the point of view of the individual or group of individuals, whereas the utilitarian principle expresses morality in terms of the group or society as a whole. The rights view forces us in our decision making to ask what is due each individual and to promote individual welfare. The rights view also limits the validity of appeals to numbers and to society's aggregate benefit.[9] However, a central question that is not always easy to answer is: "What constitutes a legitimate right that should be honoured, and what rights or whose rights take precedence over others?"

Figure 10-3 provides an overview of some of the types of rights that are being claimed in our society today. Some of these rights are legally protected, whereas others are claimed as moral rights but are not legally protected. Managers are expected to be attentive to both legal and moral rights, but there are no clear guidelines available to help one sort out which claimed moral rights should be protected, to what extent they should be protected, and which rights should take precedence over others.

Figure 10-3

A Variety of Legal Rights and Claimed Moral Rights in Society Today

Human rights	Right to life
Minorities' rights	Criminals' rights
Women's rights	Children's rights
Disabled people's rights	Fetal rights
Older people's rights	Embryo rights
Religious affiliation rights	Animals' rights
Employee rights	Right of due process
Consumer rights	Gay rights
Shareholder rights	Victims' rights
Privacy rights	

PRINCIPLE OF JUSTICE

Just as the utilitarian principle does not handle well the idea of rights, it does not deal effectively with justice either. One way to think about the **principle of justice** is to say that it involves the fair treatment of each person. But how do you decide what is fair to each person? How do you decide what each person is due? People might be given what they are due according to their type of work, their effort expended, their merit, their need, and so on. Each of these criteria might be appropriate in different situations. At one time, the view prevailed that married heads of households ought to be paid more than single males or women. Today, however, the social structure is different. Women have entered the work force in significant numbers, some families are structured differently, and a revised concept of what is due people has evolved. The just action now is to pay everyone more on the basis of merit than needs.[10]

To use the principle of justice, we must ask, "What do we mean by justice?" There are several kinds of justice. **Distributive justice** refers to the distribution of benefits and burdens. **Compensatory justice** involves compensating someone for a past injustice. **Procedural justice** refers to fair decision-making procedures, practices, or agreements.[11]

John Rawls provides what some have referred to as a comprehensive principle of justice.[12] His theory is based on the idea that what we need first is a fair method by which we may choose the principles through which conflicts will be resolved. The two principles of justice that underlie his theory are as follows:[13]

1. Each person has an equal right to the most extensive basic liberties compatible with similar liberties for all others.

2. Social and economic inequalities are arranged so that they are both (a) reasonably expected to be to everyone's advantage and (b) attached to positions and offices open to all.

Under Rawls's first principle, each person is to be treated equally. The second principle is more controversial. It is criticized by both those who argue that the principle is too strong and those who think the principle is too weak. The former think that, as long as we have equal opportunity, there is no injustice when some people benefit from their own work, skill, ingenuity, or assumed risks. Therefore, such people deserve more and should not be required to produce benefits for the least advantaged. The latter group thinks that the inequalities that may result may be so great as to be clearly unjust. Therefore, the rich get richer and the poor get only a little less poor.[14]

Supporters of the principle of justice claim that it preserves the basic values—freedom, equality of opportunity, and a concern for the disadvantaged—that have become embedded in our moral beliefs. Critics object to various parts of the theory and would not subscribe to Rawls's principles at all. Utilitarians, for example, think the greatest good for the greatest number should reign supreme.

In summary, the principles approach to ethics focuses on guidelines, ideas, or concepts that have been created to help people and organizations make wise, ethical decisions. In our discussion, we have treated the following as important components of the principles-based approach: utilitarianism, rights and justice. Such principles, or principle-based approaches, ought to cause us to think deeply and to reflect carefully on the ethical decisions we face in our personal and organizational lives. For the most part, these principles are rooted in moral philosophy and religion. On a more pragmatic level, we turn now to a series of ethical tests that constitute our third major approach to ethics.

ETHICAL TESTS APPROACH TO BUSINESS ETHICS

In addition to the ethical principles approach to guiding personal and managerial decision making, a number of practical **ethical tests** might be set forth, too. The ethical tests we discuss here tend to be more practical in orientation and do not require the depth of moral thinking that the principles do. No single test is recommended as a universal answer to the question, "What action or decision should I take in this situation?" However, each person may find one or more tests that will be useful in helping to clarify the appropriate course of action in a decision situation. To most students, the notion of a test invokes the thought of questions posed that need to be answered. Indeed, each of these tests for personal ethical decision making requires the thoughtful deliberation of a central question that gets to the heart of the matter.

TEST OF COMMON SENSE

With this first test, the individual simply asks, "Does the action I am getting ready to take really make sense?" When you think of behaviour that might have ethical implications, it is logical to consider the practical consequences. If, for example, you would surely get caught engaging in a questionable practice, the action does not pass this test. Many unethical practices have come to light where one is led to ask whether a person really used her or his common sense at all. This test has severe limitations. For example, if you conclude that you would not get caught engaging in a questionable practice, this test might lead you to think that the questionable practice is an acceptable course of action, when in fact it is not. In addition, there may be other common-sense aspects of the situation that you have overlooked.

TEST OF ONE'S BEST SELF

Each person has a self-concept. Most people could construct a scenario of themselves at their best. This test requires the individual to pose the question, "Is this action or decision I'm getting ready to take compatible with my concept of myself at my best?" This test addresses the notion of the esteem in which we hold ourselves and the kind of person we want to be known as. Naturally, this test would not be of much value to those who do not hold themselves in high esteem.

TEST OF MAKING SOMETHING PUBLIC

This is one of the most powerful tests.[15] If you are about to engage in a questionable practice or action, you might pose the following questions: "How would I feel if others knew I was doing this? How would I feel if I knew that my decisions or actions were going to be featured on the national evening news tonight for all the world to see?" This test addresses the issue of whether your action or decision can withstand public disclosure and scrutiny. How would you feel if all your friends, family, and colleagues knew you were engaging in this action? If you feel comfortable with this thought, you are probably on solid footing. If you feel uncomfortable with this thought, you ought to rethink your position.

The concept of public exposure is quite powerful. Several years ago, a poll asked managers asked would stop bribes abroad. Most managers thought that public exposure would be most effective. "If the public knew we were accepting bribes, this knowledge would have the best chance of being effective," they replied.

TEST OF VENTILATION

The idea of ventilation is to expose your proposed action to others and get their thoughts on it. This test works best if you get opinions from people who you know might not see things your way. The important point here is that you do not isolate yourself with your dilemma but seek others' views. After you have subjected your proposed course of action to other opinions, you may find that you have not been thinking clearly.

These three approaches reflect the complexity of understanding the ethics of business practices, decisions and behaviour. In the next section, we focus on how organizations may create climates that advocate ethical or unethical behaviour.

MANAGING ORGANIZATIONAL ETHICS

To manage ethics in an organization, a manager must appreciate that the organization's ethical climate is just one part of its overall corporate culture. Figure 10–4 illustrates several levels of moral climate and some of the key factors that may come to bear on the manager as she or he makes decisions. Our focus in this section is on the organization's moral climate. Two major questions that need to be considered are (1) What factors contribute to ethical or unethical behaviour in the organization? and (2) What actions or strategies might management employ to improve the organization's ethical climate?

Figure 10-4

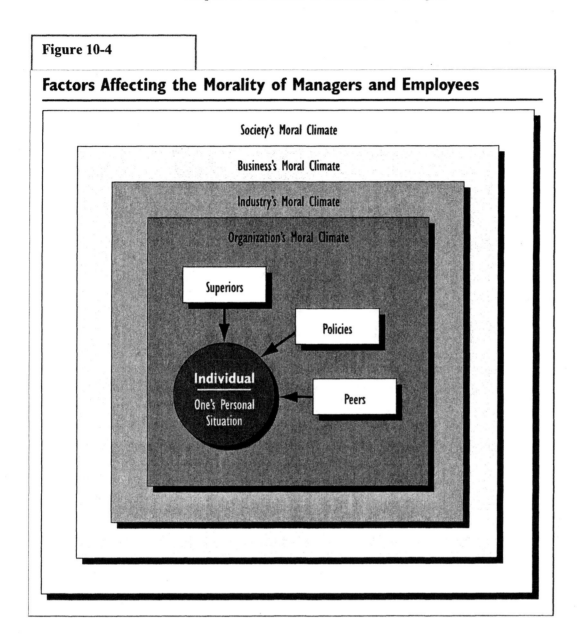

Factors Affecting the Morality of Managers and Employees

Society's Moral Climate

Business's Moral Climate

Industry's Moral Climate

Organization's Moral Climate

Superiors

Policies

Individual
One's Personal
Situation

Peers

FACTORS AFFECTING THE ORGANIZATION'S MORAL CLIMATE

For managers to be in a position to create an ethical climate, they must first understand the factors at work in the organization that influence whether or not other managers or employees behave ethically. In a recent survey conducted by the U.S.-based Society for Human Resources Management, more than half of the 462 Human Resource professionals surveyed reported that they had been pressured to act unethically in the last year, and 52 percent said they felt at least some pressure to compromise their organization's ethical standards (up from 47 percent in a similar poll conducted six years earlier). The most commonly cited sources for acting unethically included a need to follow the boss's orders (49 percent), pressure to meet overly aggressive business objectives (48 percent), and helping the organization survive (40 percent).[16]

More than a few studies have been conducted that have sought to identify and to rank the sources of ethical behaviour in organizations. Baumhart conducted one of the earliest studies, in which he surveyed over 1500 *Harvard Business Review* readers (executives, managers).[17] One of the questions asked was to rank several factors that the managers thought influenced or contributed to unethical behaviours or actions. The factors found in his study, in descending order of frequency of mention, were:

1. Behaviour of superiors

2. The ethical practices of one's industry or profession

3. Behaviour of one's peers in the organization

4. Formal organizational policy (or lack thereof)

5. Personal financial need

Brenner and Molander later replicated the Baumhart study using over 1200 *Harvard Business Review* readers. They added one additional factor to the list: society's moral climate.[18] Posner and Schmidt surveyed over 1400 managers, again asking them to rank the list of six factors in terms of their influence or contribution to unethical behaviour.[19] Figure 10-5 presents the findings of these three landmark studies.

Figure 10-5

Factors Influencing Unethical Behaviour Question: "Listed below are the factors that many believe influence unethical behaviour. Rank them in order of their influence or contribution to unethical behaviours or actions by managers."[a]

Factor	Posner & Schmidt Study[b] (N = 1443)	Brenner & Molander Study[c] (N = 1227)	Baumhart Study[d] (N = 1531)
Behaviour of superiors	2.17(1)	2.15(1)	1.9(1)
Behaviour of one's organizational peer	3.30(2)	3.37(4)	3.1(3)
Ethical practices of one's industry or profession	3.57(3)	3.34(3)	2.6(2)
Society's moral climate	3.79(4)	4.22(5)	e
Formal organizational policy (or lack thereof)	3.84(5)	3.27(2)	3.3(4)
Personal financial need	4.09(6)	4.46(6)	4.1(5)

[a] Ranking is based on a scale of 1 (most influential) to 6 (least influential).

[b] Barry Z. Posner and Warren H. Schmidt, "Values and the American Manager: An Update," *California Managemer. Review* (Spring 1984), 202–216.

[c] Steve Brenner and Earl Molander, "Is the Ethics of Business Changing?" *Harvard Business Review* (January/February 1977).

[d] Raymond C. Baumhart, "How Ethical Are Businessmen?" *Harvard Business Review* (July/August 1961), 6ff.

[e] This item not included in 1961 study.

Although there is some variation in the rankings of the three studies, several findings are worthy of note:

1. *Behaviour of superiors* was ranked as the number one influence on unethical behaviour in all three studies.

2. *Behaviour of one's peers* was ranked high in two of the three studies.

3. *Industry or professional ethical practices* ranked in the upper half in all three studies.

4. *Personal financial need* ranked last in all three studies.

What stands out in these studies from an organizational perspective is the influence of the behaviour of one's superiors and peers. Also notable about these findings is that quite often it is assumed that society's moral climate has a lot to do with managers' morality, but this factor was ranked low in the two studies in which it was considered. Apparently, society's moral climate serves as a background factor that does not have a direct and immediate bearing on organizational ethics. Furthermore, it is enlightening to know that personal financial need ranked so low.

IMPROVING THE ORGANIZATION'S ETHICAL CLIMATE

Because the behaviour of managers has been identified as the most important influence on the ethical behaviour of organization members, it should come as no surprise that most actions and strategies for improving the organization's ethical climate must emanate from top management and other management levels as well. The process by which these kinds of initiatives have taken place is often referred to as "institutionalizing ethics" into the organization.[20] In this section, we will consider some of the best practices that managers have taken to improve their organizations' ethical climate. Figure 10–6 depicts a number of best practices for creating an ethical organization climate or culture. Top management leadership is at the hub of these initiatives, actions, or practices.

Figure 10-6

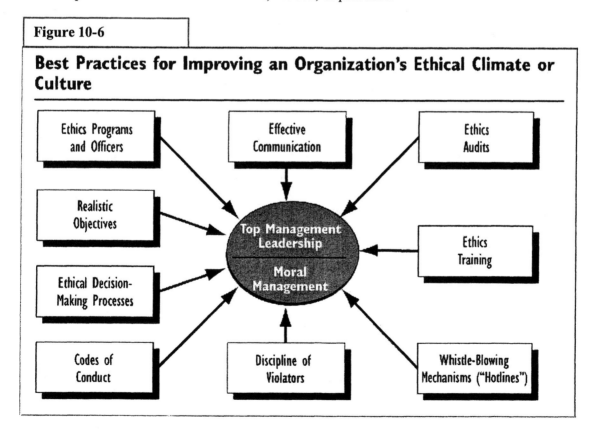

Best Practices for Improving an Organization's Ethical Climate or Culture

- Ethics Programs and Officers
- Effective Communication
- Ethics Audits
- Realistic Objectives
- Ethical Decision-Making Processes
- Ethics Training
- Codes of Conduct
- Discipline of Violators
- Whistle-Blowing Mechanisms ("Hotlines")

Top Management Leadership / Moral Management

TOP MANAGEMENT LEADERSHIP (MORAL MANAGEMENT)

It has become a cliché, but this premise must be established at the outset: *The moral tone of an organization is set by top management.* This is because all managers and employees look to their bosses at the highest level for their cues as to what is acceptable practice. A former chairman of a major steel company stated it well: "Starting at the top, management has to set an example for all the others to follow."[21]

Top management, through its capacity to set a personal example and to shape policy, is in the ideal position to provide a highly visible role model. The authority and ability to shape policy, both formal and implied, forms one of the vital aspects of the job of any leader in any organization. Trevino, Hartman, and Brown have referred to this aspect of becoming a moral manager as "role modelling through visible action." They continue by saying that effective moral managers recognize that they live in a fishbowl and that employees are watching them for cues about what's important.[22]

EFFECTIVE COMMUNICATION

Management also carries a heavy burden in terms of providing ethical leadership in the area of effective communication. We have seen the importance of communicating through acts, principles, and organizational climate. We will discuss further the communication aspects of setting realistic objectives, codes of conduct, and the decision-making process. Here, however, we want to stress the importance of communication principles, techniques, and practices.

Conveying the importance of ethics through communication includes both written and verbal forms of communication. In each of these settings, management should operate according to certain key ethical principles. Candour is one very important principle. *Candour* requires that a manager be forthright, sincere, and honest in communication transactions. In addition, it requires the manager to be fair and free from prejudice and malice in the communication. Related to this is the principle of fidelity. *Fidelity* in communication means that the communicator should be faithful to detail, should be accurate, and should avoid deception or exaggeration. *Confidentiality* is a final principle that ought to be stressed. The ethical manager must exercise care in deciding what information she or he discloses to others. Trust can be easily shattered if the manager does not have a keen sense of what is confidential in a communication.

ETHICS PROGRAMS AND ETHICS OFFICERS

In recent years, many companies have begun creating ethics programs. These programs are often headed up by an ethics officer who is in charge of implementing the array of ethics initiatives of the organization. In some cases, the creation of ethics programs and designation of ethics officers have helped reduce penalties to those companies with ethics programs that were found guilty of ethics violations.[23] Other companies started ethics programs as an effort to centralize the coordination of ethics initiatives in those companies. Typical initiatives of companies include codes of conduct (or ethics), ethics hotlines and ethics training.

Numerous major companies have adopted some kind of ethics programs, including Bell Canada, General Motors, Nortel, Texas Instruments, Xerox, and Sears.

ETHICS QUICK TEST. Companies that have endeavoured to institutionalize ethical behaviour in business practices, may include in their ethics programs some sort of ethics quick test. Using a brief set of questions to make ethical decisions has become popular in business. For example, Texas Instruments has printed its seven-part "Ethics Quick Test" on a wallet card its employees may carry. The test's seven questions and reminders are as follows:[24]

- Is the action legal?

- Does it comply with our values?

- If you do it, will you feel bad?

- How will it look in the newspaper?

- If you know it's wrong, don't do it.

- If you're not sure, ask.

- Keep asking until you get an answer.

CODES OF CONDUCT

Top management has the responsibility for establishing standards of behaviour and for effectively communicating those standards to all managers and employees in the organization. One of the classic ways by which companies and ethics officers have fulfilled this responsibility is through the use of codes of ethics, or **codes of conduct**. **Codes of ethics** are a phenomenon of the past 20 years. Over 95 percent of all major corporations have them today, and the central questions in their usefulness or effectiveness revolve around the managerial policies and attitudes associated with their use.[25] There are a number of potential values or benefits that business organizations receive as a result of their codes of ethics, including the following:[26]

1. Legal protection for the company ;

2. Increased company pride and loyalty;

3. Increased consumer/public goodwill;

4. Improved loss prevention;

5. Reduced bribery and kickbacks;

6. Improved product quality;

7. Increased productivity

Among the most common topics addressed in corporate codes are:[27] Conflicts of interest; Receiving gifts, gratuities, entertainment; Protecting company proprietary information; Giving gifts, gratuities, entertainment; Discrimination; Sexual harassment; Kickbacks; General conduct; Employee theft; Proper use of company assets.

A major study of the effectiveness of corporate codes found that there is a relationship between corporate codes and employee behaviour in the workplace, particularly to the degree that employees perceive the codes to be implemented strongly and embedded in the organizational culture. Therefore, when codes are implemented forcefully and embedded strongly in the culture, reports of unethical employee behaviour tend to be lower.[28]

SUMMARY

The recognition of the responsibilities of management to different stakeholders is a critically important task for any organization. The challenge of resolving the often conflicting interests of differing stakeholders is also an ethical challenge. Consequently, the subject of business ethics is a topic that must be addressed by any manager. While this chapter did not attempt to outline the myriad of ethical principles that managers may or may not employ, we did draw attention to the role managers play in achieving what can be viewed as three broad types or models of management ethics—moral, immoral, and amoral.

Factors were discussed that affect the organization's moral climate. It was argued that the behaviour of one's superiors and peers and industry ethical practices were the most important influences on a firm's ethical climate. Society's moral climate and personal needs were considered to be less important. Best practices for improving the firm's ethical climate include providing leadership from management, ethics programs and ethics officers and employing codes of conduct. The goal of ethics initiatives is to achieve a status that may be characterized not just by isolated moral decisions, but by the presence of moral managers and the ultimate achievement of a moral organization.

KEY TERMS

business ethics (page 183)

codes of conduct (page 195)

codes of ethics (page 195)

compensatory justice (page 188)

conventional approach to business ethics (page 185)

distributive justice (page 188)

ethical relativism (page 186)

ethical tests (page 189)

ethics (page 183)

ethics quick tests (page 194)

legal rights (page 187)

moral rights (page 187)

principle of justice (page 188)

principle of rights (page 187)

principle of utilitarianism (page 186)

procedural justice (page 188)

rights (page 187)

utilitarianism (page 186)

DISCUSSION QUESTIONS

1. From your personal experience, give two examples of ethical dilemmas in your personal life. Give two examples of ethical dilemmas you have experienced as a member of an organization.

2. Give a definition of ethical business behaviour, explain the approaches to judging the ethics of that behavior, and give an example from your personal experience of the difficulties involved in making these determinations.

3. What do you think about the idea of codes of conduct? Give three reasons why an organization ought to have a code of conduct, and give three reasons why an organization should not have a code of conduct. On balance, how do you regard codes of conduct?

4. A lively debate is going on today concerning whether business ethics can be effectively taught in business schools. Do you think business ethics can and should be taught? Be prepared to explain your reasons carefully.

ENDNOTES

1. "Partners in Crime," *Fortune Magazine* (October 27, 2003).

2. Mark Pastin, The Hard Problems of Management, Jossey Bass: Arizona, 1986.

3. Edwin Black, *IBM and the Holocaust: The Strategic Alliance between Nazi Germany and America's Most Powerful Corporation* (New York: Crown Publishers, 2001), 375.

4. Archie B. Carroll, "Principles of Business Ethics: Their Role in Decision Making and an Initial Consensus," *Management Decision* (Vol. 28, No. 28, 1990), 20–24.

5. Vincent Barry, *Moral Issues in Business* (Belmont, CA: Wadsworth, 1979), 43.

6. *Ibid.*, 45–46.

7. Manuel C. Velasquez, *Business Ethics: Concepts and Cases*, 3d ed. (Englewood Cliffs, NJ: Prentice Hall, 1992), 72–73.

8. Richard T. DeGeorge, *Business Ethics*, 5th ed. (Upper Saddle River, NJ: Prentice Hall, 1999), 69–72.

9. Velasquez, 73.

10. DeGeorge, 69–72.

11. *Ibid.*

12. John Rawls, *A Theory of Justice* (Cambridge, MA: Harvard University Press, 1971).

13. DeGeorge, 69–72.

14. *Ibid.*, 72.

15. Gordon L. Lippett, *The Leader Looks at Ethics*, 12–13.

16. Society for Human Resource Management, http://www.shrm.org/.

17. Raymond C. Baumhart, "How Ethical Are Businessmen?" *Harvard Business Review* (July/August, 1961), 6ff.

18. Steve Brenner and Earl Molander, "Is the Ethics of Business Changing?" *Harvard Business Review* (January/February 1977).

19. Barry Z. Posner and Warren H. Schmidt, "Values and the American Manager: An Update," *California Management Review* (Spring 1984), 202–216.

20. Archie B. Carroll, "Managerial Ethics: A Post-Watergate View," *Business Horizons* (April 1975), 75–80.

21. L. W. Foy, "Business Ethics: A Reappraisal," Distinguished Lecture Series, Columbia Graduate School of Business (January 30, 1975), 2.

22. Linda Klebe Trevino, Laura Pincus Hartman, and Michael Brown, "Moral Person and Moral Manager: How Executives Develop a Reputation for Ethical Leadership," *California Management Review* (Vol. 42, No. 4, Summer 2000), 134.

23. Susan Gaines, "Handing Out Halos," *Business Ethics* (March/April 1994), 20–24.

24. Texas Instruments, "Ethics Quick Test" (Texas Instruments Ethics Office), wallet card.

25. Gary Edwards, "And the Survey Said...," in Garone (1994), 25.

26. Creating a Workable Company Code of Ethics (Washington, DC: Ethics Resource Center, 1990), VIII–1.

27. Ethics Policies and Programs in American Business (Washington, DC: Ethics Resource Center, 1990), 23–24; See also W. F. Edmondson, *A Code of Ethics: Do Corporate Executives and Employees Need It?* (Itawamba Community College Press, 1990).

28. Donald L. McCabe, Linda Klebe Trevino, and Kenneth D. Butterfield, "The Influence of Collegiate and Corporate Codes of Conduct on Ethics-Related Behavior in the Workplace," *Business Ethics Quarterly* (Vol. 6, October 1996), 473.